Developing and Sustaining Successful First-Year Programs

Developing and Sustaining Successful First-Year Programs

A Guide for Practitioners

Gerald M. Greenfield
Jennifer R. Keup
John N. Gardner

Jacket design by Michael Cook

Published by Jossey-Bass
A Wiley Brand
One Montgomery Street, Suite 1200, San Francisco, CA 94104-4594—www.josseybass.com

Jossey-Bass books and products are available through most bookstores. To contact Jossey-Bass directly call our Customer Care Department within the U.S. at 800-956-7739, outside the U.S. at 317-572-3986, or fax 317-572-4002.

Wiley publishes in a variety of print and electronic formats and by print-on-demand. Some material included with standard print versions of this book may not be included in e-books or in print-on-demand. If this book refers to media such as a CD or DVD that is not included in the version you purchased, you may download this material at http://booksupport.wiley.com. For more information about Wiley products, visit www.wiley.com.

Library of Congress Cataloging-in-Publication Data
Library of Congress Cataloging-in-Publication Data has been applied for and is on file with the Library of Congress.

ISBN 978-0-470-60334-5 (cloth); ISBN 978-1-118-22070-2 (ebk); ISBN 978-1-118-23449-5 (ebk)

Printed in the United States of America
FIRST EDITION

HB Printing   10 9 8 7 6 5 4 3 2 1

The Jossey-Bass Higher and Adult Education Series

Sponsor

The National Resource Center for The First-Year Experience and Students in Transition at the University of South Carolina was established in 1986 with a small grant from the South Carolina State Commission on Higher Education. Since its founding, the National Resource Center has grown into a multifaceted organization that serves as the trusted expert and internationally recognized leader for all postsecondary student transitions. The Center's scholarship and advocacy on behalf of first-year students and all students in transition has garnered significant worldwide attention and had an impact on student success initiatives across the globe.

Building on its history of excellence as the founder and leader of the first-year experience movement, the Center's stated mission is to serve education professionals by supporting and advancing efforts to improve student learning and transitions into and through higher education. It achieves this mission by providing opportunities for the exchange of practical and scholarly information, as well as the discussion of trends and issues in this field through the convening of conferences, institutes, workshops, and online learning opportunities; publishing books, research reports, a peer-reviewed journal, electronic newsletters, and guides; generating, supporting, and disseminating research and scholarship; hosting visiting scholars; and maintaining several online channels for resource sharing and communication, including a dynamic website, listservs, and social media outlets.

Five core commitments serve as the foundation for the Center's work in pursuit of its mission. First, the Center strives to set a standard for excellence for supporting all *students in transition*—first-year students, sophomores, transfers, seniors, and new graduate students—and facilitating educational success for a diversity of students in the twenty-first century. Second, the work of the Center focuses on the *connection between research and practice*, thereby advancing and supporting both scholarly practice and applied research. Third, our dedication to *inclusion* motivates us to create a supportive and professional environment where a diversity of viewpoints is recognized and considered in the ongoing dialogue on student transitions. Fourth, the National Resource Center models effective *collaboration* and aims to create intentional and integrative connections in support of student transition and success. Fifth, it supports a climate of intellectual curiosity and provides the tools and media for educators to be *lifelong learners* and engage in an ongoing process of inquiry, exploration, and discovery.

It is our hope that this book, *Developing and Sustaining Successful First-Year Programs: A Guide for Practitioners,* will build on the Center's mission and core commitments and provide an even wider audience of higher educators with resources and ideas to assist them as they strive to improve the first-year experience for students at institutions across the United States and internationally.

Contents

Preface

It has occurred to me that there may be some readers of this book who, when they first noted its title, might have thought to themselves: *What? Another book on improving the first year of higher education! What more can there possibly be to say?* No higher educator could have thought this in 1981, the year I took my initial steps to organize the first national convening of three types of higher educators—faculty, academic administrators, and students affairs administrators—to come together to discuss one intervention to improve the success of new students: first-year seminars. And there was no scholarly literature on the first year, and certainly nothing like this book that could be used as a quick and ready reference guide. Thus, there was no literature yet on first-year "programs."

But that was then and this is now. Since that year, the first and then thirty-one more annual conferences have been held on what has come to be known as the first-year experience. And thanks to two primary sources, the University of South Carolina's National Resource Center for The First-Year Experience and Students in Transition and Jossey-Bass Publishers, there is now an impressive array of published scholarship and other resources on efforts to improve the success of beginning college students and other students in transition.

Both the study of the first year and efforts to improve the first year have become well-established, higher education mainstream lines of work. So it is hard to believe that there are still many higher educators who are new to this work who may not yet have the desired theoretical grounding, let alone a useful working knowledge, of the range of options available to improve the success of new students. But there are! Each year at the annual First-Year Experience Conference (attendance at the 2013 meeting exceeded seventeen hundred), approximately half of the attendees are first-timers. And they are not only younger and newer members of a variety of academic professions. Many of them are more senior members of the academy, especially those who have come out of traditional academic and disciplinary ranks and now find themselves in positions of academic administration and charged with responsibility for "student success" or "first-year" programs (this at one time would have been an accurate description of one of the authors of this book, Gerald Greenfield).

We, the authors, had become increasingly aware of the need for a different kind of book about first-year transition programs focused on student success. We have aspired to produce in this work a ready reference guide that creates and delivers exactly what the title proclaims: a highly focused, practical work that

- Focuses on the beginning college experiences
- Emphasizes first-year programs
- Provides a guide and, hence, is suggestive, directive, and offers what we hope and trust is good counsel
- Is for practitioners with multiple levels of responsibility for first-year programs

The three of us came together through our work on the first-year experience and involvement at related conferences. We share interests in promoting new student success and helping others, especially those new or newer to this field. One of us (Gerald Greenfield) has spent most of his professional life at one public, regional, comprehensive university as a history professor who moved into administration and was faced with the challenges of improving new student success, for example, at the level of associate provost and provost.

Another of us (Jennifer Keup) is a scholar in the discipline of the study of higher education and the administrator responsible for the operational management and strategic direction of the influential National Resource Center for The First-Year Experience and Students in Transition at the University of South Carolina (USC), especially its production and dissemination of the latest scholarship on the first year. She is in the vanguard of the emerging new intellectual leadership for the twenty-first-century evolution of the first-year experience improvement movement. This book is a tangible example of this needed leadership.

As the third member of the team, I am the founder of the National Resource Center and a former executive director of a widely replicated intervention to improve first-year student success, University 101. I also have a perspective on the need for this book by being the coauthor of five other Jossey-Bass books, none of which set out to do what this book does accomplish.

I am confident that the three of us brought to the task of compiling this work our differing knowledge, experience, and perspective bases to make this a useful tool for you, our readers. And I feel privileged and pleased to have been able to work with my two fellow authors who were not with me at the beginning of the first-year movement but are now making important contributions. It is my hope that you will join the three of us in moving this work forward to even greater levels of impact on our needy and deserving first-year students in the years ahead.

I would be remiss if I did not recognize our publisher, Jossey-Bass, and not just or even primarily for extending us the privilege of providing you this resource tool. As I look back on the now four-decades-old evolution of the first-year experience movement, I am positive that one of the most important boosts this movement received was the publishing in 1989 by Jossey-Bass of *The Freshman Year Experience*, which M. Lee Upcraft and I wrote. That work symbolized our partnership: I am a faculty member and practitioner with long experience in first-year program administration, and Upcraft was a senior student affairs administrator and higher education scholar. Of note, both of us were from flagship public universities. Since the publication of *The Freshman Year Experience*, the movement has greatly expanded and found fertile soil in all institutional sectors. Jossey-Bass, because of its reputation and imprimatur, has done much to legitimize this focus on first-year students, issues, and programs as an important field of both academic writing and action.

Jossey-Bass followed that 1989 work with *Teaching College Freshmen* (1991 by Erikson & Strommer) and *The Senior Year Experience* (1998 by Gardner & Van der Veer); and *Challenging and Supporting the First-Year Student* (2005 by Upcraft, Gardner, Barefoot, & Associates); also in 2005 *Achieving and Sustaining Excellence in the First Year of College* (Barefoot, Gardner, et al.); followed by, in 2006, a second edition of *Teaching First-Year College Students*; and then *Achieving Sophomore Success* (2009 by Hunter et al.); now the most recent addition to this genre: *Developing and Sustaining Successful First-Year Programs: A Guide for Practitioners.*

I hope that this book will be used in these ways:

- First and foremost, to make leaders and practitioners of first-year programs more successful in accomplishing student success

- As a useful tool in the conduct of institutional program reviews

- In institutional self-studies, either for reaffirmation of regional accreditation or for self-studies that comprise the basis for improvement of student success in the first year

- As a benchmarking tool to assist in either comparing what one institution offers versus another, or as simply an audit of whether a given institution does or does not engage in the practices that this work espouses

- As an incentive for aspirational planning to expand the institution's current range of offerings of first-year programs

- As a resource work in professional development, faculty development, and strategic planning exercises

- As a textbook for graduate students preparing for future careers in higher education administration and student services

- As recommended reading for informal groups of higher educators who come together to discuss the reading of shared common works to discuss their applicability for institutional improvement efforts

- As a source for inspiration and emulation for higher education work not only in the United States, from which the program concepts and illustrations are drawn, but for anywhere else on the globe that aspires to provide more support for new higher education students, the next generation of leaders in every society

- As an inspiration for uses that I was not able to envision but matter most to our creative and thoughtful readers

I have always believed that good academic published work should be the basis of the next generation of even better work. So I invite our readers to help us think about what we didn't cover that we should have. What new interventions and programs are needed that we did not describe or envision?

First-year programs have always been the foundation of my own work. The most powerful professional experience of my career was providing leadership for the University of South Carolina's University 101 first-year seminar and faculty development programs. This one program alone led to the establishment of the influential first-year experience conference series, conferences on other student transitions, a wide range of publications on student transitions, and ultimately my late-career epiphany: the need to move beyond programs to an idea that would make programs even more viable.

I have discovered that institutions must have a grand design for their first-year programs—a strategic action plan to integrate and coordinate them. Without some centralizing, coordinating gestalt, there is no glue to hold these programs together. Now, they often compete for all forms of scarce resources: staff, students, space, money, attention from institutional leaders. They also are more subject to the predispositions of the comings and goings of senior administrative leaders because these programs are less likely to be institutionalized. So I conclude by inviting our readers to think about how they could move their important work on programs so well described in this book to an even greater level of impact by developing a more comprehensive vision of what is needed for first-year student success. Look at your own institution and its versions of some or all of the programs cited in this work:

- What is your overarching philosophy and vision for this work?
- How could you better organize the coordination of these programs so that at the very least, they were better understood, supported, and executed?
- How would you develop a strategic action plan to rationalize and prioritize your programs?
- And once you develop such a plan, as several hundred institutions now have, how would you implement the plan?

As with the programs featured in this book, there is no impact, no chance of greater student success without implementation. We dedicate this work to both student success and such program implementation.

Brevard, North Carolina   JOHN N. GARDNER
Spring 2013

The Authors

Gerald M. Greenfield is emeritus professor of history at University of Wisconsin (UW)-Parkside. His introduction to teaching and learning occurred in Brooklyn, New York, where he taught for three years at an inner-city junior high school and learned the importance of establishing relationships with students and creating a sense of community to facilitate learning. He received his PhD from Indiana University, Bloomington, where he focused on Latin American and African history. In the early years of what became a thirty-seven-year career at the UW-Parkside, he participated in a national project, Institutional Renewal Through the Enhancement of Teaching, directed by Jerry G. Gaff. He became a founding member of the university's Center for Teaching Excellence and later served for several years as director of UW-Parkside's Center for Teaching and Learning and as a representative to the UW-System Office of Professional and Instructional Development. He later led UW-Parkside's participation in the Foundations of Excellence in the First College Year and organized and chaired the university's initial First-Year Committee.

Greenfield played a lead role in the development of the university's international studies program and served for many years as its director. During that time, he developed a long-running simulation, the Model Organization of American States, an enrichment program for area high schools. He also contributed to the development of an internationally focused middle school and received regional recognition for his contributions to teaching and learning for both K–12 and college students. During the final years of his career, he became a member of the university's senior administration, serving as senior special assistant to the provost, associate provost, and, for three years, interim provost.

The author or coauthor of several books and numerous journal articles in his scholarly field of Brazilian history, he also has published on issues related to the portrayal of Latin America in US public school texts and American popular culture. He coauthored a widely used middle school social studies text and a college reader that discusses international views of US history. As a result of these publications, he was invited to become a member of the Bilateral Commission on the Future of United States–Mexican Relations and published two articles focusing on that issue. He later served as a consultant to the Kellogg-Mexico Project.

He has presented on issues of teaching and learning at numerous national conferences, including the Consortium for Student Retention Data Exchange, the Annual Conference on the First-Year Experience, and the American Association of State Colleges and Universities (AAC&U); is a peer reviewer for the Higher Learning Commission; and has consulted on program development. Having developed and implemented both programs and courses, he has a practitioner's focus that emphasizes the importance of process, relationships, and sustainability. His passion for these issues in part reflects his personal educational trajectory, which included being dropped from college twice because of poor grades.

———

Jennifer R. Keup is the director of the National Resource Center for The First-Year Experience and Students in Transition at the University of South Carolina (USC), where she is responsible for all operational and strategic aspects of the center. Keup also serves as an affiliated faculty member in the Department of Educational Leadership and Policies in the College of Education at USC. Before joining the staff of the National Resource Center and the faculty at USC, Keup had professional roles in the national dialogue on the first-year experience, as well as higher education research and assessment as a project director at the Cooperative Institutional Research Program at the Higher Education Research Institute and was heavily involved in institutional assessment efforts as the director of the Student Affairs Information and Research Office at the University of California-Los Angeles (UCLA). She earned her master's and a doctorate in higher education and organizational change from the Graduate School of Education and Information Studies at UCLA.

Keup's research interests focus on students' personal and academic development during the transition from high school to college, the influence of campus programming and high-impact practices on adjustment to college, assessment, and issues of institutional impact, responsiveness, and transformation in higher education. She has been a frequent contributor in higher education as a presenter, consultant, and author. She has delivered numerous conference presentations and provided invited addresses, including recent plenary, featured, and keynote sessions for the National Orientation Directors Association; AAC&U's Institute on High Impact Practices and Student Success; the Midwest First-Year Experience Conference; and statewide first-year-experience conferences in California, Connecticut, Minnesota, Ohio, and Wisconsin. Her scholarly work has appeared in the *Review of Higher Education; Journal of The First-Year Experience and Students in Transition; Journal of College Student Retention Research, Theory, and Practice*; and *Journal of College Orientation and Transition*. Her most recent book-length publications include *Crafting and Conducting Research on Student Transitions* (2011); *The First-Year Seminar: Designing, Implementing, and Assessing Courses to Support Student Learning and Success, Volume 1: Designing and Administering the Course* (2011); the *2009 National Survey of First-Year Seminars: Ongoing Efforts to Support Students in Transition* (2011); and editorship of a volume of New Directions for Higher Education titled *Peer Leadership in Higher Education* (2012).

Keup is heavily engaged in service to the higher education field, including active involvement in the Association for the Study of Higher Education, the Association for Institutional Research, ACPA, College Student Educators International, and NASPA–Student Affairs Administrators in Higher Education. She currently serves as the assessment and evaluation chair on the Convention Planning Committee for the 2013 ACPA Convention; served on the directorate board, including as chair, for the ACPA Commission on Admissions, Orientation, and the First-Year Experience from 2003 to 2010; and is on the advisory board for the Linking Institutional Policies to Student Success national study. Keup also serves on editorial and review boards for *Journal of The*

First-Year Experience and Students in Transition, Learning Communities Research and Practice, and *Journal of Peer Learning.*

John N. Gardner is an educator, university professor and administrator, author, editor, public speaker, consultant, change agent, student retention specialist, first-year students' advocate, and initiator and scholar of the American first-year and senior-year reform movements. He is the primary architect and ongoing leader and champion of an international movement to enhance all student transitions on campuses across the country and around the world. He is founder and senior fellow of the National Resource Center for The First-Year Experience and Students in Transition and distinguished professor emeritus of library and information science at the University of South Carolina (USC). From 1974 to 1999, Gardner served as executive director of the National Resource Center and the nationally acclaimed University 101 program at USC. He is currently president of the John N. Gardner Institute for Excellence in Undergraduate Education. In his capacity at the institute, Gardner has been instrumental in the development of the Foundational Dimensions of Excellence, a set of aspirational standards in the first-year and transfer-student experience used as the intellectual foundation for a voluntary self-study and improvement process that in the decade since their being put to use, approximately 250 institutions have engaged with.

In pursuit and as the result of this work, Gardner is the recipient of numerous local and national professional awards, eleven honorary doctoral degrees, and several lifetime achievement recognitions. More specifically, Gardner has been lauded with USC's highest award for teaching excellence, the AMOCO Award for Outstanding Teaching (1975), and the Division of Student Affairs Faculty Award "for outstanding contributions" (1976). In 1986, he was selected by the American Association for Higher Education as one of twenty faculty in the United States who "have made outstanding leadership contributions to their institutions and/or American higher education." In 1996, he was recognized by the Council of Independent Colleges with its Academic Leadership Award "for exemplary contributions to American higher education." The USC Alumni Association conferred on him its highest award for a nonalum, the Honorary Life Membership "for devoted service in behalf of the University," in 1997. He was also named the 1998 recipient of USC's Administrative Affirmative Action Award "for an outstanding job in promoting equal opportunities at the University." In 1999, he was the recipient of a university award created and named in his honor, the John N. Gardner Inspirational Faculty Award, to be given henceforth to a member of the university faculty "who has made substantial contributions to the learning environment in campus residence hall life." In 2012, he and his professional and personal partner, Betsy Barefoot, were the recipients of the New American Colleges and Universities Ernest L. Boyer Award for connecting higher education theory to practice and thought to action, in and out of the classroom. Gardner also is the recipient of eleven honorary doctoral degrees recognizing him for his contributions to American higher education (from his alma mater, Marietta College, 1985; Baldwin-Wallace College, 1990; Bridgewater State College, 1991; Millikin University, 1999; Purdue University, 2000; University of Teesside, UK, 2000; Rowan University, 2001: Thiel College, 2006; Indiana University, 2008; Clarion University of Pennsylvania, 2009; and the University of South Carolina at Columbia, 2012).

A frequent presenter and speaker at national and international conferences, Gardner has authored, coauthored, and edited numerous articles and books, including *College Is Only the Beginning* (1985, 1989), *Step by Step to College Success* (1987), *Your College Experience* in ten editions (1992–2013), *The Freshman Year Experience* (1989), *Ready for the Real World* (1994), *The Senior Year Experience* (1997), *Challenging and Supporting the First-Year Student* (2005), *Achieving and Sustaining Institutional Excellence for the First Year of College* (2005), *Helping Sophomores Succeed: Understanding and Improving the Second-Year Experience* (2010), and *The Senior Year: Culminating Experiences and Transitions* (2012).

Acknowledgments

This project has had a long gestation, and we are grateful for the ongoing support from our publisher, Jossey-Bass, and especially Erin Null, editor, and Alison Knowles, assistant editor, Religion and Higher and Adult Education. We also know that this book reflects the good ideas of many of our colleagues whom we also would like to recognize.

The idea for this book grew out of our respective involvement in the Foundations of Excellence in the First College Year process at the John N. Gardner Institute Excellence in Undergraduate Education and the activities of the National Resource Center for The First-Year Experience and Students in Transition. We thank the leaders and staff members of those organizations for their support of this book, as well as for their indefatigable efforts to engage, educate, and lead higher education professionals toward the ultimate goal of enhancing the learning, development, and success of students during their journeys into and through higher education. In addition, we express our gratitude to Scott Evenbeck, an early architect of this book, who played an important role in conceptualizing the content and developing the chapter format. Jodi Koslow Martin is yet another colleague to whom we express our appreciation; she provided valuable insights, feedback, and refinements during our final phase of the writing process.

As a book focused on practice, we relied on institutional exemplars in our research and the development of campus profiles in it. We owe a great debt of gratitude to colleagues at numerous institutions who do incredible work to support first-year students, provided information about their programs, and checked the final profiles that we wrote featuring their institutional initiatives: Rosalind Alderman (St. Mary's University, Texas), Anna M. Ament (Indiana University, Bloomington), Emily Battisti, (University of Wisconsin-Parkside), Heather Bowman (Indiana

University-Purdue University Indianapolis), Kris Bransford (Concordia University), Aaron Brower (University of Wisconsin-Extension), Emily Burgess (Tallahassee Community College), Valerie De Angelis (Miami Dade College), Ricardo Diaz (Chaffey College), Lizabeth N. Doherty (Mohawk Valley Community College), Alicia Doyley (Bridgewater State University), Gesele Durham (University of Wisconsin-Milwaukee), Bill Fleming (Sam Houston State University), Dan Friedman (University of South Carolina), Dana Gaucher (Illinois State University), Michael J. Glowacki (University of Maryland), Holly Grabowski (University of North Carolina Greensboro), Kasi Jones (Purdue University), Michelle Kearns (Utah Valley University), Lisa Kovacs (Purdue University Calumet), Rob Krueger (Concordia University), Anne Goodsell Love (Wagner College), Magpie Martinez (University of Wisconsin-Madison), H. Kevin McNeelege (Hudson Valley Community College), Marc Mobley (Florida International University), Geoff Norbert (Loyola University Maryland), Stephen O'Connell (University of Central Florida), Paulette H. Patton (Ursinus College), Courtney Pepper-Owens (Jacksonville State University), Mary Perkins (Elgin Community College), Frank Reiter (Indiana University, Bloomington), Cheryl Rice (West Georgia State University), Nelljean Rice (Coastal Carolina University), Gil Rodriguez (Los Medanos College), George Sanchez (University of Southern California), Deb Satterfield (El Paso Community College), Katy Lowe Schneider (Hanover College), David Schoem (University of Michigan), Mary Ellen Shaw (University of Minnesota), Kevin P. Thomas (Western Kentucky University), Wendy Troxel (Illinois State University), Christine Tutlewski (Gateway Technical College, Wisconsin), Julie Von Bergen (Los Medanos College), Sue Weaver (Northwestern State University), Phyllis Webster (Metropolitan State University), and Diane Williams (Northern Kentucky University). We are grateful to these colleagues for their partnership on this book, their generosity with their time and expertise, and their continued advocacy on behalf of first-year students.

Gerald M. Greenfield: I express my gratitude to Betsy Barefoot and John N. Gardner for introducing me to the First-Year Experience through the Foundations of Excellence in the First College Year and for their reflections on this project in its formative stage.

My larger debt is to the authors of the works cited in the References and to the colleagues who provided information on their institutions. It has been a joy to work with my coauthors, who combine professionalism and knowledge with good humor and friendship. Finally, I express gratitude to my wife, Susan Smith Greenfield, for her patience, encouragement, and good cheer while living with a man she dubbed "the gnome in her basement" because of the long hours I spent researching and writing this book.

Jennifer R. Keup: I thank my coauthors for the opportunity to collaborate with them, contribute to a rich dialogue, and learn from them through the process of writing this book; it has been a privilege to work with these gentlemen. I also recognize my former and current colleagues at the National Resource Center and the University of South Carolina for their involvement in and support of this book, especially Jessica Hopp, Cindy A. Kilgo (currently at the University of Iowa), Ryan D. Padgett (currently at Northern Kentucky University), and Tracy L. Skipper. In addition, I express my gratitude to colleagues at the John N. Gardner Institute for Excellence in Undergraduate Education—most notably John Gardner, Betsy Barefoot, and Drew Koch—for their contributions to the research for this book. On a more personal level, I extend my sincere gratitude to my family. The support of my parents, Patricia and Sal Rinella, has been instrumental to my personal, academic, and career development and success since birth. My sons, Aidan and Shane Keup, provide me with unbelievable joy, represent the future first-year students for whom I work, and are very excited to see their mother's name on the front of a "real" book. To my husband, Peter Keup, I humbly express my gratitude for his patience with my writing process and for being such a wonderful partner every day.

John N. Gardner: I acknowledge especially all of my mentors and supporters at the University of South Carolina who made the launching of the first-year-experience movement possible. I also acknowledge with grateful appreciation colleagues and first-year advocates at the nearly 250 institutions I have had the privilege of working with in the Foundations of Excellence processes and have given me the vision for the next major directions in my career.

Introduction: Where Have We Been, and Where Are We Going?

In the academy, we often start by looking back at the well-traveled road of our history to examine precedents and previous practices as we consider our current crossroads and potential future pathways. The topic of this book, the first-year college experience, and our disciplinary backgrounds—we are two historians and a social scientist—cause us to follow this reflective practice. Although the study of the first year and efforts to improve the transition from high school to college is now well established, it was not so long ago that this work lacked a place in higher education practice, a literature base to support it, or even a lexicon to guide discourse about it. First-year success used to be viewed solely as a function of the innate qualities and social privilege of students rather than as the result of institutional commitment to creating and supporting effective educational processes. The ingredients for this paradigm shift date back to early eras of American higher education, but they did not fully coalesce until the second half of the twentieth century.

The democratization of higher education that began after World War II changed the face of higher education in terms of both the number and types of postsecondary institutions. The expansion included significant growth in the number of community and technical colleges and expanding state college systems to complement the long-standing plethora of private and church-affiliated institutions. More recently, for-profit institutions and online learning opportunities have emerged and further diversified the landscape of higher education institutions. In addition, dual-enrollment programs and transfer pathways have created structures in which more than one institution may serve as the foundation for students' learning. Together these trends challenge historic assumptions about traditional baccalaureate learning environments.

To a significant extent, these shifts in higher education institutions both reflected and responded to a diversification of the college-going population in terms of race, gender, religion, sexual orientation, ethnicity, and social class. This dramatically changing student demography was impelled in large measure by the impact of generations of civil rights activists and the resultant legislation and policy focused on access, equity, and social justice at the local, regional, and national levels. Once the doors of higher education were opened to all, many new populations of students stepped through the entryway.

Although higher education has not yet achieved parity with respect to the students it serves, there is substantial evidence that the characteristics of students entering and navigating the baccalaureate experience have diversified significantly. For instance, the Latino population in higher education doubled between 1980 and 2000 (Saenz, 2004), women have emerged as the new majority on college campuses (Pryor, Hurtado, Saenz, Santos, & Korn, 2007), and the percentage of students who grew up with a parent born outside the United States or speaking a language other than English at home has increased among incoming college students (National Center for Education Statistics, 2005; Western Interstate Commission for Higher Education, 2008), and the proportion of multiracial students continues to increase. Furthermore, the diversity has broadened to include students from different physical and learning ability levels, first-generation-student status (i.e., neither parent earned a college degree), students who are working or drawing need-based financial aid, and non-traditional-aged students.

Beset by internal and external demands resulting from these shifts, the academy reconceptualized the nature of its educational role. More specifically, colleges and universities began to examine their responsibility for engendering a student-centered campus culture and to design and implement programs that would both challenge and support first-year students (Sanford, 1967), which also was reflected in the higher education research literature. Based on their encyclopedic reviews of scholarly literature on the impact of college on students, Pascarella and Terenzini (1991, 2005) concluded that institutions should "focus on the ways they can shape their academic, interpersonal, and extracurricular offerings to encourage student engagement" (2005, p. 602). In addition, Kuh identified the need to "provide sound evidence for the effectiveness of undergraduate teaching and learning that could be used to help both colleges and universities improve" as one of the motivators for the development of the National Survey of Student Engagement, which is administered by hundreds of colleges and universities each year and serves as the data source for numerous research studies on the learning experiences and outcomes of college students (in National Survey of Student Engagement, 2007, p. 3). Shortly after, scholars at the University of Texas at Austin developed the Community College Survey of Student Engagement (CCSSE) with the intention of "producing new information about community college quality and performance that would provide value to institutions in their efforts to improve student learning and retention, while also providing policymakers and the public with more appropriate ways to view the quality of undergraduate education" (2012, para. 12). Since its launch in 2001, the CCSSE has served as a primary engine of institutional assessment and higher education research on the quality of undergraduate experience in community colleges. Clearly higher education scholarship and practice began a redirection toward how to foster student success.

In concert with these efforts, educators rediscovered many practices that encouraged student engagement and success in their transition to college and thus positioned them well in their educational trajectory toward timely graduation, learning and skill development, employability, and responsible citizenship. Such interventions included curricular and cocurricular initiatives, many of which have a long history in higher education. For instance, residential learning experiences and informal welcome and orientation rituals have been in place since the colonial era (Dwyer, 1989). Similarly, vestiges of academic advising can be found in the seventeenth century, and evidence of first-year seminars is traceable to the late 1800s (Gordon, 1989). Cohort-based learning strategies, the precursors to modern learning communities, date back to the 1920s (Tinto, 2000), and service-learning emerged from the experiential education and social activism movement of the 1960s and 1970s. However, these respective efforts were not always formalized, rarely brought to scale, and often administered in isolation rather than in an integrated fashion. Tinto (2009) characterizes these programs for first-year students as having a "piecemeal" approach, which left them "at the margins of institutional life," as if they were merely "add-ons" to the real business of the university (pp. 9–10).

The origins of the modern first-year experience movement coincide with the democratization of higher education with respect to both institutional type and student access; a renewed interest in previous student success structures such as orientation, advising, learning communities, and residential learning; and the emergence of new strategies such as service-learning. This renaissance is widely attributed to the development of the University 101 course at the University of South Carolina (USC), a first-year seminar that combined an extended orientation model with a credit-bearing course and a holistic, humanistic, and student-centered approach to learning and student support. This course resonated with so many faculty, student affairs professionals, and academic affairs administrators both inside and outside the university that it sparked the development of similar first-year seminars at many other campuses across the United States as well as in other countries. These courses often served as the anchor for other first-year strategies, support initiatives, and student success efforts, thereby establishing a precedent for multifaceted, comprehensive, intentional, and integrated programs as the standard of success in supporting the transition to college for new students (Barefoot et al., 2005). As a result, a modern definition for the term *first-year experience* emerged:

> The first-year experience is not a single program or initiative, but rather an intentional combination of academic and co-curricular efforts within and across postsecondary institutions . . . [that represent] a purposeful set of initiatives designed and implemented to strengthen the quality of student learning during and satisfaction with the first year of college—the stage in American higher education during which the largest proportion of university dropout occurs. (Koch & Gardner, 2006, p. 2)

Thus, the first-year experience became codified, matured into a movement, and incorporated myriad student success practices under its umbrella. Ultimately the institutional efforts at USC led to the development of an internationally recognized organization to provide expertise, resources, and leadership on the topic of student transitions: the National Resource Center for The First-Year Experience and Students in Transition, a cosponsor of this book.

Despite the convergence of the democratization of higher education from the perspective of institutional type and student access, the rediscovery and development of several student success initiatives, and the maturation of the first-year experience into a national and international movement, there is still more work to be done with respect to the support of learning, development, and success of first-year students. For instance, national data indicate that new students frequently enter college with inadequate academic preparation, a history of disengagement in their final year of high school (e.g., coming late to class, declining rates of studying and doing homework, lower levels of interaction with high school teachers), and an inflated sense of their academic abilities, all of which can put them at a disadvantage for first-year success (Pryor et al., 2007). Similar data show that some degree of academic disengagement persists into the first college year (Ruiz, Sharkness, Kelly, DeAngelo, & Pryor, 2010). In addition, involvement in learning and student support programming during the first year of college tends to vary significantly by personal characteristics among students, such as race, ethnicity, or gender; major; financial stress; and social connections (National Survey of Student Engagement, 2012), thereby suggesting that equity issues remain a concern with respect to student success.

In addition, statistics on sophomore return rates have remained relatively unchanged over the past several decades (ACT, 2010a). While educators strive for much more than a "heartbeat in the seat," persistence metrics do represent a baseline of success and often serve as the coin of the realm in discussions of college impact and student success. Yet too many students are not making it past this important hurdle or are doing so on academic probation or in some other state of educational or personal distress. Furthermore, national research studies show that institutions still tend to "attribute attrition to student characteristics [rather] than to institutional characteristics," which suggests that there is still room for colleges and universities to take up the mantle of leadership in the student success equation (ACT, 2010b, p. 2).

New student success also is contingent on the ability to inform and engage a growing number of first-year student advocates among educators and professionals on college campuses. With a central goal of organizing or, often, reorganizing the academy with student success as critical to its mission, the power of partnerships and a collaborative approach to student success has become a standard of practice (Barefoot et al., 2005; Kuh, Kinzie, Schuh, Whitt, & Associates, 2005). Both historically and currently, faculty members are often the primary drivers and champions of first-year-student success initiatives despite common disciplinary, departmental, and institutional barriers to the support of and reward for their service in these roles. Student affairs professionals, directors and coordinators of various student success programs, academic advisors, orientation professionals, and residential life coordinators have been long-standing supporters of first-year efforts and are welcoming the next generation of leaders in these roles. There are also national trends toward the engagement of other campus constituents in student success initiatives, including librarians, mental health counselors, assessment and institutional research professionals, career center staff members, financial aid officers, admissions and enrollment management colleagues, and fellow students. Furthermore, higher education has become far less insular, and off-campus partners such as parents and families of students, common employers of undergraduates, community partners, state and federal agencies, and other colleges and universities are common collaborators in student success initiatives. All of these examples illustrate that first-year-experience efforts model a horizontal structure in higher education and reach across perceived boundaries in the academy (Keeling, Underhile, & Wall, 2007). Therefore, it is important to educate and involve both long-standing and emerging partners in efforts toward first-year student success, which may include addressing historic, cultural, and structural barriers to such widespread collaboration, as well as to a student-centered approach.

This book seeks to build on our history, address current issues, and provide a resource to first-year student educators and advocates. We have aspired to produce a ready reference guide that will achieve the following goals:

- Provide a primer on program essentials for new entrants to the field at the entry, supervisory, and senior administrative levels
- Offer a practical hands-on, how-to guide to successful program leadership and execution
- Provide a compendium of valuable resources for readers to selectively draw on
- Aid in the development, refinement, and sustainability of first-year programs
- Apply to the interests and responsibilities of a wide array of campus constituents and leaders tasked with the oversight of first-year-student initiatives
- Offer advice on effective organizational structures
- Provide guidance on attracting valuable partners to support the work of first-year initiatives, recognizing that these programs do not exist on an island
- Offer counsel and strategies for assessment and evaluation
- Highlight the value to the institution for adopting and sustaining this work
- Provide examples and profiles of successful programs from a wide variety of institutions with respect to size, control, type, selectivity, and culture

In pursuit of these goals, this book is heavily informed by scholarly literature and higher education theory, but ultimately it emphasizes practice. As the title suggests, it focuses on the beginning college experiences and emphasizes the first-year programs and initiatives that aim to facilitate the transition, learning, development, and success of new students. Thus, our first task in conceptualizing this book was selecting the specific programs, practices, and initiatives that represent components of a first-year experience. Note that we avoided using "the" when referring to first-year experience and instead used a broader, more inclusive article in referring to "a" first-year experience. This is purposeful and represents our beliefs and experiences that there is no one formula for first-year student success. A first-year experience is a flexible construct that must reflect institutional characteristics and history, campus culture, resource parameters, and, most important, the needs of the students who enter and progress (or do not progress) through the college or university. Regardless of these important considerations, certain initiatives nevertheless represent common support structures for new students and serve as the foundation for many first-year-experience programs. We examined these common programs, drew from both curricular and cocurricular structures, and arrived at a list of twelve interventions to feature in this book:

1. *High-impact pedagogies* are included because for the majority of first-year students, especially nonresidential students, the common forum for the first-year experience is the classroom. And what often matters most to student success is *how* students are taught even over and above *what* they are taught in their first year.

2. *Summer bridge programs,* which have existed in concept and practice since the launch of the federal Upward Bound program in 1965, have had a positive influence on millions of Americans with respect to college access and success and are being replicated both with and without government funding.

3. *New student orientation* is a long-standing and vital program that serves as a critical initiation for new students and represents an important vehicle for disseminating information, is a catalyst for building community, and serves to both communicate and define campus culture.

4. *Advising approaches and strategies* have evolved from mere course scheduling into a developmental and holistic process for first-year students as they forge, explore, and pursue their academic and career goals, thereby making academic advisors critical advocates for new student success.

5. *First-year seminars,* the most ubiquitous archetypal first-year program, often serve as the curricular anchor for other first-year initiatives and have a robust scholarly and assessment literature base documenting their positive impact on student success.

6. *Learning communities* (linked or paired courses for small cohorts of students coenrolled in two or more courses) have been enthusiastically adopted in all types of institutional settings and have established a body of empirical evidence for their effect on a wide array of student outcomes.

7. *Residential learning programs* capitalize on the benefits that residential experiences have on students as demonstrated by the key first-year outcomes that they realize, such as engagement, community building, and degree completion. They also represent the advancement of "housing" beyond an auxiliary service toward a key environment for learning that is rich with opportunities to connect to the curriculum.

8. *Developmental education* is necessary for a large proportion of new students, with a majority of new American college students requiring at least one course at a developmental level. The viability and sustainability of these programs, however, is under high levels of public policy scrutiny and attack.

9. *Early alert warning systems* identify and help chart a corrective course for students who are experiencing academic difficulties in their first term and seek to do better and avoid being put on probation for the next term.

10. *Probation initiatives* serve as a second-term support structure and corrective intervention for students who remain enrolled after they have demonstrated substantial levels of underperformance and are often the last attempt to right the trajectory of these students toward academic success and persistence to the second year.

11. *Peer leadership* is included because research has shown that the greatest influence on students during the college years is other students and because we want to encourage our readers to prepare and place more outstanding undergraduates in positions of influence on entering students.

12. *Second-year transitions* are not only the culmination of the first year but also represent the first key transition of student identity within the institution (from the newest participant in the community to a more experienced member) and serve as a springboard for future success in the undergraduate experience.

In truth, any one of these topics could be, and in many instances has been, the focus of an entire book. However, our intent is to provide a current, comprehensive resource that provides breadth and serves as a "greatest hits" guide to the oversight of an efficient and effective first-year experience. Therefore, each chapter in this book is dedicated to the discussion and development of one of these interventions. The chapters are loosely organized in a chronological framework around when a new student might experience the programs during the first year. However, this order is not critical to understanding the material. In fact, the chapters were written to be used as both stand-alone pieces as well as integrated into the larger book. It is also important to note that we intend this list of programs to be suggestive, not prescriptive, of the variables that may be included in a formula for first-year-student success. Readers may choose to read the book cover to cover, select only chapters that are relevant to their respective institutional and student needs, or read the chapters in an order that better reflects the delivery of support services on their campuses.

Regardless of how readers choose to approach reading this book, it is important to understand that we firmly subscribe to the belief that a first-year experience is ideally multifaceted, integrated, and comprehensive. Thus, it must include more than one, and preferably many, of these programs to reach its true potential (Koch & Gardner, 2006; Barefoot et al., 2005). Any one of these areas of support may represent an institution's premier first-year intervention or serve as a starting point for a fledging program. However, a true first-year experience includes more than just one "star" program and, instead, represents a constellation of support programs.

The structure within the chapters is intentional. Each chapter is organized in a similar fashion beginning with a general introduction to the program that includes a historical, descriptive, and scholarly background on the intervention. Thereafter, content is arranged under the same seven sections for each first-year intervention: "Approaching the Work/Critical Partners," "Organization/ Implementation Process," "Leadership Roles/Communication," "Resource Needs/Personnel," "Assessment," "Benefit Analysis," and "Institutional Practices." These sections represent the critical aspects of any program development, implementation, and administration process. (See Figure I.1.)

Figure I.1. Envisioning, Implementing, and Sustaining Student Success Programs

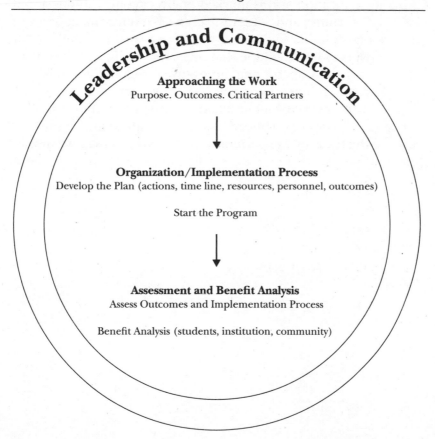

We believe that it is nearly impossible to create a successful and sustainable program without including each of these components and that it is often an area of programmatic weakness when one or several of these areas are overlooked or ignored. The template for each chapter also allows readers to see a general pattern to the creation and oversight of first-year initiatives. As such, it is possible to look across different first-year programs in certain areas to see trends, note differences, identify similarities, and create economies of scale with any one aspect of program development, implementation, and administration or to blend these processes across several programs.

While we hope that this book facilitates the development and refinement of first-year programs, we do not see it as an end of the dialogue on these practices. Innovation remains a constant in higher education and is marked by lively conversations about teaching, learning, and student success. We offer the content of this book as a guide for current practice but also as fodder for lively conversations. We hope that higher education professionals will use this book in forging innovative programs for new student success, embrace their role as first-year-student advocates, engage in the discourse on student success, make this work central to the mission of colleges and universities, and ultimately improve the transition experiences of current and future first-year students.

Developing and Sustaining Successful First-Year Programs

Chapter One

High-Impact Pedagogies

Supporting a high-quality undergraduate learning experience has long been a goal of colleges and universities. However, there has not always been agreement on the definition of *quality* in those discussions. Chickering and Gamson (1987) were among the first to help operationalize this concept with their Seven Principles for Good Practice in Undergraduate Education, guidelines for teaching, learning, and classroom practices:

- Encouraging contact between students and faculty
- Developing reciprocity and collaboration between students
- Promoting active learning within and outside the classroom
- Maintaining a timely feedback loop for evaluation processes
- Emphasizing time on task
- Communicating high expectations
- Respecting diverse talents and learning styles

These principles provided a framework for an effective teaching and learning experience and became the foundation for engaging pedagogies such as group learning strategies, integrated courses, team projects, peer review, team teaching, and the use of multiple instruction models in class (Erickson, Peters, & Strommer, 2006). They also paved the way for the use of new instructional tools, including portfolios, electronic communication, and online learning modules.

Swing (2002) added to this list of important teaching practices in his research on first-year seminars. Calling them "engaging pedagogies," he empirically validated Chickering and Gamson's principles by identifying five teaching strategies that were highly correlated with students' satisfaction and achievement of learning outcomes in first-year seminars:

- Use of a variety of teaching methods
- Challenging assignments
- Productive use of class time
- Encouragement for students to speak in class and collaborate
- Meaningful discussion and homework

More recent research by Goodman, Baxter Magolda, Seifert, and King (2011) continued to advance this notion of high-impact teaching strategies. From their work, they conclude that "fostering student learning calls on faculty and student affairs educators to focus on the design of courses, programs, and services in ways that maximize challenge and high expectations, diversity experiences, and good teaching/high-quality interactions with educators" (p. 9). These researchers also provide specific examples of each of the areas that they identify as critical to student learning. For instance, they note that academic challenge and high expectations include rigorous in-class activities, assignments, and exams that require higher-order thinking, and helping students integrate knowledge across multiple sources. They identify diversity experiences as both informal interactions such as meaningful conversations with diverse individuals and formal incorporation of content in class lectures or attendance at events about cultural diversity. Good teaching and high-quality student interactions with educators may consist of faculty interaction outside the classroom, organized syllabi and class sessions, clear expectations for student learning and performance, prompt feedback, and the perception that faculty are genuinely interested in students and student learning.

The Association of American Colleges and Universities (2007, 2011) has identified ten curricular and cocurricular structures that tend to draw on high-quality pedagogies and practices in pursuit of twenty-first century learning outcomes (Kuh, 2008). Defined as "teaching and learning practices that have been widely tested and have been shown to be beneficial for college students [toward] increase[d] rates of retention and student engagement"

(Kuh, 2003, p. 9), research continues to show positive results associated with these educational experiences, programs, and approaches (Brownell & Swaner, 2010; Koch, Foote, Hinkle, Keup, & Pistilli, 2007; Troxel & Cutright, 2008):

- First-year seminars and experiences
- Common intellectual experiences
- Learning communities
- Writing-intensive courses
- Undergraduate research
- Collaborative assignments and projects
- Diversity and global learning
- Service-learning and community-based learning
- Internships
- Capstone courses and projects

The common characteristics of these high-impact practices overlap significantly with the models put forth by Chickering and Gamson (1987), Swing (2002), and Goodman et al. (2011) and include an investment of time and energy, interaction with faculty and peers, diversity experiences, frequent feedback, reflection, integrative learning, and high expectations (Kuh, 2008). When they are implemented effectively and organized in a timely and integrated fashion, students' experience with two or more of these high-impact practices becomes the benchmark for a quality undergraduate experience (Kuh, 2008). Seven of the Association of American Colleges and Universities (AAC&U) high-impact practices are tightly connected to the instructional experience and classroom setting—first-year seminars, common intellectual experiences, learning communities, writing intensive courses, collaborative assignments and projects, service-learning and community-based learning, and diversity and global learning experiences—and thus may be construed as high-impact pedagogies (Association of American Colleges and Universities, 2007, 2011; Brownell & Swaner, 2010; Kuh, 2008).

Institutional strategies with respect to high-impact practices vary. For example, a campus may choose to focus its energies around one high-impact practice or pedagogy that serves as the anchor for their student experience, as is the case at Kapiolani Community College (KCC), a two-year institution in the University of Hawaii system that serves approximately ninety-three hundred undergraduates. KCC specifically identifies service-learning in the institutional mission statement and uses opportunities to pursue service-learning and community engagement as pathways through the university curriculum, the foundation of campus-community partnerships, and the framework for other integrated and applied learning strategies in the classroom and to facilitate faculty-student interaction. Similarly, the University of Maine, Farmington, a public liberal arts institution with approximately two thousand students, has a dedication to experiential education that features internships and service-learning initiatives prominently and is the foundation of the undergraduate experience for 70 percent of its students.

Conversely, a campus may connect many of these high-impact practices and pedagogies into a constellation of student success initiatives, as is typically the case for the host of institutions featured in the Documenting Effective Educational Practices study conducted by the Center for Postsecondary Research (Kuh, Kinzie, Schuh, Whitt, & Associates, 2005) and that elect to participate each year in the Foundations of Excellence process sponsored by the John N. Gardner Institute for Excellence in Undergraduate Education (Barefoot et al., 2005).

Only one of these high-impact practices and pedagogies is, by definition, tied to the first year. However, since experiences in the first year often set the tone for students' entire undergraduate experience, it is important that colleges and universities expose new students to these practices and set high expectations for their learning experiences at the institution. Consequently, several of these high-impact practices are common components of an integrated, comprehensive, and intentional combination of academic and cocurricular initiatives that comprise a first-year-experience program and forge a successful pathway through the undergraduate years (Koch & Gardner, 2006; Barefoot et al., 2005). National research shows that institutions are using at least one, and often many, of these seven structures for high-impact pedagogies among first-year students, and a growing literature base provides evidence of their positive impact (Barefoot, Griffin, & Koch, 2012; Brownell & Swaner, 2010; Koch, Foote, Hinkle, Keup, & Pistilli, 2007; Leskes & Miller, 2006; National Survey of Student Engagement, 2007; Padgett & Keup, 2011; Pascarella &

Terenzini, 2005; Troxel & Cutright, 2008). Several of these practices and pedagogies represent the topic of chapters in this book.

Approaching the Work/Critical Partners

Throughout this book, we discuss the notion of response to student needs and consideration of institutional mission and culture as starting points for nearly all first-year student support initiatives. Not surprisingly, student needs are central to the development and implementation of high-impact pedagogies. In fact, they are paramount to creating a student-centered model of teaching and learning in which high-impact pedagogies can be effectively organized and supported.

Student-centered learning is consistent with the overall shift in higher education from an emphasis on teaching content, which places the professor at the center of the learning experience, to a focus on student learning, which elevates the student to a position of responsibility and prominence in the educational process (Barr & Tagg, 1995). As such, student-centered learning "is an approach to focusing on the needs of the student rather than needs of others involved in the process, such as teachers and administrators...[and] places their needs and learning outcomes at the forefront of the resources offered and the course material presented" (Keup & Petschauer, 2011, p. 16). While it may appear simple, the culture of higher education has not always fostered an environment where the student is at the center of the learning experience. Even at smaller institutions or at campuses committed to teaching over research as the focus of the faculty, the classroom often still emphasizes the sage-on-the-stage model. The consideration and adoption of high-impact pedagogies are often catalysts for a change in institutional culture rather than a reflection of the status quo.

Whenever one is adopting student support strategies that represent a potential departure from current culture and practice, as may be the case with high-impact pedagogies, it is important to fully assess both the barriers and points of momentum for the change. The most cited argument against effective implementation of high-impact pedagogies relates to physical and environmental structures such as an institutional focus on graduate education and research at large research-focused institutions, a preponderance of large classes for undergraduates in general and especially for first-year students, an overreliance on lecturing as the delivery method for introductory and gateway course material, decentralized administration and programming, and institutional or disciplinary rewards structures for faculty that deemphasize teaching (Pascarella, Cruce, Wolniak, & Blaich, 2004). Since professors are often primary agents in the development and delivery of high-impact pedagogies, issues such as unionized faculty and a high number of part-time instructors will also have relevance to the consideration and implementation of these practices. Despite these challenges, and even because of them, it is prudent to engage leadership from the faculty senate, centers for teaching excellence, campuswide committees on teaching and learning, and faculty and staff from academic departments as partners in the effort to create a student-centered learning environment and promote the use of high-impact pedagogies. It is imperative to the institutionalization and sustainability of the effort to forge early collaborations with faculty and staff from areas of the campus that have been historically resistant to the effort, have a high attrition and failure rate among first-year students, and house common gateway courses for lower-division students.

Although the challenges to effectively implementing high-impact pedagogies are significant, they are not insurmountable and may be effectively addressed with the assistance of various resources on campus and trends in higher education. First, over the past few decades, first-year seminars, learning communities, and service-learning have gained a foothold in American higher education and a significant presence on many colleges and universities across the country. These programs are themselves high-impact practices and a hotbed of activity with respect to engaging pedagogies and faculty development strategies. Thus, there are likely initiatives already in place on campuses that are engaging high-impact pedagogies and providing training on these strategies. The directors of these programs are critical partners in the wide-scale consideration and adoption of high-impact pedagogies and can offer leadership in the administration, application, and assessment of these pedagogical principles.

Second, advancements in technology and the dawn of peer education provide low-cost tools to help create new learning environments that may be more appropriate to certain students' learning needs as well as to mediate the negative impact of large classes on pedagogy. Since the basic tenets of high-impact pedagogies are highly transferable (Brownell & Swaner, 2010), it is possible to creatively construct online learning modules and peer-led instruction models that incorporate and complement high-impact pedagogies. As such, university technology offices and peer-led student support services such as supplemental instruction, tutoring, and peer advising are likely to provide valuable partnerships for high-impact pedagogies.

Third, many accreditation processes have turned their focus to student learning, development, and success, particularly in the first year of college. Given the connection of high-impact pedagogies to student gains in these areas, there may already be a built-in need that has been established on the institutional level. Colleagues from the offices of institutional research, student assessment, and program review, as well as members of accreditation committees, may be able to help highlight the value of high-impact practices to the campus community.

Finally, there continues to be significant investment—institutional, regional, and national—in professional development options in the area of high-impact pedagogies. Leadership from campus-based centers for teaching excellence and for teaching and learning, institutional colleagues who oversee new faculty orientation and faculty development efforts, and interinstitutional partners forged by connections at national conferences are other key collaborators in any effort to incorporate high-impact practices. Numerous professional networks provide resources, research, training, and support in these various high-impact pedagogies, including the National Resource Center for The First-Year Experience and Students in Transition, the Washington Center for Improving the Quality of Undergraduate Education, and Campus Compact, as well as the work of AAC&U, which draws these bodies of work together. Several professional associations within the disciplines also provide resources and recognition for teaching and learning and the high-impact pedagogies associated with those efforts.

Organization/Implementation Process

High-impact pedagogies span different academic areas of the campus, often engage student support units, and may leverage student affairs partnerships, which also imbues them with incredible potential to cross historic boundaries in higher education and break down organizational silos. Therefore, it is important to gain high-level support for these initiatives early in the process. Whether it is selected as the focus of an accreditation process, is a grassroots effort by the faculty and staff, or represents a campuswide initiative to improve student learning, performance, and retention, the effort toward implementing high-impact practices is most effective and has the greatest impact with support from the institution's senior leadership: the president, chancellor, provost, vice president of academic affairs, or assistant or associate provosts. Buy-in generated at the level of deans will create even more of an impetus toward change. As such, a first step is to engage support, in the form of buy-in and financial resources from institutional leadership.

A valuable resource toward generating and maintaining such support is to conduct an institutional audit of current high-impact practices and pedagogies. As we already noted, there are often pockets of student-centered teaching and high-impact pedagogies on campus that can provide momentum and leadership toward more widespread adoption. Common areas for these activities are first-year-experience programs, university colleges, centers for teaching excellence, and academic departments. The high-impact pedagogies used in these programs can then be examined for scalability across new areas on campus or serve as a template for other efforts.

The creation of a task force or steering committee is advisable to oversee the implementation of high-impact pedagogies. The critical partners mentioned in the previous section and the faculty and staff overseeing areas that currently use high-impact pedagogies are a logical fit for membership in this group. Although these early adopters and supporters are natural leaders of the effort, it is also advisable to include partners from areas of campus that have faced structural or cultural barriers to the incorporation of high-impact pedagogies. By including some objectors in the effort, it is possible to gather information about challenges, address concerns, and begin to create new advocates for the effort. Furthermore, while pedagogy may feel as if it is solely an academic domain, the cocurriculum is a significant learning space as well. Therefore, student affairs colleagues represent a pool of knowledgeable partners who often oversee support programs and structures that are instrumental to the success of high-impact pedagogies and should be represented on any committee related to their implementation and organization. This committee may choose to work as a whole or divide the expertise of the group into subcommittees related to different high-impact pedagogies or different aspects of implementation (e.g., administration and logistics, campus communication, assessment). Regardless of the approach that is selected, the committee should commit to regular meetings and electronic communication between meetings to facilitate momentum around the effort toward widespread adoption of high-impact pedagogies.

Once members of the committee have been selected and a communication and meeting strategy identified, the first task of the group should be to determine the desired outcomes of the effort to advance high-impact pedagogies. As part of this effort, it is essential to develop common definitions for the high-impact practices themselves and student-level and program-level performance metrics. As referenced in the summary of literature and program descriptions contained in this chapter, there are many high-impact practices and pedagogies and each of them represent a highly-flexible structure. So it is important to operationalize what is meant by the umbrella term, what will count as a high-impact experience, and how the effectiveness of these strategies will be gauged. Once these definitional issues have been clarified, the committee can turn its attention to the identification of a reasonable time line, leaders and support personnel, appropriate resources, and assessment strategies for implementation and scalability of high-impact pedagogies for first-year students.

Leadership Roles/Communication

Leadership for the implementation of high-impact practices is likely to be a shared endeavor, and much of it will come from the collective energy of the members of the task force or steering committee. However, as with many other student success efforts, collective ownership and shared leadership is not always an efficient and sustainable model. Therefore, institutions should identify an individual to lead the development, implementation, and oversight of high-impact pedagogies.

Candidates for this leadership role include faculty members or academic staff with proven experience with high-impact practices and pedagogies. This person may be a vice provost or vice president overseeing undergraduate education initiatives that typically include high-impact practices and pedagogies, or an assistant or associate vice president or director-level position reporting to one of these senior roles. If the effort is connected to an accreditation process, the leader may be drawn from the institutional accreditation committee. Similarly, if the implementation of high-impact practices is coupled with an emphasis on the first-year experience, the director or dean of the first-year experience or seminar may be tapped for leadership with respect to high-impact pedagogies. Finally, high-level administrators in a university college may be nominated for this leadership position. Regardless of the professional role of the leader who will oversee the effort around high-impact pedagogies, she or he should remain connected to the core academic activities of the institution in physical proximity and with respect to reporting lines so that his or her efforts are not easily marginalized.

Once identified, this leader will need to be an active representative of the effort. He or she will likely serve as the head of the task force or steering committee on high-impact pedagogies and practices, the primary vehicle for cross-campus collaboration and communication. This leader also must create other channels of communication with various stakeholders, such as faculty, academic support staff, student affairs colleagues, alumni, parents, common employers of graduates, and community partners. Regular written reports to campus constituents, websites, and electronic communication channels can highlight achievements, current trends and issues, training resources, and assessment results as they relate to high-impact pedagogies. In addition, in a campuswide effort such as the adoption and support of high-impact pedagogies, communication must flow both ways. The leader of the effort and the task force or steering committee should create opportunities for critical partners, members of the campus community, students, and external entities such as employers, alumni, or community partners to provide feedback on both process and outcomes with respect to high-impact pedagogies.

Resource Needs/Personnel

Since high-impact pedagogies are generally a decentralized, campuswide effort, costs for core staff, office space, and operational expenses are not likely to be as significant as for other first-year student success initiatives. However, these budget items may come into play if the efforts to advance high-impact pedagogies include the development of an institutional teaching support center or the creation of a centralized faculty development program or if structures that currently exist in these areas need supplemental funding. As with other initiatives, these types of expenses can be managed with an initial infusion of funds from an internal budgetary reallocation or an external grant. However, the leader of the effort needs to work with campus administration and staff to plan for a transition to sustainable long-term funding and a recurring budgetary source.

A primary area of budgetary investment with respect to high-impact pedagogies is in the area of professional development, training, and faculty support. While faculty are experts in their respective fields and highly trained in their content area and research practices, their academic and professional backgrounds do not often include instruction in pedagogy and classroom practices. Even if an institution maintains a campus center related to teaching support, extra funds will probably need to be dispersed to the respective departments for professional development in these practices. Funds may be used to organize specialized training at the department level, send faculty to regional and national conferences on the topic of high-impact practices and engaging pedagogies, or create a library of print and electronic resources related to this topic. Given the diversity of opportunities to address the need for professional development on high-impact practices and engaging pedagogies, funding must be budgeted appropriately on the department level to cover conference registration fees and travel expenses; purchase of books, online modules, and other instructional materials; and compensation for consultants and speakers to come to campus.

The investment in professional development with respect to high-impact practices will be successful only if it is paired with incentives and rewards structures that allow, and even encourage, faculty and instructional staff to take advantage of these opportunities. Thus, funds should be directed toward the development of internal grants for professional and course development, opportunities for sabbaticals to advance teaching as well as research goals, and course buyouts to create time and space for faculty to reconsider their courses and the pedagogies they have been using. Whenever possible, these opportunities should be structured in a way that is consistent with the tenure and promotion standards and rewards structures that are meaningful in a faculty career, including acquisition and award of grants, a focus on scholarship, and involvement in the larger disciplinary community. Furthermore, investing in the development of institutional rewards and recognition programs focused on excellent use of high-impact practices and highlighting notable teaching is recommended. There are national awards for teaching excellence in the first year that often include the use of high-impact pedagogies as a criterion for which institutions should consider nominating faculty. These awards include the Outstanding First-Year Student Advocate Award and Excellence in Teaching First-Year Seminars Award that are sponsored by the National Resource Center for The First-Year Experience and Students in Transition and awarded annually. Although it requires the investment of human and fiscal resources, institutions should organize efforts to nominate campus colleagues for these awards or even use them as a template for the development of campus, systemwide, or regional awards that recognize similar areas of excellence in use of engaging pedagogies, effective use of high-impact practices, and support of first-year student success.

Another area of resource need for high-impact pedagogies is related to the provision of faculty mentorship, especially for new professors. Identifying experienced faculty members who effectively integrate these pedagogies in their courses and then pairing them with more junior faculty will help model these desired practices, communicate a strong institutional investment in these strategies, and forge faculty connections and collegiality that will add momentum toward the integration of high-impact practices and pedagogies. Often these efforts are most effective when they mirror the very practices that they are promoting in the classroom among students. For example, the creation and facilitation of faculty learning communities focused on the topic of learning strategies and student-centered classrooms will help professors at all levels with their continued development in this area and do so using the structure of a high-impact practice. Similarly, it may be possible to identify a common reading on these topics that new professors are asked to read, reflect on, and discuss. Although these efforts require an outlay of valuable human resources, opportunities for collaboration and learning among faculty will pay dividends in the creation of a student-centered culture, the successful adoption of high-impact pedagogies, and the quality of the learning experience for students.

Assessment

Assessment activities are one of the primary ways for individuals to provide input and improve any process, including the adoption and oversight of high-impact pedagogies for undergraduate education and first-year-student success. One of the challenges of assessing high-impact practices and pedagogies is the general overreliance on easily acquired but limited outcomes such as retention, grade point average, and satisfaction (Padgett & Keup, 2011). High-impact pedagogies are intended to promote a host of learning experiences, skill acquisition, career training, and preparation for responsibly citizenry. Therefore, it is essential to use assessment measures that truly capture student learning outcomes and not just retention, grades, and satisfaction measures.

Schuh, Upcraft, and Associates (2001) identify six learning outcomes that are common measures of student learning: complex cognitive skills, knowledge acquisition, intrapersonal development, interpersonal development, practical competence, and civic responsibility. These same items are mirrored in the general guidelines for the Council for the Advancement of Standards in Higher Education (CAS) (2009) and are noted in the Association of American Colleges and Universities' 21st Century

Learning Outcomes (2007, 2011), which also include intercultural knowledge and competence, information literacy, written and oral communication skills, and ethical reasoning.

Once the appropriate outcomes are identified for high-impact pedagogies, it is important to consider how to measure the achievement of these metrics. The Association of American Colleges and Universities created a set of rubrics for assessing achievement of skills related to its twenty-first-century learning outcomes (Rhodes, 2010). These rubrics provide benchmark measures, interim milestones, and capstone levels for fifteen learning outcomes of undergraduate education, such as quantitative literacy, creative thinking, teamwork, problem solving, civic engagement, and integrative learning.

Similar rubrics of assessment are offered for information literacy through the American Library Association and on excellence in the first year and for transfer students in the Foundations of Excellence self-study process by the John N. Gardner Institute for Excellence in Undergraduate Education. Finally, certain theoretical frameworks in the higher education and student affairs literature offer guidelines for the development of rubrics for student outcomes. In particular, stage theories of psychosocial and cognitive-structural development of students provide useful definitions and descriptions of incremental change and progress toward student learning, adjustment, and success (Skipper, 2005). These all represent valuable tools, but these guidelines and rubrics should not be adopted wholesale. Instead, they should serve as a template and be adapted to the institutional context, student characteristics, and elements of the high-impact pedagogy.

Other methods of data collection are also useful to the assessment of high-impact practices. Course and teaching evaluations, which are widely administered but vastly underused as a source of assessment data, can provide a valuable means to gather information about students' experiences with high-impact pedagogies. Inclusion of supplemental items can provide constructive feedback to instructors about how their student-centered teaching efforts were received, generate ideas for improvement, and even collect self-ratings of learning and development among students. E-portfolios are another way to gather data on students' growth and development as the result of high-impact pedagogies.

These collections of student work are not only valuable to the faculty and the institution with respect to the outcome of efforts related to high-impact practices but can communicate to potential employers the level of achievement based on students' learning experiences.

In addition, several national assessment instruments have adopted items that measure students' experiences with high-impact practices and pedagogies, as well as measures of outcomes associated with these experiences. Examples of such instruments include the National Survey of Student Engagement, the Community College Survey of Student Engagement, the suite of surveys from the Cooperative Institutional Research Program (i.e., the Freshman Survey, Your First College Year Survey, and College Senior Survey), and assessments of individual high-impact practices, such as first-year seminars, from Educational Benchmarking Inc. (EBI). These national tools provide an efficient and effective method to capture institutional data and compare them to institutional peer groups and national trends on high-impact pedagogies and related student outcomes. However, the desired outcomes of high-impact pedagogies are complex and will likely require qualitative methods of assessment (e.g., open-ended responses, student reflections and journals, focus groups, individual interviews) as a complement to quantitative assessment tools.

Benefit Analysis

The effective implementation of high-impact pedagogies often represents a significant cultural shift for a campus, which can be challenging and requires time as well as human and fiscal resources. However, institutional assessments and higher education research show that high-impact pedagogies yield substantial gains when they are implemented individually and even greater positive results when they are offered early in the undergraduate experience and administered as an integrated web of support structures for first-year students. Students who experienced high-impact practices and pedagogies tend to record higher persistence to the second year, higher graduation rates overall, and better grades (Brownell & Swaner, 2010; Koch et al., 2007; Troxel &

Cutright, 2008). Research has also shown that student-centered practices and pedagogies foster a sense of community on campus and greater satisfaction with college (Brownell & Swaner, 2010). These practices had a substantial positive effect for historically underrepresented minorities, low-income students, and first-generation college students (Brownell & Swaner, 2010; Cruce, Wolniak, Seifert, & Pascarella, 2006; Santiago, 2008). Accordingly, high-impact pedagogies can help advance an equity agenda on campus as well as increase the performance of all students.

While retention and grades are of common interest to campus stakeholders, it is valuable to note that high-impact practices and student-centered pedagogies are meaningful predictors of other outcomes. For example, Pascarella et al. (2004) found that these practices and pedagogies in undergraduate education are linked to the increase in cognitive and personal development during college, which was validated in several other studies (Cruce et al., 2006; Kuh, 2003; Mayhew, Wolniak, & Pascarella, 2008). More specifically, Brownell and Swaner (2010) summarize the evidence found in several studies of high-impact pedagogies to show that they generally improve students' academic engagement, intellectual development, writing and reading skills, critical thinking, and integrative learning. Leskes and Miller (2006) found consistent relationships between the use of "powerful educational practices" and inquiry learning, global learning, and civic learning (p. 32). These practices not only foster the development of skills and learning outcomes but help students develop more positive learning orientations, lead to greater intellectual curiosity, and foster an interest in graduate degree plans (Cruce et al., 2006; Mayhew et al., 2008).

High-impact practices and pedagogies were also found to have an impact on noncognitive measures, such as greater self-efficacy and identity development. In addition, research shows that these practices and pedagogies contribute to higher levels of civic engagement and social responsibility, appreciation for diversity, and intercultural awareness (Brownell & Swaner, 2010; Mayhew et al., 2008). Finally, these studies show that students who have high-impact learning experiences tend to have meaningful and positive interactions with faculty, fellow students, and peers from diverse backgrounds.

Institutional Practices

LaGuardia Community College

LaGuardia Community College is a two-year public institution on Long Island, New York, with over eighteen thousand students who represent a wide array of constituents such as freshmen, transfers, veterans, and adult learners. It has an established history of commitment to student success and the first-year experience and was an early participant in the Foundations of Excellence self-study process sponsored by the John N. Gardner Institute for Excellence in Undergraduate Education and a frequent institutional contributor to publications by the National Resource Center for The First-Year Experience and Students in Transition. As part of this commitment to first-year-student success, LaGuardia Community College offers multiple high-impact learning experiences for students that create "opportunities that rival those at most four-year institutions" (Barefoot et al., 2005, p. 75).

A robust learning community program provides a primary structure for high-impact pedagogies and student-centered educational practices for first-year students at LaGuardia. Several learning communities are offered, including liberal arts and sciences introductory clusters, which have been in place since 1976. These clusters adopt a traditional coenrollment learning community model with thematic connections and interdisciplinary readings and assignments. English as a Second Language learning communities provide students an opportunity to connect their English language instruction with introductory content in major courses. In yet another example, learning communities called "first year academies" are offered in business and technology, applied health, and liberal arts. These programs connect developmental courses, introductory courses in the respective majors, e-portfolio construction, and a connection to social and global issues. Faculty coordinators for each of these learning community programs ensure student-centered experiences that feature high-impact pedagogies and tight connection with twenty-first-century learning outcomes as defined by AAC&U.

High-impact practices and pedagogies are also supported at LaGuardia through its Cooperative Education Department, which provides experiential learning and internship opportunities for students. This department has been part of the campus learning experience for over thirty years and maintains a mission "to engage students in a process of active learning that links work experience with opportunities for critical analysis and reflection" (LaGuardia Community College, n.d.a). Working closely with local employers, the department uses three-month internships to help provide learning experiences that complement education occurring in the classroom and cocurriculum. Many associate degree programs require an internship, and the connection between the academic departments and the Cooperative Education Department is strong at this institution.

In addition, high-impact pedagogies are supported in multiple opportunities for LaGuardia Community College students to study abroad, which are coordinated by the Office for International Connections. Understanding the vast potential of diverse and global learning experiences as a high-impact pedagogy, the Office for International Connections seeks to "identify, organize, and promote activities at home or abroad that will prepare students to function in the globally interdependent world of the 21st century" (LaGuardia Community College, n.d.b). Close connections between this office and faculty ensure ample opportunities for students to collaborate across cultures, develop intercultural awareness, appreciate diverse viewpoints, and engage in internships that provide a global focus.

Drury University

Founded in 1873, Drury University is a small (sixteen hundred undergraduates), private liberal arts college located in Springfield, Missouri. It seeks to prepare students to find personal meaning, advance career success, and foster engaged citizenry through the infusion of diversity and global learning across the undergraduate experience. More specifically, the institution's Global Perspectives 21 Curriculum is a required core component for all students, thereby advancing intercultural competency and "resulting in a global studies minor for all students" (Leskes & Miller, 2009, p. 52). The six-course program combines a focus on mathematics and science literacy (Scientific Perspectives) with a focus on critical writing, language skills, and the study of cultural heritages (Global Studies). The outcomes of this program of study include "facility with a second language, communication, reasoning, and problem-solving skills related to global issues; and substantial awareness and appreciation of other cultures" (Leskes & Miller, 2009, p. 52).

While Drury's commitment to global and diverse learning is itself a high-impact practice as defined by AAC&U, the university engages a host of other high-impact pedagogies and structures in support of global and diverse learning, many of them featured in the first year of college. For example, Drury supports a first-year seminar that lasts two terms with the same students and instructor. These seminars focus on connecting students to the university, Springfield, and global communities; use a common interdisciplinary reader; and strive to advance students' interdisciplinary understanding, analytical skills, and oral and written communication proficiency (Schroeder & Swing, 2005). The goals, themes, and student groupings of the first-year seminar also serve as the foundation for various orientation activities such as an early summer registration day, a common reading experience, welcome week activities, and convocation. Therefore, Drury's first-year seminar affords several opportunities for common intellectual experiences and serves as "a gateway to the Global Studies 21 curriculum" (Schroeder & Swing, 2005, p. 149).

In their case study of this institution's first-year program, Schroeder and Swing (2005) noted, "A critical ingredient in the success of Drury is reflective, evidence-based practice . . . [and a] well-developed and comprehensive assessment of skills and knowledge drives innovations" in the first-year seminar, core curriculum, and orientation activities (p. 160). Value-added models of assessment (pretest and posttest) are used for writing, oral communication, and critical thinking, and various measures of multicultural competence provide a feedback loop to students to enhance their skills. In addition, historic and ongoing administration of the National Survey of Student Engagement "clearly indicate that Drury students exhibit a considerably higher level of engagement in academic and intellectual experiences than students at peer institutions" and gains in a host of student skill areas measured by the instrument such as "reading and writing, . . . quality undergraduate experiences, time use, and educational and personal growth" (Schroeder & Swing, 2005, pp. 161–162).

University of Southern California

The University of Southern California (USC) is a highly selective, four-year private institution located in Los Angeles. It maintains an institutional mission dedicated to being a "global university" and serves over seventeen thousand undergraduate students. Despite its size, USC offers a number of high-impact practices and student-centered learning experiences for its undergraduates, especially its population of low-income and historically underrepresented students. Examples include a rich array of diversity courses as part of general education requirements, numerous opportunities for undergraduate research, various study-abroad initiatives, and a recently implemented first-year seminar. Two of the institution's premier programs, the Joint Education Program (JEP) and a Writing in the Community course, feature high-impact pedagogies and are especially worthy of note (Sanchez, 2011).

The JEP is one of the oldest and largest service-learning programs in the country and connects USC to the surrounding community. Over two thousand students engage in service experiences in greater Los Angeles, which includes many disadvantaged and low-socioeconomic areas. These experiences in the field are then combined with undergraduate course work to facilitate integrated and applied learning, as well as global and diversity learning principles. High levels of faculty interaction, weekly personal and intellectual reflections, mentorship from student program assistants, technology, and active learning strategies in the classroom ensure that the service and academic components are tightly coupled to create meaningful learning experiences for the students.

USC's general education requirements include a writing program, which generally consists of a first-year writing and critical reasoning course, a course related to social issues, and an advanced writing course (WRIT 340). Writing in the Community is one variation of WRIT 340 and includes a community engagement component within the course. This version of the course draws its content from the social, economic, and political landscape of the Los Angeles community and incorporates reflection into the writing process. Similar to USC's service-learning initiative, students in this course partner with community groups to place their writing in a real-world context and identify and address social issues through their instruction on composition and rhetoric. "Although the tenets of good writing remain the central focus of the course, the semester will culminate in a media-driven, documentary-style final project, which will use writing, research, and personal experience to communicate these issues in a way meaningful to a broader public audience" (University of Southern California, 2013, para. 2). Through this connection, students develop not only their written communication skills but also their civic engagement and diversity and global skills.

Chapter Two

Summer Bridge Programs

Throughout the history of American higher education, there have been eras of expansion and diversification with respect to college entry (Cohen & Kisker, 2010; Thelin, 2004), including "during the early 1800s when access expanded to include more 'common men' in higher education,...the late 1800s when women and blacks entered higher education in larger numbers," and in the middle of the twentieth century as a result of the civil rights movement and the GI Bill (Kezar, 2000, p. 1). Toward the end of the twentieth century and into the new millennium, several other populations gained greater access to higher education. Cohorts of new students now include greater numbers and proportions of previously underrepresented racial and ethnic groups, first-generation college students (neither parent earned a college degree), students with physical or learning disabilities, nonnative English speakers, adult and returning students, low-income and working students, and international students (Crissman Ishler, 2005; Kezar, 2000; Pryor, Hurtado, Saenz, Santos, & Korn, 2007).

In order to ensure that access to higher education is tightly coupled with success in college, institutions often develop support programs to assist new populations of students with their transition and achievement in college. Outside of financial aid, bridge programs represent the most common type of support program for historically underrepresented and potentially at-risk students entering higher education. These "academic programs offered for students before the first year of college" are now available at nearly 45 percent of institutions across the country, although they are far more common at larger institutions and public institutions

(Barefoot, Griffin, & Koch, 2012, p. 4). In addition to their growing prominence, bridge programs are widely believed to be a cost-effective (Barefoot et al., 2012) intervention with a high impact for new college students (summarized in ERIC Clearinghouse on Higher Education, 2001; Koch, 2001; Koch, Foote, Hinkle, Keup, & Pistilli, 2007; Myers, 2003; Pascarella & Terenzini, 2005).

Summer bridge programs range widely in general type, duration, focus, and content. However, they are generally designed to assist entering college students with their development of academic and study skills and ease their transition from high school or community college to a four-year institution (ERIC Clearinghouse on Higher Education, 2001; Garcia & Paz, 2009; Pascarella & Terenzini, 2005). The ultimate goals of these programs are to retain these new students within higher education and "provide them an equal footing with other students" (Kezar, 2000, p. 1). Bridge programs also help provide support to overcome some of the most common barriers to college success for historically underrepresented students (Kezar, 2000; Terenzini et al., 1996):

- Lack of self-confidence
- Unrealistic and inappropriate expectations about college
- Low levels of interaction with faculty
- Uninformed or inexperienced precollege support groups, most notably family
- Poor integration and connection to the campus community
- Underdeveloped academic skills

The content of summer bridge programs typically focuses on offering instruction in common areas of developmental need such as mathematics, reading, and writing; the provision of study skills information such as note-taking strategies, time management techniques, and assessment of individual learning styles; and forging connections with the institution through the introduction of key personnel, orientation to campus resources, and individual mentorship (Kezar, 2000). Since students participating in summer bridge programs are frequently first-generation college students, content often addresses the goals and purposes of higher education.

These programs may also provide an introduction to certain institutional characteristics that may define new students' educational experience, such as attending a research university, minority-serving institution, or liberal arts college. Programming for parents, family, spouses, children, and other members of the students' personal support system has become a regular component of summer bridge programs. Less universal but still common elements of summer bridge programs are connections to certain majors, disciplines, or careers through preprofessional programming and career counseling, computer and information literacy, and community service opportunities. Finally, summer bridge programs may also engage community partners such as local businesses and neighboring schools and colleges.

Another defining feature of summer bridge programs is the target population for the initiative. Most of these programs are intended for minority, low-income, and first-generation college students, including the Search for Education Elevation and Knowledge summer bridge program at CUNY's Brooklyn College and the Accelerated Student Support Through Integrated Success Teams Program at the University of Texas at El Paso. National data indicate that 29 percent of institutions offer summer bridge programs to all students but that participation is optional. However, these same data show that provisionally admitted students, students eligible for Educational Opportunity Programs, and developmental students are most often required to participate in these programs (Barefoot et al., 2012). Bridge programs may also target students on the basis of gender, as do the Men of Vision in Education and Women Invested in Securing an Education programs at Goodwin College.

Other bridge programs are designed for honors students or academically gifted students who may also come from at-risk backgrounds such as the Academic Advancement Program at the University of California-Los Angeles. Furthermore, 7 percent of institutions indicate that students in STEM fields were required to participate in summer bridge programs and 24 percent of colleges and universities offer optional bridge programs for STEM students (Barefoot et al., 2012; Barefoot & Koch, 2011), including the Tennessee Louis Stokes Alliance for Minority Participation summer bridge program at the University of Tennessee at Knoxville.

As the number of students who begin their higher education journey in community colleges increases, more summer bridge programs are targeting new transfer students as well as those entering directly from high school (Poisel & Joseph, 2011). Specific examples of transfer summer bridge programs include the Transfer Summer Program as part of the Academic Advancement Program at UCLA and the Exploring Transfer program at Vassar College. Given the flexibility of summer bridge opportunities to address the needs of different groups of students, many institutions offer more than one type of these programs (Kezar, 2000).

The funding pathway for summer bridge programs provides further differentiation among these offerings. Some programs are one aspect of a larger transition and support program offered through state or federal aid programs. One such program is Upward Bound, a federal TRIO program that provides opportunities to low-income, historically underrepresented, and first-generation college students in their pursuit of a college degree. Another example is GEAR UP (Gaining Early Awareness and Readiness for Undergraduate Programs), which provides discretionary grants to states and partners to provide early intervention programs and financial support to middle school students through high school and in preparation for college (US Department of Education, 2011). Other summer bridge programs are developed by grants or private corporations to provide generalized support for underrepresented students or to facilitate undergraduate access and preparation for specific careers. For instance, the Hyatt and HBCU Hospitality Management Consortium's Hyatt Hotels Summer Bridge Program for High School Students focuses on supporting promising minority high school students to explore educational pathways and future careers in hospitality and tourism (Hyatt Hotels Corporation, 2011). In another example, the National Science Foundation partnered with Alabama A&M, Morehouse College, and Xavier University to provide a six-week program that emphasizes academic skills related to science, technology, engineering, and mathematics (STEM) fields. However, the most common source of sponsorship for summer bridge programs is still at the institutional or, for public institutions, the systemwide level.

Finally, summer bridge programs also vary in timing and duration. Some programs are as short as a few days, and others span a full six weeks of the summer prior to enrollment. Resources certainly play a role in the decisions regarding program length, but the most critical factors are the needs of the students who are the target of the program and the goals that the initiative seeks to address.

Although this chapter focuses on summer programs, higher education institutions are also engaging in bridge programs much earlier in the educational pipeline. In her survey of precollege academic outreach programs, Perna (2002) found that 25 to 35 percent of such programs focused on low-income, underrepresented minorities, first-generation, and low-performing students in middle school, and another one-quarter to one-third targeted these same groups in outreach efforts for ninth and tenth graders. Conversely, summer bridge programs also are becoming an integrated component of orientation and first-year experiences on college campuses, reflecting the new standard of a comprehensive and seamless approach to the college transition for new students (Barefoot et al., 2005). Therefore, as bridge programs begin to mature and merge with early-outreach and first-year-experience initiatives, they may no longer remain solely in the summer prior to enrollment.

Approaching the Work/Critical Partners

Throughout this book, the notion of fit between student success initiative, institutional culture, and student needs is a constant theme and one that applies to summer bridge programs too. Although there are myriad choices with respect to content, duration, sponsorship, and target populations, "what should become apparent is that individualization of the program to the campus is critical . . . [and] conducting an audit of your own campus' needs is essential" (Kezar, 2000, p. 2).

A review of institutional vision, mission, strategic plans, student learning outcomes, and student trends is necessary at the outset of any summer bridge initiative. Unlike other first-year programs, it is important to examine these cultural artifacts and the empirical evidence with a critical eye on two specific issues when considering them in light of summer bridge programs. First, most of these programs are intended to advance the access, achievement, and success of a specific student population, most often at-risk and underrepresented student groups. Therefore, it is important to understand not only what the institutional audit and data review communicates but also what or, more specifically, who is missing from this information:

- Which groups have not yet reached parity in their representation on campus in general and in certain programs such as STEM majors or honors colleges?
- Are certain student groups missing with respect to their presence on and integration with the campus community? If so, who are these students?
- What are the factors that account for their absence? Could these issues be effectively addressed through summer bridge programs?

Second, it is imperative to disaggregate the information and data gathered through the campus audit such that general trends do not overshadow conclusions specific to certain subpopulations that are often the impetus and focus of summer bridge programs:

- What are the differential rates of performance, adjustment, and completion for students by identity group (e.g., racial/ethnic designation, income status, age, first-generation student status, ability level, residential versus commuter), academic preparation, or interest area (e.g., major, career plans, community service orientation, desire to conduct undergraduate research)?
- Which student subpopulations seem to underperform compared to their peers?
- How do students' pathways through college and time to degree differ by demography, personal experiences, academic background, educational goals, and career aspirations?

When these issues are addressed during the institutional audit, these data communicate more relevant information to guide the development, implementation, and outcomes of the summer bridge program.

Critical campus partners will emerge throughout the data audit and in consideration of the variety of options for a summer bridge program. Some common collaborators for these programs are colleagues in early outreach, admissions, TRIO programs, testing and placement, developmental education, enrollment management, and institutional research. These colleagues can usually provide valuable insight into which students are captured in institutional outreach, application, selection, and course placement procedures, as well as individuals and groups that are frequently overlooked. They will be pivotal partners in any process to raise interest in admission to the institution and success thereafter.

Clearly faculty members are among the important collaborators in this work. Given the focus on academic preparation in summer bridge programs and the common goal of academic readiness for the first year as stated by 93 percent of institutional respondents to a national survey in 2011 (Barefoot et al., 2012), these initiatives could not achieve even their most basic outcomes without high-quality faculty to teach the content of the course work that comprise these programs. Yet faculty involvement in successful summer bridge programs goes far beyond content delivery. As with many other curricular-based first-year programs, summer bridge programs typically have small classes; maintain educational environments that draw on the principles of high-impact pedagogies; focus on the process as much as the products of learning; and engage faculty as mentors, models, and coaches (Erickson, Peters, & Strommer, 2006; Swing, 2002). Therefore, the selection of faculty who are engaged in these programs must account for these particular skills on top of their knowledge of the subject matter.

Faculty members who participate in summer bridge programs should truly represent the most engaged first-year advocates as well as experienced instructors. Therefore, those who have received teaching awards, have received high teaching evaluations from undergraduate students, and have a history of engagement in professional development activities related to teaching and pedagogy on campus, such as with Centers for Teaching Excellence, or off-campus, including participation in conferences related to teaching and learning, are primary targets for teaching opportunities in summer bridge programs.

Depending on the content and structure of the summer bridge program, other campus units may be sources of collaboration, including housing and residential life for programs that allow or require students to live on campus; parents' associations or offices of parent and family programs for summer bridge opportunities that engage students' personal support networks; and placement and career services for summer bridge content related to preprofessional programming and career pathways. In addition, the target population for the summer bridge initiative may suggest other campus units with which to collaborate. For instance, financial aid, work-study, and student employment offices are critical for bridge programs for students from lower socioeconomic levels. Similarly, programs that target students from particular identity areas may rely on the support of women's centers, student disability services, international student offices, transfer student support units, and multicultural affairs and student organizations dedicated to diversity or specific identity areas. Finally, much like orientation, there are likely to be a number of offices and departments on campus either engaged in the delivery of summer bridge content or that are introduced on the program, including the library, information technology, tutoring, the writing center, supplemental instruction, first-year experience programs, and advising. Representatives from these units must be engaged early in the planning process in order to develop and provide high-quality programming to summer bridge participants.

Critical partners for these programs also reside outside academe. Students' parents and families may be the beneficiary of summer bridge programming, but they also are important partners in the success of this initiative. Their support, both emotional and financial, is an important factor in students' participation in these programs and a source of reinforcement of the utility and application of the skills learned therein. Many summer bridge programs include a service component and strive to create connections with the city or town in which the institution is located. Therefore, community partners can be key collaborators and advocates for the program. Given that the basic premise of summer bridge programs is to smooth the transition to college, connections with high schools and community colleges that are sending a large proportion of students from the target populations to the campus are another source of collaboration. Finally, engaging representatives from the system (for public institutions), appropriate consortia (for private colleges and universities), and at the state level in the planning and administration of summer bridge programs will help the coordinating staff at the institution to remain up to date on college access policies, K–12 and higher education partnerships, and systemic plans for facilitating college student success.

Organization/Implementation Process

The wide variation in approaches to and characteristics of summer bridge programs makes it difficult to identify a single implementation formula. Since these programs have been present in American higher education for so long, many institutional examples are available for different types of programs. In addition, federal programs such as TRIO's Upward Bound and state equal opportunity programs like New York's Higher Education Opportunity Programs and CUNY's Search for Education, Elevation, and Knowledge provide vetted templates for success. Kezar (2000) recommends the Council for the Advancement of Standards general guidelines to direct the development and implementation of summer bridge programs. Although each of these resources is valuable, none of them can be adopted wholesale for institutional application; each must undergo revision and refinement to fit the campus culture, student needs, and individual program goals.

This initiative typically runs on an annual cycle that begins in winter with staff recruitment, training, and program planning. The cycle continues through spring when the program participants are recruited, program staff members accept and review applications for competitive programs, and participants are selected. Students are brought to campus for the program in the summer, and assessment data are collected from the students throughout their experience. These data are then analyzed after the close of the program and results are disseminated in the fall. Finally, data-informed decisions and program improvements are implemented in fall and winter. Then the cycle begins again for a new cohort of summer bridge instructors and students.

Summer bridge programs may be housed in a number of different units on campus. The most common administrative homes for these programs are the university college, first-year programs, orientation and testing, specific academic departments, the admissions office, TRIO offices, and offices of multicultural affairs. Bridge programs for academically talented students sometimes are administered by honors programs. Although the program will ultimately reside in one specific area, it is much more likely to represent numerous collaborations among campus and community partners, thereby generating a sense of shared ownership.

Identifying the target group and the general purpose of the bridge program will provide valuable information to guide decisions regarding organization, structure, and implementation strategies. For example, credit-bearing academic courses may be the backbone of summer bridge programs for students interested in STEM fields. However, other types of programs directed toward academically underprepared students may focus on academic success workshops or remedial or developmental education courses that will not apply to graduation. Programs for first-generation college students may rely heavily on the development of peer networks and family programming as opposed to bridge programs for academically gifted students, which typically include greater emphasis on faculty mentorship, or programs for exploring or undecided students in which the primary relational emphasis is the academic advisor. More often than not, a variety of individuals will serve as instructors and mentors in summer bridge programs. Summer bridge programs commonly adopt a coaching team model that includes faculty, academic advisors, peer leaders, librarians, and academic support staff.

Beyond determining the scope, scale, content, structure, and instructional staff for the program, it is important to create channels of promotion and communication with potential participants. A key step in any promotional strategy is the development of a clear and accessible program statement and a strong connection with the university's identity, mission, and goals. Next, it is important to find avenues to disseminate this information. Recruitment efforts can include electronic communication, letters, websites, hosting students for campus visits, promotional events in the community, and other outreach efforts to high schools and community colleges.

Leadership Roles/Communication

While summer bridge programs are often a collaborative initiative, they generally have a designated coordinator, dean, or director. Program leadership may represent the entire role for this individual or be one aspect of a larger set of responsibilities for the position. Like most other program administrators, this individual maintains organizational authority for the summer bridge initiative, articulates and upholds a vision and mission for the program, oversees programming, manages fiscal processes, supervises staff, and represents the program to internal and external constituencies (Council for the Advancement of Standards, 2009). The leader needs to maintain a current and relevant knowledge base in the area of student access and success, particularly with respect to the target population and goals of the specific program. Also, this individual needs to be conversant with institutional, state, and federal policies as they relate to the summer bridge program.

The leader of the summer bridge program must initiate and maintain collaborative relationships with internal and external partners in support of the program. A number of critical campus and community partners need to be engaged in program planning, implementation, and delivery in order to ensure success. Therefore, formal and informal collaborations and open channels of communication are necessary with admissions; testing and placement; orientation; advising; residential life; the office of institutional research; academic departments; first-year experience programs; student success centers; libraries; and academic support units such as tutoring, supplemental instruction, and writing centers.

The leader of the program must facilitate communication among these campus partners, which may happen in formal structures such as through an advisory board structure and regular meetings or through more informal channels such as an informative website or newsletter as well as social media. This person should be prepared not just to provide information but to advocate for the program and the students it serves within the larger campus community. As the leader of a program that often serves an at-risk or historically underrepresented student population, he or she must use the position of authority on the campus to be an activist for these students who have historically been overlooked and underserved. The ability to understand and disseminate assessment data and programmatic results is fundamental to the success of the initiative and the leader overseeing the program. Skills and credibility in these areas can be gained by a personal history with a summer bridge or a similar outreach program; professional experience and expertise in the areas of student access, learning, development, and success; and the strong support of campus leaders such as senior administrators, faculty, and student leaders. Thus, it is likely that the position will be filled by an experienced professional. Finally, it is critical that this position can command the resources and institutional buy-in necessary to advance the goals of the program and institutional efforts toward access and equity.

Resource Needs/Personnel

Summer bridge programs require attention to several types of operating expenses that are common for most student success initiatives, such as marketing and communication for the program, office space, supplies, computers, and technological support. Funds for instructional facilities, residential space, and recreational activities are typical in summer bridge programs and must be budgeted as baseline items. Program staffing is also a consideration. In addition to a director or coordinator, many programs employ an assistant director, professional support staff, and student paraprofessionals to serve as undergraduate advisors, mentors, and tutors. It is important to remember that the investment of human and fiscal resources per student for summer bridge programs is often greater than for other student support initiatives given the high needs, at-risk, and academically underprepared character of the target population and the intensity of these programs. Therefore, the overall budget allocation for staffing these programs is likely to be larger than for other student success initiatives.

Program promotion and participant recruitment and selection can be a significant expense for summer bridge programs. It is a time-intensive process to identify students who are eligible for the program, gather their contact information, and gain access to appropriate communication channels through high schools, community colleges, and their homes. The development and dissemination of informational, recruitment, and application materials for the program requires a significant investment of human and fiscal resources. If admittance to the program is competitive, it will be necessary to secure personnel to review applications and make selections among the candidates, which will likely require professional staff, cross-campus partners, and other volunteers to participate in the review and selection process.

Finally, the success of many of these programs relies on financial support for its participants. Given that the target audiences for summer bridge programs are frequently low-income students, students of color, and first-generation college students, the cost of college and related programming may be of significant concern. These same target groups are often wary of taking out loans for higher education expenses, may be generally unaware of financial aid options, and have concerns about the issue of lost income from not working the summer before college. Therefore, while almost one-third of summer bridge programs pass on some of the operational costs to participants, nearly all programs provide at least some financial assistance. Examples of aid include waiving tuition and fees for the courses taken in the summer, providing stipends or summer employment to participants, covering room and board for residential programs, underwriting the costs of books and instructional materials, or funding the entire cost of the program.

Institutions address these resource needs in various ways. Recent national data on efforts to improve undergraduate student success and retention (Barefoot et al., 2012) indicate four primary funding streams for summer bridge programs, although these institutional programs often draw from more than one of these sources. Approximately 15 percent operate on private donations from individuals or corporations and grants from foundations. About 30 percent of survey respondents reported that at least some of the costs are paid by participants in the program. State or federal funding models are present for half of the programs. However, the largest proportion of programs, nearly 60 percent, draws from institution or unit-level funding.

Assessment

Given the significant resource investment of summer bridge programs, it is critical to evaluate their impact on student outcomes and overall program effectiveness through a comprehensive assessment plan. Yet 15 percent of institutions responding to the 2010 National Survey of Efforts to Improve Undergraduate Student Success and Retention reported that they did not conduct any research on the outcomes of these programs, and a similar proportion of respondents were unfamiliar with the empirical evidence on their effectiveness (Barefoot et al., 2012). Assessment and reporting is especially important, and often mandated, for programs that are funded with external dollars, such as corporate partnerships, foundation grants, or private donations. However, it is equally important to show that summer bridge programs yield a return on investment when they draw from unit-level, institutional, or systemwide funding (Garcia & Paz, 2009).

As with any other first-year student success effort, assessment activities for summer bridge programs should be tightly coupled with program outcomes and connected to institutional goals and student needs. On the most basic level, assessment activities should include a program evaluation to gauge participants' general satisfaction, ideas for improvement, and direct measures of learning from the experience. Faculty, staff, and peer leaders who participate are likely to have valuable formative feedback and should be given voice in the program assessment as well. Common assessment outcomes also should include student performance measures such as successful matriculation to the institution; improved persistence rates to the second term of the first year, the sophomore year, and graduation; grades that are at least comparable to or greater than the general first-year student population; greater familiarity with college expectations; interaction with faculty; and the foundation of an academic and personal support network in the form of faculty, peers, and staff (Barefoot et al., 2012; Kezar, 2000).

Several assessment principles are particularly meaningful for summer bridge programs, especially when addressing the student learning and performance outcomes. First, expectations for program outcomes and the duration of the assessment plan must be consonant with the nature and length of the summer program as well as its target population. When these factors are considered, a longer time line is typically necessary to assess the effect of summer bridge programs. Like many other preenrollment and first-year programs, summer bridge experiences establish a foundation for future success. Given that these programs last at most a few months and many times span only a few days, it is reasonable to assume that fulfillment of such lofty goals as engagement, skill development, academic achievement, and the establishment of support networks will not be achieved by the end of the program or even in the first year. In addition, persistence and graduation outcomes require a multiyear assessment model. As such, it is important to chart the progress of summer bridge participants during the first year of college and even throughout their entire undergraduate experience in order to fully understand the range of benefits that these programs provide.

Similarly, it is important to fully understand the audiences for the program and organize assessment processes accordingly. If the summer bridge program is required for some students and an elective for others, these differences must be noted in the data and comparative analyses conducted on these subgroups. Similarly, just as data disaggregation is critical when evaluating data regarding campus culture and student needs when approaching and implementing summer bridge programs, these steps are equally necessary when examining the data for program effectiveness. So if multiple groups are targeted in program recruitment and selection (e.g., low-income students, first-generation students, historically underrepresented minority groups), assessment instruments and analyses should be structured to capture students' affiliation with each of the identity areas of primary interest to the program. Students' identity is multifaceted, and they are likely to affiliate with more than one of the target areas for the program. Thus, assessment plans should not structure these options in mutually exclusive categories but be flexible enough to allow for multiple identities.

Third, assessment plans for bridge programs should adopt a value-added model (Astin, 1993a). In this assessment model, pretests are used to determine a baseline level of performance, and posttests are administered to determine change and progress from the performance on the pretest. This value-added approach is particularly important for summer bridge programs since the target populations for this student success initiative often are at-risk or underprepared students. Therefore, the performance level of summer bridge completers may only equal that of the general first-year student population. However, that level may represent significant improvement over their baseline or expected performance given the degree of risk and lack of academic preparation prior to summer bridge participation. Although the administration of surveys at two time points may seem daunting, many summer bridge programs require extensive application materials and placement tests for participation, which can provide valuable baseline data for student performance metrics and program outcomes.

Finally, many summer bridge programs engage qualitative assessment strategies to complement quantitative methods. Surveys are useful tools to collect data on retention, grades, understanding and use of campus resources, and even self-ratings of academic and social self-confidence. Other outcomes such as a sense of belonging, depth of interpersonal relationships, breadth of social and academic support structures, and understanding of college-level expectations may be better examined through narrative data collected in focus groups, individual interviews, and written reflections. These qualitative strategies allow a more nuanced examination of affective and psychological outcomes of summer bridge experiences to add to the understanding provided through quantitative data on the programs.

Benefit Analysis

Summer bridge programs require a significant investment of time, money, and effort and are typically focused on a smaller group of first-year students than other programs. However, institutional and scholarly research has shown that they have high success rates in a number of areas.

The most commonly cited outcomes are increased retention rates, higher grade point averages (GPA), and smoother transitions to college. Although studies report mixed evidence on the effect of these programs on GPA (Ackerman, 1991; McLure & Child, 1999; Wolf-Wendel, Tuttle, & Keller-Wolff, 1999), most published research shows that the programs have a positive effect on retention overall (Ackerman, 1991; Garcia, 1991; Kezar, 2000; Logan, Salisbury-Glennon, & Spence, 2000; Walpole et al., 2008), especially for underrepresented and low-income students (Ackermann, 1991; Oseguera, Locks, & Vega, 2009). Furthermore, research on the impact of summer bridge programs on general transition experiences indicates positive results for academically talented students (Glennan, Martin, & Walden, 2000), as well as for underrepresented and low-income students (Ackermann, 1991). Other research provides empirical evidence for the positive effect of program participation on academic adjustment (Paul, Manetas, Grady & Vivona, 2001) and engagement (Walpole et al., 2008), as well as social and emotional adjustment (Paul et al., 2001; Walpole et al., 2008).

Additional research shows that summer bridge programs facilitate other outcomes that are precursors and correlates of student success. For instance, there is evidence that program participants report greater ease using technology (Logan et al., 2000). In another example, students were more confident in their choice of major and felt more comfortable expressing a need for student support services than their peers who did not participate in the program (McLure & Child, 1999). The programs also tend to enhance academic skill development and are positively related to earning math credits (Evans, 1999) and higher scores on tests of reading comprehension, essay composition, and algebra (Fitts, 1989). These programs appear to facilitate student interaction with peers, faculty, and staff (Robert & Thomson, 1994) and even contribute to collaboration among faculty (Bowles, Falk, & Strawn, 1994).

Although the majority of this work has taken place with students who are going directly to four-year colleges and universities from high school, the success of summer bridge programs has led to their development for entering transfer students. Analyses of these programs also produce statistically and practically significant positive results for transfer students (Chenoweth, 1998). In an examination of several student success initiatives for transfer students at four four-year colleges and universities, summer bridge programs were "the only examples of a support program that has proven to be valuable and successful in the retention, persistence, and graduation rates of transfer students" (Eggleston & Laanan, 2001, p. 95).

Although there is ample evidence of the effectiveness of these programs for students and even faculty who are involved in them, it is important to frame the discussion of benefits beyond individual impact on the program participants. By facilitating the transition and success of participating students, especially those from at-risk or underrepresented populations, the institution has the potential to gain in representation among these student groups. As such, there is vast potential to increase structural, behavioral, and psychological diversity at the institution (Hurtado, Dey, Gurin, & Gurin, 2003) and advance educational equity and social justice.

Institutional Practices

Indiana University-Purdue University Indianapolis

Awarding degrees from both of its namesakes, Indiana University and Purdue University, and located in Indianapolis, Indiana University-Purdue University Indianapolis (IUPUI) is an urban, comprehensive, public research university that serves over twenty-two thousand undergraduates and welcomes approximately twenty-five hundred new students each year. Housed in University College, the Summer Bridge Program, established in 2001 with 18 students, served approximately 575 students in 2012. The program lasts two weeks with an optional residential component. Some incoming students, such as Twenty-First Century Grant recipients and Summer Success Scholarship recipients, are required to attend the program. Other students may elect to participate and are accommodated on a first-come, first-served basis.

There is no fee for the program, but students are required to pay for their food and housing expenses during the program. Students who sign up for the program before July are allowed to move into university housing early in order to accommodate the residential component of the program, help them develop a sense of belonging, and ease their transition into the start of the fall term. The overall goal of the program is to create an academic and social community at the institution for new first-year students.

Summer Bridge Program participants are divided into groups of twenty-five based on their interest in a particular major, with undecided and exploring students placed together in groups. Each group is assigned an instructional team comprising a faculty member, academic advisor, peer mentor, and a librarian, thereby maintaining a low ratio of instructional staff to students for the program. Classes in English, math, and presentation skills represent the primary course work for the program. Programming, curriculum, and student outcomes of the two-week program are intended to address students' needs for adjustment and achievement, such as "establish networks for success with faculty, advisors, student mentors, and librarians; make friends with other students; learn about college-level expectations for reading and writing; receive individualized support for math; begin connecting with a school and major; become acquainted with the campus; and gain experience in using instructional technology" (Indiana University-Purdue University Indianapolis, n.d.).

Given the intensity of the program and the high investment of the instructional team in the success of participants, very few students drop out. Further, "Student Success Scholarships are awarded to eligible students who successfully complete the IUPUI Summer Bridge Program and actively participate in academic support programs during the fall semester following their Summer Bridge experience" (Indiana University-Purdue University Indianapolis, n.d).

Adding to the success of the program is a comprehensive assessment plan that includes students, faculty, and staff feedback. Findings from these assessment data include evidence that Summer Bridge participants at IUPUI earn higher GPAs than their nonparticipating peers and that 58 percent of students from the 2010 cohort of the Summer Bridge Academy earned a GPA of 3.0 or higher. These data also show that Summer Bridge students perceive that program participation increases their confidence about college success. More specifically, 96 percent of participants from 2010 said that "the program provided them with the resources and information to succeed in college" (Indiana University-Purdue University Indianapolis, n.d.). Positive results are not limited to the student participants in this program; IUPUI faculty members also believe that participants are better prepared for college-level work.

Ursinus College

Ursinus College is a highly selective, private, liberal arts college located in Collegeville, Pennsylvania, with an undergraduate population of under two thousand. As one of the more diverse liberal arts colleges in the country, Ursinus includes students from thirty-five states and twelve countries; 20 percent of its students are students of color. This commitment to diversity extends beyond structural representation, and the institution strives "to build and maintain a vibrant multicultural community" (Ursinus College, n.d.).

The summer prior to a student's first year at Ursinus College is a time of both anticipation and preparation. Among the wide array of programs, the college offers a summer bridge program: the W. R. Crigler Institute (named for Ursinus's first African-American graduate). Designed for incoming first-year students from historically underrepresented groups, the institute is a three-week summer program of academic, leadership, and social development. Students live in the residence halls and participate in a credit-bearing, intensive course that begins in the summer and continues through the fall term, which provides "a way to acclimate to Ursinus's academic demands and campus culture" (Kuh, Kinzie, Schuh, Whitt, & Associates, 2005, p. 117). Students also participate in community service projects, connect with Ursinus alumni, become acquainted with Ursinus faculty and facilities, attend workshops, and build peer networks and lasting friendships. During the Crigler Institute, students engage with others whose perspectives and backgrounds may differ from their own, build leadership skills and resourcefulness in a college setting, deepen their social consciousness in theoretical as well as practical contexts, and lay the foundation for academic excellence in college. The Crigler Institute provides an extraordinary opportunity for incoming first-year students to step closer toward full transition from high school to college.

The mission of Ursinus College is "to enable students to become independent, responsible and thoughtful individuals through a program of liberal education. That education prepares them to live creatively and usefully, and to provide leadership in their society in an interdependent world." With these ideals in mind, the Crigler Institute at its core aims to enrich the academic and personal development of students who are the first of their families to go to college, come from low-income households, or demonstrate interest in multicultural affairs. The number of participants is limited. The institute's goals are to provide a positive initial college experience; promote intellectual development; support meaningful friendships and active participation in campus life; promote peer interaction to facilitate social development, communication efficacy, and the building of a support network; and engage students in programs that foster the value of intercultural awareness (such as study abroad, summer fellow, or community service) and reinforce the importance of hard work and persistence. Institutional assessment data provide evidence of success on many of these measures, as well as retention rates that are comparable to the general population of entering Ursinus students (Kuh et al., 2005).

Louisiana State University

As the state's flagship institution, Louisiana State University (LSU) is a large, selective, public, four-year institution located in Baton Rouge that serves over twenty-eight thousand students in bachelor's, master's, and doctoral programs and enrolls well over five thousand new first-year students each year. In 1991, it developed the Summer Scholars Program (SSP) to recruit and retain its African-American students. Housed in the University College/Center for the Freshman Year and directed by an SSP Coordinator, the program selects fifty to fifty-five students who participate in an eight-week residential program in the summer prior to their first term of enrollment at the institution. The ultimate goal of the program is to provide participants "with the academic, social, and cultural tools . . . needed to assimilate and succeed in college life" (Collins, 2007, p. 3).

While the program is primarily focused on academic success, it takes a more holistic approach by also including social, cultural, and career aspects in the program. Students participate in six to nine hours of regular college classes, engage in academic skills workshops, receive tutoring, and are introduced to academic support units on campus such as advising, the library, computing services, and the Center for Academic Success. Social aspects are addressed in personal counseling sessions, peer support among the program participants, and mentorship provided by program leadership and former Summer Scholars. Leadership development workshops and career counseling help prepare Summer Scholars for these aspects of the undergraduate experience. Given that the target population of the program typically comprises low-income students, financial assistance is provided through the program.

Over the course of the program, both qualitative and quantitative assessment strategies have provided empirical evidence for its effectiveness and informed decisions about program improvements. Quantitative data have shown a 98 percent retention rate to the second year for SSP participants, as well as an 80 percent six-year graduation rate, higher than rates for all LSU students (Collins, 2007). These same data indicate that participants earned an average GPA of 3.1. Results from the qualitative assessments reveal high levels of student satisfaction and the perception of program value to their transition and success.

Chapter Three

| New Student Orientation

The process of welcoming and integrating new members to a community is a rite of passage in many environments, including higher education. Early in the history of American higher education, new students were informally received into the university by older students in the form of mentoring or hazing and more formally by faculty in their supervision of students in a residential setting (Ganser & Kennedy, 2012; Mack, 2010).

The first formal orientation programs took place at Boston University and Harvard University in the late 1880s. The purpose of these early programs was to "acquaint new students with college life," facilitate faculty interaction, and "indoctrinate new students into the college and to conduct basic transactions that needed to occur prior to the start of classes" (Mack, 2010, p. 3). By 1940, more than one hundred institutions had adopted similar orientation and transition programming to address these goals, thereby leading to more formalized oversight that shifted away from the faculty and into the hands of deans of men, deans of women, and other student affairs personnel. By the 1960s and 1970s, "orientation programs became a college-wide effort as the material covered spanned services and resources from across the institution" (Mack, 2010, p. 5) and often engaged the staffing and leadership of student paraprofessionals (Ganser & Kennedy, 2012). Since that time, orientation has undergone an era of professionalization, become almost ubiquitous in higher education institutions, and evolved and diversified in structure and form.

Goals of Orientation

Because orientation has been part of the fabric of higher education for such a long time, its mission and purpose, as well as guidelines for best practices, have been firmly established. Based on the body of work on this student intervention, Mullendore and Banahan (2005) define *orientation* as "a collaborative institutional effort to enhance student success by assisting students and their families in the transition to the new college environment" (p. 393). The Council for the Advancement of Standards in Higher Education (2009) establishes a fourfold mission for orientation programs that includes "facilitating the transition of new students into the institution; preparing students for the institution's educational opportunities and student responsibilities; initiating the integration of new students into the intellectual, cultural, and social climate of the institution; and supporting the parents, partners, guardians, and children of the new student" (p. 324). In pursuit of this mission, Jacobs (2010) identifies three common activities in and goals of orientation: building community, disseminating information, and defining campus culture.

Among these three, the most frequently acknowledged outcome of orientation is for the new student to build community (Jacobs, 2010). It may not be possible for an individual to forge a deep and meaningful support structure within the limited time frame of an orientation program. However, it is critical that during orientation, a student begin to envision himself or herself within the social fabric of the institution and start to spin the strands of connection that will ultimately result in a strong web of support during college. It is also important to ensure that the academic realm is represented in this foundation of community in order to provide the scaffolding for academic success (Jacobs, 2010). The inclusion of faculty and other academic support staff and a focus on the intellectual community of the campus and classroom are valuable components of the orientation experience.

A second widely acknowledged purpose and outcome of orientation programming is to disseminate information (Jacobs, 2010). Orientation agendas are rife with administrative tasks and logistical details for new students, and it is a stereotypic image of the precollege experience for students to collect massive amounts of handouts, referrals, advice, guidelines, policies, and procedures. While technology has rendered paper catalogues and handouts largely a thing of the past, students are often still barraged with information about how to successfully navigate the next four (or five or six) years of college. When this process of providing information is done without intentionality or an eye toward integrated as well as comprehensive coverage, the impact of all of the valuable information is likely to be lost on an overwhelmed student. Furthermore, it is vital that these materials be accurate, appropriate to the stage of the students' development, and relevant to students' most pressing concerns and questions. When these issues are taken into account, the outcome will reduce the number of costly errors in students' educational trajectory (Jacobs, 2010) and result in an orientation program that extends "beyond the provision of information per se to the establishment of early contacts for new students not only with other members of their entering class but also with other students, faculty, and staff . . . to help new students make the often difficult transition to the world of college" (Tinto, 1993, p. 159).

Third, orientation programs have the potential to introduce, clarify, and even change campus culture (Jacobs, 2010). Orientation is not the first interaction that a student has with the institution, but it is often among the earliest experiences that he or she has as a full-fledged member of the campus community. Orientation thus represents a prime opportunity to outline the basic tenets of the campus community, communicate institutional expectations of students, and help students identify their expectations for college, which can facilitate alignment and increase the chances of students' adjustment and success (Jacobs, 2010). However, since incoming first-year students have limited knowledge of institutional history and campus culture, orientation also represents an opportunity to communicate new expectations or introduce emerging cultural norms. Thus, messages at orientation need to balance both current and aspirational views of campus culture to ensure student success and advance the vision of the institution.

Orientation Programming

Historically, the most common programming to achieve the goals of orientation has been in the form of on-campus activities prior to the start of college, which typically range from a half-day to a week in duration. Approximately 80 to 85 percent of institutions offer orientation programs that include several one- to three-day sessions staggered across the months prior to the start of the fall term (Barefoot, Griffin, & Koch, 2012; Mann, Andrews, & Rodenburg, 2010). Students may select one of these sessions based on scheduling preferences or student characteristics (e.g., special sessions offered for honors students, student athletes, bridge program participants).

Northern Arizona University uses this model and provides a residential, two-day orientation that teaches traditional first-year students to manage logistical aspects of their transition to college. It also highlights academic resources, facilitates student involvement in the campus academic and social communities of campus, and engages students' parents and families.

Another model for preterm orientation is to bring students together in the days immediately before the start of their first term at the institution. Commonly called "Welcome Week" and coupled with moving into campus housing at residential campuses, such programming may serve as an alternative or complement to summer orientation activities. For example, Princeton University orients its entire cohort of entering students with a one-week residential program that begins just before classes start and extends to the second day of the fall term.

Although summer programs and welcome week activities represent the bulk of orientation activities, new models for orientation practice are emerging. These new iterations include different formats for shared orientation experiences such as service experiences or common reading programs; alternative settings, including outdoor orientation experiences and online formats; and engagement of new constituencies such as adult learners, students' families, and transfer students. Many programs now conceptualize orientation as an ongoing process for new students that is integrated with other programming for a comprehensive first-year experience. The content and goals of orientation are often highly connected to residential life initiatives, first-year seminars, learning communities, and convocation.

As one example of emerging practices, outdoor orientation experiences have gained a foothold in new student programming over the past few decades with examples found at Dartmouth, the site of one of the earliest outdoor orientation programs, founded in 1935; HoneyRock Camp at Wheaton College; and the University of New Hampshire, the current home of the leadership for the national organization called Adventure Orientation Programs. Born out of a foundation in camping education and relying heavily on a renewed interest in integrated and applied learning (Association of American Colleges and Universities, 2011; Kuh, 2008; Rhodes, 2010), outdoor orientation is a structured program for small groups of students that uses adventure experiences and peer interactions to facilitate an active learning orientation experience (Bell & Vaillancourt, 2011). Camping, wilderness training, and adventure activities such as ropes courses are common types of outdoor orientation activities. National data indicate that just over 20 percent of institutions across the country engage in this type of orientation programming (Barefoot et al., 2012). Other research studies provide strong evidence that outdoor programs not only advance the common goals of orientation but are especially effective at facilitating social support among peers (Bell, 2006a, 2006b; Gass, Garvey, & Sugerman, 2003) and developing individual students' self-confidence and self-esteem (Galloway, 2000).

Another emerging model for orientation programming, common reading programs, are present at over 40 percent of campuses across the country (Barefoot & Koch, 2011) and involve the selection of a book that all incoming students are either encouraged or required to read prior to arrival on campus. Reading the selected text creates an immediate commonality among new students and can facilitate community building. The text is typically selected for its connection to an institution's mission, values, or strategic initiatives in an effort to communicate campus culture. Selection criteria may also consider the capacity for the text to engender intellectually rigorous and critical discourse that will introduce and model college-level academics (Skipper, Latino, Rideout, & Weigel, 2010). Programming around a common reading initiative typically includes a culminating event held during preterm orientation that consists of a convocation event, keynote speaker, or small discussion groups led by upper-division students, staff, librarians, and faculty. These programs often go well beyond a single event and may include social media activities such as Facebook groups and online discussion forums, incorporation of the book as a required text for first-year seminars and introductory English classes, and other related events such as film festivals, essay contests, speaker series, and art exhibits (Laufgraben, 2006; Skipper et al., 2010).

A final emerging model is online orientation, which is becoming more prevalent as a complement to, or replacement for, traditional in-person delivery methods. The most often cited reasons for incorporating information technology in any aspect of higher education are to increase access, support relevant competencies, and maximize cost efficiency for both the student and the institution (Brown & Hernandez, 2010). However, recent national data on college students' facility with and desire for technological tools suggest that implementation of online resources and technologically enhanced academic environments represents a student-centered approach to information acquisition and learning (Johnson, 2012). In addition, higher education is experiencing increasing college participation among students from demographic backgrounds for whom traditional in-person orientation models may be neither appropriate nor accessible, such as working and low-income, first-generation, commuter, and older students (Crissman Ishler, 2005; Wilson & Dannells, 2010).

Successful delivery of online orientation rests on a technology platform that provides log-in capabilities; tracking of student involvement, progress, and completion of the program; connection to other web-based and technological resources, including course management systems used by the campus and academic advising; incorporation of external media, including YouTube and Facebook; high levels of graphic and visual content; and synchronous as well as asynchronous capabilities. Although the goals of an online orientation may differ from an in-person model, they should strive to model "campus-based orientation, transition, and retention programs [in their tendency] to involve multiple avenues for direct interpersonal contact" and "provide an active learning environment that allows students to truly connect with the campus culture'' (Brown & Hernandez, 2010, p. 120).

Approaching the Work/Critical Partners

Nearly all components of first-year-experience programs draw from multiple campus constituencies and communities. In fact, a hallmark of successful first-year-experience programming is the involvement of faculty, student affairs, academic affairs, academic support, and current students (Barefoot et al., 2005). However, even among programs that cut across institutional boundaries, new student orientation rises to the top in terms of its sense of shared responsibility and collective investment. Given the breadth of this intervention, orientation is likely to draw information, expertise, and buy-in from all of the campus communities, offices, programs, and resources that orientation staff members cover in their sessions. Whether through gathering print materials, verifying the accuracy of online resources, being involved as a presence on the program for orientation, or sharing budgetary resources, staff, or space, cross-campus collaboration is a foundation of successful orientation programming.

The key partners for orientation vary according to the structure, goals, and content of the program, as well as institutional size and structure. For instance, offices of university computing and information technology will be key partners for online orientation components but may be less invested in outdoor orientation models. Similarly, residential life, housing, and other campus facilities are highly involved colleagues in traditional summer orientation models, as well as welcome week activities, but may not be as engaged in convocation or common reading programs. In yet another example, parking services and community partners are likely to be involved in orientation at a commuter institution, although such information may represent little more than a print piece in a folder of material for students at a highly residential campus. Furthermore, smaller institutions may have fewer cross-campus colleagues involved in the orientation experience since each campus professional may represent multiple institutional functions as opposed to larger institutions that have a more decentralized administration model.

Despite the variation across institutional characteristics and program goals, certain campus partners have been historic fixtures in the delivery of efficient and effective orientation programs:

- Academic advising
- Representatives from academic departments
- Placement and testing services
- Registrar and enrollment services
- Campus activities and student life
- Dean of students office
- Offices of student conduct and judicial affairs
- Campus safety and crisis management

Specially trained upper-division students also are critical partners for orientation programs. Most notably, these students serve as permanent or volunteer staff of orientation programs, representatives of the respective campus units engaged in orientation, or individual or group mentors for incoming students. These peer leaders are much closer to the student experience and are highly accessible to fellow students, thereby serving as a relevant resource to new students and a valuable channel of feedback to the staff of orientation programs (Keup, 2012).

Emerging trends in orientation programming have identified other communities and advocates to engage on behalf of new students. For example, there has always been an interest in connecting new students with faculty members. However, it is becoming even more apparent that "involving faculty in orientation programming helps to promote an environment where students want to belong and contribute" and that "to reinforce these benefits, student and faculty interaction should be encouraged and scheduled during the orientation process" (Mann et al., 2010, p. 46). There also is a greater move toward comprehensive and integrated programming for new students, thereby necessitating communication, involvement, and planning across admissions and enrollment management, orientation, and first-year-experience programs. Gone are the days when students are handed off from one unit to another in their selection of, orientation to, and transition through an institution. Instead, the emergent standard of practice is a highly integrated delivery of student support structures with goals, staff, and programs that cross over campus units dedicated to new student selection and success (Barefoot et al., 2005).

Orientation also is no longer the sole province of a single campus community. More frequently, external constituents are becoming engaged in the process of new student orientation and included as key partners. One example is the inclusion of parents and families in orientation programming over the past several decades (Mack, 2010; Ward-Roof, Page, & Lombardi, 2010). Yet another is collaboration among institutions regarding new students whether it is with respect to records, transfer agreements, or dual-enrollment programs. As the diversity of new students grows, the orientation process for many new members of the campus community necessitates the inclusion of outside entities such as military and veterans' services for current or former members of the military, various federal agencies and offices of foreign affairs for growing numbers of international students, and campus connections with community partners or corporate entities for working or adult students.

Organization/Implementation Process

As with any other student intervention, the first step of orientation program development and delivery is gaining an understanding of the institutional environment and identifying student needs. The purpose of new student orientation may feel universal and its implementation prescribed by guidelines set forth by the Council for the Advancement of Standards and information provided by the National Orientation Directors Association. However, the articulation and actualization of the goals of orientation must ultimately fit the specific mission and culture of an institution. Orientation programming "must be intentional and coherent; guided by theories and knowledge of learning and development; reflective of developmental and demographic profiles of the student population; and responsive to needs of individuals, special populations, and communities" (Council for the Advancement of Standards, 2009, p. 324). An environmental scan is recommended and should include a review of campus mission, vision, and value statements; recent and current accreditation reports;

campus strategic planning information and goals; campus policies and procedures; and current assessment data at the institutional, program, and student levels. This information should present a picture of institutional and student needs, as well as campus culture. It should provide a clear vision for what orientation programs can do to sustain campus strengths, address areas of challenge, advance institutional goals, clarify and communicate policies and procedures, provide an accurate portrayal of institutional norms and cultural cues, preempt student concerns and historic risks, and forge a path for both student success and institutional advancement. One element of this process is to be honest in the evaluation of institutional strengths and weaknesses, as well as the assessment of the student profile. Too often educators are distracted by a romanticized notion of the institution as it "used to be" or the students they wished they had rather than the current reality.

After this initial step, orientation leaders should carefully identify student learning outcomes for their programs. These outcomes provide guideposts for program development, service delivery, and the collection of data to illustrate program effectiveness and impact. Again, the Council for the Advancement of Standards (2009) provides guidance by suggesting a list of domains for orientation learning outcomes, including "knowledge acquisition, cognitive complexity, intrapersonal development, interpersonal competence, humanitarianism and civic engagement, and practical competence" (p. 324). These guidelines also provide a description of student success for each of these outcomes, which may be used as a rubric for learning outcome assessment. Selection of student learning outcomes for orientation must capitalize on connections of the program to the institutional mission and to student needs and must be linked to a process by which student progress toward the outcomes is captured. Therefore, it is prudent for orientation programs to focus on fewer learning outcomes—fewer than ten is advisable—that are measurable and intimately connected to the campus, orientation program, and the students.

Once an institutional scan is completed and student learning outcomes established, campus personnel in orientation must address decisions to be made with respect to program development and delivery. The question of "Which populations do we serve in orientation?" is a significant area of consideration for program organization and implementation. The population of entering college students has become more diverse with respect to age, race/ethnicity, national origin, religion, native language, and family background and includes a greater proportion of women and students who are transfers, low-income, first-generation, disabled, and nontraditional (Crissman Ishler, 2005; Knox & Henderson, 2010; Wilson & Dannells, 2010). In response, orientation programming has become more specialized and targeted in its content and delivery to meet the needs of such a wide variety of entering college students. Some examples of specialized programming include orientation sessions for transfers, commuters on a predominantly residential campus, international students, and veterans. Beyond the growing diversity of students is a trend toward including advocates and support agents for new students in the orientation process, most notably parents and other family members. It therefore becomes important to identify the target populations of orientation efforts and whether the needs of these populations will be addressed within a single orientation model or various specialized programs in order to provide effective adjustment experiences for all students.

The selection of program components for orientation also requires consideration. While orientation primarily focuses on students' introduction and integration to the campus, this process is multifaceted and needs to address a range of logistical, personal, academic, interpersonal, and developmental issues. According to Mullendore and Banahan (2005) and Mann et al. (2010), these issues fall into four typical categories:

- *Safety and well-being*, which consists of health, physical and emotional security, self-esteem, a safe and comfortable residence, and a community of respect.
- *Academic activities*, which include an introduction to academic structures and requirements, registration, advising, academic assistance resources, the library, classroom procedures and etiquette, and interactions with faculty.

- *Cocurricular activities*, such as social events, introduction to student organizations and leadership opportunities, and networking opportunities
- *Student services* available to new students such as residential life and housing, career services, counseling, health centers, parking and commuter resources, campus safety, wellness programs, and multicultural affairs.

Such a wide range of issues and topics can be overwhelming to organize and address within the duration and context of orientation programs. The use of student development theory can assist in the organization and application of orientation program components. Commonly used examples include Sanford's balance of support and challenge; Chickering's theory of identity development; Schlossberg, Waters, and Goodman's theory of transition; Maslow's theory of motivation; and Tinto's theory of retention (Mann et al., 2010; Pascarella & Terenzini, 2005; Rode & Cawthon, 2010; Tinto, 1993). Any one or a combination of these student development theories can provide an effective way to make difficult decisions about which topics to include, how to organize them, and what represents a meaningful outcome of the orientation experience in these areas.

Leadership Roles/Communication

Although the orientation process is one with widespread institutional investment, it should have specific leadership. In other words, orientation may involve many colleagues but ultimately must be owned by an individual or office. In fact, without the identification and wide acknowledgment of such leadership for orientation programs, the inclusion, integration, and coordination of multiple partners is likely to falter. Thus, it is not surprising that the majority of orientation programs have a dedicated office to oversee and administer these programs. However, where this office falls within the institution's organizational structure varies by institutional size, control, funding models, and missions. Common locations for orientation programs include student affairs, academic affairs, admissions and enrollment management, dean of students offices, student development, and advising (Mann et al.,

2010; Mullendore & Banahan, 2005). National data indicate that nearly three-quarters of orientation programs are located within student affairs, and oversight by academic affairs and enrollment management is present at only about 10 percent of institutions (Mann et al., 2010).

Leadership by professional staff is the norm in orientation programs. Data from the National Orientation Directors Association Databank indicate that over 60 percent of respondents have a director-level position overseeing orientation programs (Mann et al., 2010). The Council for the Advancement of Standards states that the qualifications for this person must include "an earned graduate degree in a field relevant to the position they hold" or that he or she "must possess an appropriate combination of educational credentials and related work experience" (2009, p. 326). Other useful competencies for this position are excellent written and oral communication skills, ability to work with diverse individuals and collaborate across multiple stakeholders, strong organization skills and attention to detail, supervisory and management skills, and experience with budgetary and financial oversight. Given the wide range of professional expertise necessary for the position, it is recommended that the orientation director be an experienced professional (Mann et al., 2010).

The leadership of the orientation effort on any campus must develop, implement, and maintain a complex communication plan. These efforts should include a current, accessible, and informative website for prospective and current participants, various print materials to serve outreach and informational purposes, a host of integrated and comprehensive educational materials to distribute during orientation activities, and the dissemination of program updates and outcomes to campus stakeholders. Many directors form an advisory committee to facilitate communication with the campus community about orientation programming as well as to inform strategic decisions. Orientation draws on a number of campus and external constituencies, which need coordination and communication. Inclusion of individuals from these groups on an advisory committee provides a channel for communication, a steady pool of resources for idea generation, an accountability measure, and a feedback loop for evaluation.

Resource Needs/Personnel

Orientation staff members typically fall into three categories: professional, support, and student. Orientation staff can take on a range of titles, including associate or assistant director, coordinator, full-time assistant, orientation leader, team captains, and orientation interns (Ganser & Kennedy, 2012; Mann et al., 2010). Much like the position of director, individuals in a professional position must have appropriate academic credentials, as well as experience and training commensurate with their role in the program.

Student paraprofessionals, including in supervisory roles, are common and critical staff members for effective delivery of orientation programs. Undergraduate students are often used in the role of peer leaders and typically oversee the experience of a small group of students within the overall orientation session. Their duties include facilitating new students' navigation through the content of the session; providing an introduction to the physical structure and resources on campus; and offering individual mentorship, counseling, and support to new students. Orientation leaders also provide a model of student success in the campus community and can articulate and illustrate institutional expectations of students (Ganser & Kennedy, 2012). Peer leaders are a valuable resource to a successful orientation program because they relate to students as both an expert and a peer, thereby serving as a more accessible authority figure to new students (Mann et al., 2010). Thus, the recruitment of orientation leaders should strive to capture a diverse group that is representative of the population of incoming students and can relate to them. They must receive comprehensive training, ongoing supervision, and clear expectations for their positions, particularly with respect to their authority among peers (Council for the Advancement of Standards, 2009; Ganser & Kennedy, 2012).

Support staff are another valuable member of the orientation team. While professional staff plan and oversee the orientation program and student staff members are instrumental in its delivery, support staff members are typically the first point of contact for new students and their families. Their role as customer service agents sets the tone for the program and is an introduction to the ongoing relationship that the student and his or her family will have with the institution. Their role is so critical that the Council for the Advancement of Standards (2009) guidelines state that orientation programs "must have technical and support staff members adequate to accomplish its mission" (p. 326). These staff members should "be technologically proficient and qualified to perform their job functions, be knowledgeable of ethical and legal uses of technology, and have access to training," as well as have reasonable workloads, adequate training, ongoing feedback from supervisors, and a plan for professional development (p. 326).

Certainly one of the greatest resource investments of effective orientation programs is in the remuneration and benefits for professional, student, and support personnel. Additional costs may include recruitment, initial training, and ongoing professional development support of these staff members. While such expenses are an issue for all staff members, the reliance of new student orientation on a large pool of student personnel that must be replenished each year makes recruitment, training, and support a substantial and recurring line item in any budget. Ongoing professional development opportunities for professional and support staff are another substantial investment, but one that is likely to pay dividends in the development and maintenance of a relevant program that serves the needs of a diverse student body with efficient use of the most current tactics and technologies. Finally, when accounting for the costs associated with personnel, it is also important to consider the small but significant expenses that are invested in an advisory board, campus partners, or other external agents that support the program. These expenses may include conference call costs, facilities and support for in-person meetings, parking for outside visitors, and small tokens of appreciation for the service of this group.

In addition to funding for staff, an orientation program budget must include items related to operating expenses and facilities. If a program has an office on campus, the costs of running such an office should include recurring expenses for facilities; utilities; supplies; furniture; and information technology hardware, setup, and maintenance. If there is no central office for orientation programs, the cost to outsource typical office operations is a critical variable in the budgetary equation. Orientation programs tend to use many facilities on campus in their delivery, such that facility rental and use fees must be a factor in funding models for the program. Also, program supplies, marketing materials, and the development and maintenance of online and technical components of orientation are common resource elements (Mann et al., 2010). Ultimately funding priorities must relate to the institutional mission, student needs, and orientation program goals, as well as exist within fiscally responsible resource parameters.

Financial resources for orientation programs may be generated in a variety of ways. The guidelines set forth by the Council for the Advancement of Standards (2006) identify "institutional funding, . . . state appropriations, student fees, user fees, donations, contributions, concession and store sales, rentals, and dues" as possible funding streams to support orientation programs (p. 328). Some costs of orientation programming, such as room and board, can be passed directly to the program participants, although financial assistance should be a program priority for low-income students who are unable to afford the cost. Finally, since orientation has such a wide base of support and benefit for units across campus, resource and budgetary sharing with one or many of the critical partners may be an option.

Assessment

Given the substantial investment of human and fiscal resources, orientation program staff must prove that the "flurry of activity designed to help students make a successful transition to college" in fact, meets its goal (Crissman Ishler & Upcraft, 2001, p. 262). High-quality assessment and evaluation activities are the primary vehicle to make the case for program effectiveness.

The reasons for assessing orientation programs are similar to those for any campus initiative and "can be summarized into the following categories: (a) habit, (b) requirement/expectations, (c) conformity, (d) politics, (e) accreditation, (f) planning, and (g) improvement and development" (Schuh & Upcraft, 2001, summarized in Schwartz & Wiese, 2010, p. 218). The standards of good practice for assessment of orientation programs are identical to those for all other campus initiatives

(Crissman Ishler & Upcraft, 2001; Schwartz & Wiese, 2010; Upcraft, Crissman Ishler, & Swing, 2005):

- The use of appropriate quantitative, qualitative, and mixed-methodology approaches
- A strong connection between assessment activities and student learning outcomes
- Inclusion of all constituencies involved in the program
- Use of both direct and indirect measures
- Selection or development of psychometrically sound instruments
- Wide dissemination of findings
- Use of assessment results for program improvement

And yet there are specific assessment issues to consider with respect to new student orientation programs (Council for the Advancement of Standards, 2009). First and foremost, assessment of new student orientation must address the stated learning objectives and program outcomes. National data reveal a list of common orientation outcomes that are in alignment with the mission and purposes of these programs: more knowledge about the institution, facilities, and services; building connections with students, faculty, and staff; celebrating and commemorating the arrival of new students; completion of testing, registration, and advising; and improved retention rates (Barefoot et al., 2012). Crissman Ishler and Upcraft (2001) highlight the importance of these outcomes when they state that "ultimately, the worth of an orientation program must be measured by whether the orientation efforts resulted in students making a successful transition to college, doing well academically, . . . and persisting to graduation" (p. 263). Given the nature of some of these outcomes, orientation professionals should incorporate both short-term and long-term time lines for their assessment plans. Orientation programs may yield immediate results in students' preparation to achieve these goals, but it will likely take months and years to determine the effectiveness of programs on outcomes such as academic achievement, adjustment, development, and retention.

Another common outcome of orientation efforts is satisfaction with the program itself, an important measure in a comprehensive assessment plan for orientation and among the easiest outcomes on which to gather data. Over 60 percent of institutions participating in the National Survey of Efforts to Improve Undergraduate Student Success and Retention administered by the Gardner Institute for Excellence in Undergraduate Education indicated that satisfaction with the program itself was a key outcome of interest (Barefoot et al., 2012). Although it would be inappropriate to rely solely on satisfaction to determine program effectiveness, data collected on this measure help determine the relevance of the program to student needs. As the primary consumers of the program, what new students say is done well and their perceptions of areas of weakness provide valuable information to guide program improvement.

Because orientation is one of the first points of contact with new students, it provides a key moment to collect data on the background, needs, expectations, and initial perceptions of entering students (Crissman Ishler & Upcraft, 2001). This can be done on an individual basis to determine student needs or on a collective level to assess issues of campus climate (Crissman Ishler & Upcraft, 2001; Upcraft, 2005). While admissions and registrar data are useful sources of this information, orientation assessment provides another opportunity to collect more nuanced data on the newest cohort of students. These data are useful in program planning; evaluation of students' perceptions of the campus climate as welcoming, safe, and inclusive; and understanding and illustrating institutional responsiveness. They are also important baseline data for longitudinal assessment of curricular and cocurricular initiatives offered later in the first year and throughout the undergraduate experience (Upcraft et al., 2005). Thus, orientation is not only an assessment end point, as is the case for orientation outcomes and student satisfaction; it also represents the starting point for long-range assessment of the first-year experience at large.

The current era of assessment and accountability in higher education has led to the proliferation of national survey instruments; services, resources, and tools for the development and administration of local surveys; enhanced data analysis software; and numerous print resources on assessment and evaluation. Although not all of these tools are specific to orientation, many are easily adapted to orientation activities. Standardized national assessment tools provide national or interinstitutional comparisons. Conversely, locally developed instruments allow the leadership of orientation programs to address programmatic elements and student experiences that are unique to their institution. Finally, qualitative approaches such as "focus groups, small-group discussions, and other similar methods can be used to obtain" information about the experience in and impact of orientation programs (Robinson, Burns, & Gaw, 1996, p. 65).

Benefit Analysis

Orientation programs require a healthy investment of time, staff, and financial resources. Beneath the basic issues of resource allocation and expenditures is a larger notion of value and return on investment for the funds dedicated to new student orientation. While this is particularly crucial in lean economic times, fiscal responsibility and cost-effectiveness is a standard of practice regardless of the state of the economy.

Ultimately the effectiveness of a program is measured by its ability to achieve its goals and meet the learning objectives identified for orientation, notably through assessment findings. However, "in order to make the case that the cost of orientation is warranted and, further, that the cost to produce a quality program is imperative" (Jacobs, 2010, p. 30), many orientation directors must draw some common arguments. First, it is important to note the role of orientation in the effective and efficient communication of accurate and broad-scale information on campus programs, services, and resources that help students adapt to the campus environment academically, personally, and socially. Orientation also serves as a vehicle to reduce costly errors for both students and the institution by helping avoid "missing deadlines, registering for unnecessary classes, and demonstrating poor academic performance," which can increase persistence and graduation rates (Jacobs, 2010, p. 31). It also communicates institutional expectations of successful college students, identifies appropriate strategies, and influences early habits that ultimately lead to higher student performance, satisfaction, and retention among students. Finally, orientation programming is crucial in building connections among and across campus units and minimizing redundancy among new student success programming. Jacobs (2010) goes on to identify levers of influence in making the case for orientation, including "staying abreast of changes in the [orientation] field and the institution, knowing the students admitted to the institution, creating a sense of urgency, being aware of competing interests, building allies, and assessing the program" (p. 34).

The body of scholarship on orientation programs provides substantial evidence for their impact and support for their return on investment. Many research studies on orientation use first-year grade point average, persistence to the second year, and graduation rates as metrics of success, and most show positive effects on these outcomes among students who participate in orientation activities (Busby, Gammel, & Jeffcoat, 2002; Erikson, 1998; Fabich, 2004). Other studies indicate that students who engage in orientation programs show higher rates of academic and social integration (Nadler, Miller, & Dyer, 2004; Robinson, Burns, & Gaw, 1996), which contributes to the positive outcomes of higher grades and greater retention rates (Fox, Zakely, Morris, & Jundt, 1993; Pascarella, Terenzini, & Wolfe, 1986; Zakely, 2003). Orientation experiences typically are associated with greater involvement in the campus community during the first year (Gentry, Kuhnert, Johnson, & Cox, 2006; Prola, Rosenburg, & Wright, 1977), declaration of major (Donnelly & Borland, 2002), and positive feelings about the college (Nadler et al., 2004; Stripling & Hinck, 1993). Overall, the positive impact of orientation remained robust regardless of institutional features, student populations, and programmatic structures.

Institutional Practices

Purdue University

Purdue University is a large, selective, public research university that serves over forty thousand students on its main campus in West Lafayette, Indiana. It currently has one of the largest orientation programs in the country, named Boiler Gold Rush for the university mascot, the Boilermakers, and founded in 1993. It serves over five thousand new students each year and is housed in the nationally renowned Student Success at Purdue office at the university. The mission of this program is to "instill excitement in being a

Purdue student through an engaging and enriching environment that provides opportunities to partake in meaningful activities, traditions, leadership development and conversations with students of various backgrounds and experiences" (Jones, 2011, p. 1).

Boiler Gold Rush (BGR) is a six-day program that is held on Purdue's campus the week before classes begin. Students move into the residence halls two days prior to orientation; those who commute and live off-campus are also encouraged to participate in BGR. Orientation activities include an introduction to academic success strategies, interaction with faculty and staff in new students' respective majors, campus tours, social events, and learning about campus culture and traditions. Activities are guided by three sets of goals for the program: learning-oriented goals, program and service goals, and developmental goals.

Boiler Gold Rush relies heavily on a large number of student paraprofessionals who serve as orientation leaders and orientation supervisors. Over 450 undergraduate staff members contribute to the program. The experience of orientation leaders is so embedded in BGR that there are established learning outcomes for these students as well as the new students they serve. For example, as a result of being a BGR student leader, students will develop communication, facilitation, and organization skills; develop an understanding of academic resources and support structures on campus; and gain an appreciation for diversity. Their service as orientation leaders often leads to engagement in other peer leadership positions on campus such as through supplemental instruction, campus activities, executive board positions in student organizations, and student mentor roles for early outreach programs offered through the Student Success at Purdue office.

A strong program of assessment is woven throughout the BGR process and informs its continuous improvement. First, program participation is tracked, and student enrollment, retention, and graduation rates are analyzed based on BGR participation. Second, students are asked to rate their satisfaction with the program, as well as engage in reflections on their experience in orientation activities. Third, special attention is given to the experiences of international students who are asked to participate in focus groups about BGR. Results of these assessment activities show that students who participated in BGR have significantly higher retention rates than students who did not participate, especially among women and underrepresented minorities. Furthermore, students who went through orientation at Purdue tend to graduate at a higher rate than their nonparticipating peers.

Tallahassee Community College

A public, two-year college located in Tallahassee, Florida, Tallahassee Community College (TCC) enrolls over thirty-eight thousand students, although only about twenty thousand of them are earning credits toward a degree. The institution is committed to promoting "the intellectual, social, and personal development of students; to assist students in developing the ability to think critically, creatively and reflectively" and preparing students for university transfer, to meet economic and workforce needs, and to "live productive and satisfying lives" (Tallahassee Community College, n.d.). To begin their educational journey toward these goals, all new TCC students are required to participate in orientation.

While TCC has engaged new students in some orientation activities for many years, a departmental reorganization allowed the institution to hire its first full-time orientation director in 2009. With a reporting line up through enrollment services and student success, which falls under student affairs, the director engages the assistance of twenty academic advisors and twelve to fourteen student paraprofessionals to serve approximately ten thousand new students who enter the institution in the fall, spring, and summer terms. New students are required to complete an online component that provides a general introduction to policies, procedures, and student services. After successful completion of this web-based orientation module and an online assessment of their learning, students must enroll in one of several day-long on-campus orientation sessions, which are offered in the months prior to the term when they will enroll as a first-time, first-year student or new transfer student.

The agenda for the on-campus orientation activities includes a campus tour, presentations about campus resources, course registration, completion of an individual learning plan, and information about living in Tallahassee. The core of the on-campus orientation experience is a group appointment with an academic advisor. Advising groups are determined by performance on academic placement exams, which allows students with similar concerns, questions, and academic pathways to meet with an advisor together, thereby introducing administrative efficiency and leveraging peer group support. After orientation, new students can schedule follow-up appointments with the advisor as well as revisit the online orientation information to help address any additional or emergent issues in their transition to TCC.

Assessment activities at TCC have found a direct link between participation in orientation and several key student outcomes. First, 98 percent of students who attend orientation activities transition to paid enrollment at the institution and remain enrolled in classes for the first semester. Seventy percent of these students are retained to the second semester of the first year, and 65 percent persist to the second year of college. While these are promising metrics for matriculation and retention, orientation staff members at TCC also evaluate other aspects of new student transition and success. For instance, assessment results indicate that over 90 percent of students who participate in orientation were able to articulate one personal and one career goal, which helped them narrow their field of study, select their major, and be thoughtful in their course selection process, all of which contribute to students' adjustment and success at the institution. TCC students who completed orientation also have a clearer idea of the institution's expectations of them and can navigate these expectations more successfully toward year-to-year persistence and, ultimately, degree completion and transfer.

Metropolitan State University

Metropolitan State University, a public four-year institution, was founded in the Twin Cities area of Minnesota in 1971 as a "university without walls" that held classes at facilities throughout Minneapolis and St. Paul. The institution has grown to serve eleven thousand students, many from historically underrepresented and underserved student populations such as transfers, minority students, adult learners, and nontraditional students. Since its founding, Metropolitan State University has established four campuses and maintains a robust online education program.

The university's orientation program reports to enrollment management and is designed to be consistent with its commitment to access and excellence and to achieve its mission to provide "innovative student-centered programs that enable students from diverse backgrounds to achieve their educational goals" (Metropolitan State University, 2011). The bulk of new student orientation is offered in an online format. Academic planning is a major component of the program. The format allows students to indicate their major or program of study, take advantage of interactive explanations for some majors, and engage in additional advising tools to help students plan their program. The majority of the online orientation content is organized into seven web-based modules that address welcome, program planning, learning resources, student rights and responsibilities, success strategies, library information, and registration. At the completion of each module, students are administered a quiz on the information that they learned. The extensive quiz tool in the Desire to Learn (D2L) system automates the grading process, and a code is entered into the student's academic record indicating she or he successfully passed the quiz. Orientation and student support staff members send an e-mail to the students congratulating them on successfully completing orientation, outlining the next steps for getting registered, and providing their advisor's contact information. A three-hour on-campus orientation is offered as a complement to the online modules and is required for all first-year students, students on probation, and students in a bridge scholars program, the Power of YOU.

In order to gather formative and summative information on their online orientation, Metropolitan State University hired an outside agency to conduct an assessment of the program. Responses to an online survey showed that over 80 percent of students were satisfied or extremely satisfied with the online orientation experience. These same data indicated that students found the orientation information on student services, university policies, and campus procedures particularly helpful. Data collected in the online survey also showed that 82 percent of the students who completed orientation contacted their advisor at least once after that, a practice that is positively related to student transition and success. Finally, the results of this survey also have been used to identify areas for refinement in the program, which have been implemented and are being considered for future cohorts of new students.

The online component of Metropolitan State University's new student orientation has received national attention and accolades. It was the recipient of the 2007 Advising Technology Innovation Award, which is given by the National Academic Advising Association for recognition of the most creative and unique uses of technology in support of academic advising and support. It also was acknowledged with a Center for Transforming Student Services Best Practice Award in 2006, which is awarded to a program for creative use of tools, strategies, and ideas to design, implement, and maintain innovative online student services toward positive and measurable outcomes.

Chapter Four

| Advising

Advising stands at the heart of the educational process: it provides services to all students and plays an important role in almost all first-year success initiatives (Tinto, 1998). Habley (1994) suggests the uniqueness of advising in that it is "the only structured activity on the campus in which all students have the opportunity for ongoing, one-to-one interaction with a concerned representative of the institution" (p. 10), a point that Drake (2011) affirms. These interactions are especially relevant to first-year students as they adjust to a new educational environment. For many students, especially those in their first year, advisors are the face of the university (King & Kerr, 2005). Respondents to an ACT survey of retention programs identified advising as a critical component in first-year student success (Habley, 1994), a finding reconfirmed by the 2010 ACT survey (Habley, McClanahan, Valiga, & Burkum, 2010).

A seminal work by O'Banion (1972) identified five "dimensions" of academic advising: "exploration of life goals; exploration of vocational goals; program choice; course choice; and scheduling classes" (p. 62). The Council for the Advancement of Standards in Higher Education (2005) affirms that the primary purpose of academic advising programs is to assist students in the development of meaningful educational plans, which include "relevant and desirable student learning and development outcomes" across multiple domains, such as critical thinking, and "understanding and appreciation of cultural and human differences" (p. 4). With its broad student-centered focus, good advising has a positive impact on student success and retention (Allen & Smith, 2008). Habley (2005) noted that despite the Council for the Advancement of

Standards in Higher Education statement, advising mission statements often lack clarity and evidence confusion with regard to terminology. In terms of process, he suggested the importance of fit between institutional mission and the advising mission, the need to engage multiple constituencies, and using assessment to inform mission revisions. He also emphasized that mission should inform decision making.

Writing in 1990, Boyer noted the teaching-learning dimension of advising. That applies to advisors themselves as well as to the students with whom they interact (Campbell & Nutt, 2008), and best practice emphasizes student learning (Grites & Gordon, 2000; Hemwall & Trachte, 2005; Appleby, 2008). The National Academic Advising Association identifies learning outcomes as an integral aspect of academic advising and suggests they should enable students to

> craft a coherent educational plan based on assessment of abilities, aspirations, interests, and values; use complex information from various sources to set goals, reach decisions, and achieve those goals; assume responsibility for meeting academic program requirements, articulate the meaning of higher education and the intent of the institution's curriculum; cultivate the intellectual habits that lead to a lifetime of learning; [and] behave as citizens who engage in the wider world around them. (NACADA, 2012)

There are four major models of advising approaches: prescriptive, developmental, intrusive, and appreciative. Additional iterations, such as integrative advising and strengths-based advising, combine elements from two or more models (Church, 2005). In prescriptive advising, once the dominant mode, the advisor-student relationship harkens to that between a knowledgeable master and new apprentice. Advisors know what students need to learn. They explain university regulations and requirements, including the general education program, major declarations, and number of credits needed to progress toward a degree in a timely fashion. The prescriptive approach's similarity to high school advising makes it familiar to entering students and may facilitate their initial transition to college (Brown & Rivas, 1994). It remains a common approach in advising for underperforming first-year students and those on probation.

The developmental model "focuses on the needs of the student" as the critical factor structuring the relationship between student and advisor (Hagen & Jordan, 2008, p. 20) and is foundational for both intrusive and appreciative advising. Crookston (1994) remarks on the interdependence of the personal and academic dimensions in successful advising. From a developmental perspective, the teaching-learning relationship embedded in a holistic approach helps students clarify goals and develop the skills they need to achieve them. The Developmental Advising Inventory, a survey instrument, enables self-assessment by students along multiple dimensions, such as intellectual, emotional, spiritual, and social (Dickson & McMahon, 1989). In this student-centered perspective, the advisor functions as a facilitator-teacher who helps students clarify their goals (Burton & Wellington, 1998).

The intrusive approach (also referred to as intentional or proactive advising) often is used with students who are at risk of failure or on probation and combines elements of both prescriptive and developmental advising; it rests on establishing a strong relationship with students, which can create additional incentives for them to succeed (Molina & Abelman, 2000). Its effectiveness depends on a delicate balance in which advisors facilitate students' recognition of the factors that caused their poor academic performance, including those for which students are largely responsible, but also focuses on actions students can take and the services available to support their efforts to be successful (Gehrke & Wong, 2007). Smith (2007) suggests that collaborative intrusive advising that involves advisors and faculty has the potential to increase retention, and Austin, Cherney, Crowner, and Hill (1997) discuss the use of intrusive advising with groups. The origins of appreciative advising date to 1987 in the work of Cooperrider and Srivasta that launched the theory of appreciative inquiry (AI). As AI developed, it identified a multistage process—"disarm, discover, dream, design, deliver, don't settle"—that begins with a focus on relationship building. AI initially became an important perspective for organizational development and, subsequently, for advising, and it has particular relevance for entering student populations identified as at risk. Bloom and Martin (2002) note that one of AI's founding principles is that people generally "respond more favorably to people who are optimistic thinkers and who help us create positive images of our futures, rather than to people who are negative and disapproving of our plans" (n.p.). Advisors try to create a positive initial interaction that will enable students to move beyond various negative feelings toward themselves and the institution, which facilitates productive conversations about their desired future and ways to get there, including the relevance of different majors.

The appreciative approach, then, stresses the importance of fostering "a deeper personal relationship between advisors and students through an emphasis on the intrinsic, ontological value of each student encountered" (Bloom, Hutson, & He, 2008, p. 7). Another approach, strengths-based advising, is a concept that arose from psychology and has been applied to the business world. It suggests that the tendency to focus on and remediate weaknesses has less power than one that identifies strengths and then works to develop them (Buckingham, & Clifton, 2001; Clifton & Anderson, 2002). Incorporating this perspective into academic advising is especially effective with first-year students and those having difficulty experiencing academic success (Schreiner, 2005). Student development theory suggests the importance of assisting students to discover and define their core beliefs, thereby raising their sense of self-authorship (Baxter-Magolda, 2004).

Advising once was exclusively a faculty responsibility, and it was common for entering students to already have identified a specific major and career objective. Attempts to ameliorate societal issues, especially inequalities related to racial, religious, gender, and ethnic identities, resulted in the influx of new student populations, the majority of whom came from families with little or no experience with higher education.

One response to the perceived needs of these new cohorts was the professionalization of various student support services, including advising (Kuh, 2008; Cohen & Kisker, 2010; Rouse, 2011). Advising then became a shared function in which professional advisors played the major role with first-year and undecided students and faculty assumed responsibility when students declared a major. Programs in music, theater, and fine arts often require auditions or portfolios for admission, and it is common for staff or faculty in those departments to advise students. Advisors also became part of the staff of professional programs, for example, in business and the health sciences.

The faculty role in advising undeclared students has continued to change, in part because of a recognition of the link between positive student-faculty relations and student success and retention (Glennan, 2003). In addition to providing academic advice, faculty can contribute to student development (Baker & Griffin, 2010) and how students approach learning (Cruce, Wolniak, Seifert, & Pascarella, 2006). Sacred Heart University's Freshman Advising Program emphasizes the student-faculty relationship. Faculty advisors teach at least one of the courses taken by the students, thereby facilitating multiple opportunities for interactions and conversations about academics. Through these interactions, they become the "go-to" people for students' academic concerns. Faculty at SUNY-Oswego also engage in first-year advising. Incoming students receive an advisement mission statement that stresses the importance of developing a relationship with their advisor, not only for course selection but also to enable them to "clarify goals for career and life; utilize his or her personal strengths and the strengths of the college; [and] explore career options, educational opportunities, and resources" (SUNY-Oswego, 2010).

Peer advising has become an important and growing initiative at many institutions (Habley, 2004). Koring and Campbell (2005) identified six roles for peer advisors:

> Help new students transition to and through the institution or a specific school or department within the institution by offering a friendly peer contact; help advisees master basic academic processes such as scheduling classes or declaring majors; teach and reinforce student skills for success, such as time management or study skills, either in individual conferences or in workshops and group advising sessions; act as referral sources for their advisees; enrich faculty or staff advising by offering a different but complementary point of view from faculty or staff advisors' perspectives and by providing advising at alternative times (evening or weekend) and in alternative venues (residence halls or student center lounge areas); and are role models for successful students. (p. 11)

Students serving as peer mentors also benefit from their participation, as do the faculty and staff with whom they work (Koring &

Campbell, 2005). A peer advisor at Madison's Edgewood College reflected that she "spent almost two years learning everything from meeting with students, to communicating effectively with faculty, to developing a strong professional base" and concluded that "overall I think it has made me a much better advisor, student, and member of the college community" (Rothberger & Zabel, 2012).

The increasingly complex world of advising suggests the importance of professional activities for faculty advisors to develop expertise and the ability to support student success (Kramer, 2003). Nutt (2003) recommended that institutions consider creating in-house programs that reflect the nature of their student population and advising model. Given the variations among institutions in terms of missions, student populations, and the range of majors and programs, an institution may decide to customize one of the major advising models to meet its needs. Regardless of the specific advising home, effective communication and collaboration among advisors, student and academic support services professionals, and faculty who work with first-year students play a powerful role in the effectiveness of any advising model. The Bloomington Advisor's Council at Indiana University brings together advisors, counselors, faculty, administrators, and other members of the university community who share an interest in advising. The group sponsors a professional development series that runs throughout the academic year. Fall and spring conferences take place at the beginning of those semesters, and the program also includes five workshops. Academic advisors who participate in at least four of the year's programs receive a certificate, and the council notifies their immediate supervisors.

Approaching the Work/Critical Partners

The Council for the Advancement of Standards in Higher Education affirms the importance of an ongoing institutional review of the mission, objectives, and outcomes of academic advising programs, but Habley (2005) cautions that lack of clarity and direction often exists with regard to implementation. Kuh, Kinzie, Buckley, and Associates (2009) suggested that advising becomes more effective when it is integrated with academic support and is "sensitive to the developmental needs of diverse students" (p. 59). Advising networks, one of the practices that contributed to the success of Developing Effective Educational Practices institutions, brought together "the combined resources of professional advisors, faculty members, peers, and others" (Kuh, Kinzie, Schuh, Whitt, and Associates, 2005, p. 246). The collaborative approach becomes especially challenging and important at complex universities that use a highly distributed advising model. For example, at East Carolina University, ten advising centers support different programs, but an advising collaborative co-locates all their services.

Developing a formal mission, including specific outcomes, can be an important step in revising an existing advising system to enhance its work with first-year students and should also facilitate ongoing assessment of both process and outcomes. Habley (2005) points to advising's tendency to "focus on the *what* and the *how* of advising" and remarked that while these are important considerations, they often are seen as a central part of a mission statement rather than as a result of and support for the mission statement (n.p.). Developing a specific mission or set of goals for first-year advising can provide an opportunity to focus on the needs specific to that general population and its major cohorts. In addition to a general mission statement, Ithaca College lists specific goals for first-year students, including ones related to transitions, major selection, and "encouraging reflection on their intellectual challenges" (Ithaca College, 2012). Mission and goals provide the basis for collaborative discussions on student success, while also facilitating both assessment and professional development. Advisors typically play multiple roles (Petress, 1996), and in the absence of a specific guiding mission and specific goals and objectives, advisors may independently define their roles, priorities, and approaches. When that occurs, an ostensibly centralized advising system becomes fragmented.

Drafting a mission and structure for a new model for first-year advising might form part the responsibilities of an advising task force. The task force's membership should reflect those campus areas whose participation would evidence and promote the development or enhancement of a collaborative system. Messia (2010) notes a three-category typology of stakeholders identified by

Harney (2008): "internal core stakeholders, internal but indirect stakeholders, and external and indirect stakeholders" (n.p.). Faculty, staff advisors, students, and administrators formed the core group. The internal but indirect category included the registrar, enrollment management, and the offices of student affairs and academic affairs. Citing Varney (2008), Messia (2010) identified external stakeholders as those who might "influence the institution"; among others, they included "parents, alumni, employers, and accrediting bodies" (n.p.). Business management theorists have produced more complex stakeholder models that identify additional constituencies (Freeman & Evan, 1990; Freeman & McVea, 2001).

The advising task force should begin its work by posing questions, doing research, and then designing a new approach (Smith & Troxel, 2008). It might review and discuss stakeholder concepts and the existing system, including its structure, programs, working relationships, funding, personnel, and assessment data. Miller (2011), using the phrase *four-dimensional models*, suggests the utility of four critical questions: "who is advised; who advises; where is advising done; [and] how advising responsibilities are divided" (p. 4). Within that schema, the task force could focus on the institution's existing practices for advising first-year students and its capacity to provide the ongoing contact and communication needed to build relationships with first-year students and foster a sense of connectedness to the university. It might also review its current partners and their roles, the extent to which classroom instructors participate in advising first-year students, and whether their participation is part of an overall advising plan. Additional concerns might include assessment practices and results and campus satisfaction with the system. A focus on these multiple issues will likely raise awareness of the importance and complexities of first-year advising and help to identify campus stakeholders who should be part of efforts to alter the existing system. This review also could identify other offices that might help develop and support the revised campus program, which also should stimulate broader campus interest in advising.

Given this initiative's central purpose, conversations with students become important, especially with those who have been retained and are in leadership positions. Their stories and reflections will likely add new perspectives to the discussion by grounding it more fully in the student experience. At the same time, data on students who were not retained are vital as well, particularly to understand how they experienced the college and why they decided to leave. At a minimum, representation from all offices and individuals who participate in advising, including faculty, should be encouraged. Looking for exemplary programs at other campuses, particularly peer or aspirational institutions, should help identify organizational models that are potentially good fits. Those models may also suggest additional individuals and offices whose inclusion would enhance the initiative. The National Academic Advising Center website (www.nacada .ksu.edu/) is a good place to begin.

Organization/Implementation Process

The advising task force's discussions of potential missions and outcomes should inform others in the institution of the wide range of organizational models and delivery systems for advising (Habely & Morales, 1998; King, 2003; Pardee, 2000). While many task force members are likely to participate in this next phase, adding new members, especially those who bring needed expertise such as strategic planning skills or are in an administrative role, will facilitate implementation. Since some professional advisors may view reform as a criticism of their work and have misgivings about ownership of their professional area, it becomes even more important to honor their knowledge and dedication to student success by making sure they are appropriately represented in this new group, which should be identified with a new name and given a specific date for producing a set of recommendations. Sustained communication with the campus community and attention to perceptions of change as having winners and losers should ease the transition to a revised advising approach. To emphasize the importance of their work, the new group, which might be named the advising implementation task force, should have a direct report to the relevant senior administrator, who might be in either academic or student affairs. Ideally, collaboration between student affairs and academic affairs will characterize the work of the new task force, and that might be honored by having a dual-report line.

Advising Models

As noted, advising models vary, often reflecting institutional history, mission, complexity, and the size and characteristics of the student population. In addition to various distributed models, common iterations include advising centers, advising and career centers, and advising and counseling centers. First-year advising may also be housed in a first-year center, student success center, or university college. At large, complex universities, advising may follow a distributive model in which all advising, including that of new students, is located within individual schools, colleges, and programs. Advising for specific programs, such as study abroad and community-based learning may also follow that model.

Since multiple models can prove successful, it becomes critical to identify one that fits an institution's culture, resource base, and the demographics of its first-year student population. In addition to the mission, goals, and outcomes identified by the earlier task force, the selection of a new model should be informed by internal strategic planning documents related to recruitment, retention, and resources, along with program reviews and accreditation reports. For example, an institution with little or no on-campus housing that plans to move more aggressively toward a residential model might want to integrate residence-based advising into its plans. Similarly, potential changes to entrance requirements, plans to develop new academic programs, or plans to target new student populations would factor into the choice of a program suited to meet the needs of students. Fiscal issues become especially critical in times of tight budgets, so the cost-effectiveness of a specific advising model will likely be a relevant consideration. Incorporating a peer advisor or peer mentor program should be considered, as students receiving that assistance view both of those positively (Mottarella, Fritzsche, & Cerabino, 2004).

Effective Implementation

At many institutions, an advising syllabus helps guide advisors' sessions with students. The syllabus communicates a variety of information, including the institutional advising mission or approach and expectations and anticipated outcomes for both students and advisors (Trabant, 2006). Advising handbooks outline institutional policies and procedures related to advising and serve as "the cornerstone of a well-developed and implemented academic advising program" (Ford, 2003, n.p.). The task force should review the current campus advising syllabus and handbook and identify potential revisions. Ford also provides valuable suggestions for developing or revising an advising handbook. The task force might also review handbooks from other institutions. For example, the provost's office at Tuskegee University issued the *Academic Advising Handbook for Undergraduates* that serves as the official policy guide for the entire university community. It discusses numerous topics, including mission, goals, objectives, and advising responsibilities. The data and conversations we have already noted should create a broader sense of the positive outcomes a revised system might produce for students, advisors, faculty, and the institution.

Habley (2005) suggests that lack of clarity and direction often exists with regard to implementation, but even with that concern addressed, the feasibility of any proposed change often becomes a critical issue. It is important to document how cognate models function at similar or aspirational institutions, including outcomes for both students and advisors. Those data might help address campus concerns regarding potential downsides of a new approach, including its fit with the institution and its students. Honoring the dedication and achievements of those already associated with advising and providing leadership opportunities for them in the new system should minimize negative talk and ownership concerns. While focusing on first-year students, it also makes sense to consider student transitions to the second year. A campus second-year experience program could add those perspectives to the discussions.

Since advising has multiple stakeholders, effective implementation requires broad campus support. This is especially important for staff and faculty who might see their roles or authority as adversely affected by the change. Faculty members often believe that their participation in advising is not valued by their colleagues (Dillon & Fisher, 2000). At many institutions, faculty advise only students who have declared a major in their discipline or indicated their intent to do so. Even then, they may focus only on the major and suggest that students consult with professional advisors for general graduation requirements. Tenure and promotion guidelines may focus mainly on teaching and research, and after that on general university service, and annual reviews used to determine salary raises and promotion may ask for little more than the number of advisees assigned to a faculty member.

Revising position descriptions to emphasize the importance of advising, particularly of first-year students, and including that in salary and tenure decisions could promote greater faculty engagement with entering students. In 2011, Beloit College revised expectations for faculty participation in advising and, among other things, suggested that they discuss what they have done to help students "connect with the mission, goals, programs, and resources of Beloit College" and to report on specific efforts they have made to assess both advising and mentoring (June, 2011). Campuses might also recognize and reward such activities as working with student organizations or becoming a member of a campus committee whose purview relates to advising. Faculty members might also experiment with a new advising practice, such as individual meetings to follow up on group advising (Sprague, 2008).

The task force's final report should provide an overview of the proposed approach to advising first-year students and examples from cognate institutions, including assessment data related to student success and satisfaction, supplemented by surveys of staff and faculty satisfaction. That report also should provide an implementation time line that indicates required approvals, space requirements, and personnel needs, including a dedicated director for the new program. Transition issues are important when implementing a new system, and these are likely to retain importance beyond the new model's initial year. A phased approach can ease those issues by serving as a pilot test, while reducing initial resource needs. For example, rather than beginning with all first-year students, the program could first focus on high-risk populations and add other cohorts as resources become available.

Leadership Roles /Communication

Given the variability of practices and models, it may be useful to conceptualize leadership and communication in terms of three phases: the process through which the model is selected and approved, its initial implementation, and its ongoing assessment and development. Consensus among senior administrators contributes to the probability of successfully establishing any innovation, and is especially important if the new model requires changes in the report line for first-year advising or in its relationships with other campus offices. For example, if first-year advising no longer will be housed in the campus advising center, the director of that center needs to endorse the change and work to ensure that the center's staff also understand and support it. Identifying all the critical constituents and meaningfully engaging them in the conversation should ease transition issues, and frequent updates and progress reports to all staff and faculty committees with an interest or stake in advising and student success will help to normalize the process and increase the initiative's transparency. Communication often becomes even more important once a new model is in place. An overall strategy for providing ongoing information to the campus community might include multiple forms of communication, such as e-mail, social media, a first-year advising newsletter, open houses, and presentations to relevant campus committees. This communication should promote general awareness of the program and convey a sense of transparency.

Communication among all those engaged in advising and teaching first-year students also is vital to the effectiveness of the new system. While advising models may lodge primary responsibilities differently, collaborative collegial relationships across campus will lead to positive outcomes. For example, professional advisors may suggest that a student speak with one of his or her classroom instructors. Good practice suggests that the advisor notify the instructor. In turn, that instructor should communicate with the advisor, perhaps before the scheduled meeting and certainly after. In general, it is important for advisors to know whether a student took the initiative to request a meeting or was responding to a suggestion from the course instructor. Within the limits of confidentiality, instructors should get a general sense of what was discussed and what, if anything, was agreed on. Referrals to other campus professionals, for example, the staff of residence halls, counseling, or developmental education, should, to the extent possible, reflect that same open, collaborative working relationship in which it is assumed that all parties are committed to the student's success. This will help to ensure that students receive consistent messages and that key campus constituencies know that the program has continued to move ahead.

Resource Needs/Personnel

Program costs will vary depending on the advising model and mission, the size of the student population served, and the need for additional personnel. An effective program must have a full-time director, and, depending on institutional size and student needs, it might also need an assistant director. Programs need a sufficient number of advisors; in determining that figure, being realistic about case loads, especially when dealing with a large population of at-risk students, is crucial. The advising approach also may have personnel implications. For example, programs that require multiple student-advisor interactions may exceed the capacity of existing staff, especially given the need to monitor student compliance and maintain accurate records. Other expenses might include professional development activities for advisors and faculty participants and costs for duplicating and distributing new materials, such as an advisor handbook. Housing the new program might require expenditures for remodeling to ensure the confidentiality of advisor-student meetings and provide meeting space.

Active faculty participation in the new model might have implications for teaching load, which could increase adjunct faculty costs and expenses for overload payments. A more robust program may also create higher demands for other services, such as counseling, developmental educators, and career counselors. Organizing and supervising a peer advising program is likely to create some staffing needs and may require additional funds for student development and perhaps student stipends. More robust assessment, both formative and summative, could exceed existing capacity, especially if it entails focus groups. Increased cost for professional development for advisors, faculty, and staff participants may include attending regional and national workshops and participating in conferences.

Since advising exists at all colleges and universities, an initial step is to assess the existing allocation of resources and personnel for that function and determine what might be shifted to the new model for first-year advising without adversely affecting advising services for other students. That audit can provide an empirical base for identifying the scope and nature of new resource needs and might also identify cost-effective synergies. It should also include personnel and resources engaged in other services primarily geared to first-year students, with an eye toward the possibility of dedicating some of those to the new model. However, new initiatives are unlikely to succeed if they beggar other important services, so offices identified by the scan should be given an opportunity to respond and suggest alternatives prior to the implementation of any changes. The results of these exercises then become the fiscal or personnel baseline for implementing a new model.

Comparing that baseline to the projected needs facilitates the development of a plan for ramping up the new program. The size of the resource and personnel gap will determine the reach and time frame for fully implementing the program. There are likely to be both one-time and continuing costs to initiate and maintain the program, including ongoing assessment, additional personnel, and expenses associated with professional development and dissemination activities.

Assessment

Nutt (2004) suggests that "the first and often overlooked step in assessing academic advising is the development of an institutional mission for academic advising" (n.p.); therefore, program mission, objectives, and outcomes should be at the heart of the assessment process (Aiken-Wisniewski, Smith, & Troxel, 2010; Troxel, 2008). As conceptualized by Maki (2002, 2004), the overall assessment cycle begins with the identification of outcomes and then moves to gathering and interpreting evidence, which is followed by implementing changes (Robbins & Zarges, 2011). While acknowledging the importance of assessing student perceptions and satisfaction with their advising experience, Nutt (2004) also points to the need to assess specific student learning outcomes, as does Maki (2004), who defines learning as "a process of constructing meaning, framing issues, drawing on strategies and abilities honed over time, reconceptualizing, understanding, repositioning oneself in relation to a problem or issue, and connecting thinking and knowing to action" (p. 2).

The advising process might seek to assist students in identifying appropriate courses, assume responsibility for their own learning, and develop behaviors conducive to academic success. In turn, that suggests the need to focus on potential career objectives and link those to specific majors, which then promotes a discussion of both required courses and skill sets. Of necessity, advising objectives would also focus on required general education courses for the institution and their relationship to students' proposed areas of interest. In addition, institutional and departmental regulations or standards regarding drops, adds, course withdrawals, and grade point averages would need to be discussed. Much of this conversation can be captured in learning outcomes. Nutt (2004) provides an example: "Students will be able to read and utilize a degree audit in their educational planning; Students will develop an educational plan for successfully completing their degree goal; Students will demonstrate an understanding of the value of the general education requirements; [and] Students will demonstrate the ability to make effective decisions concerning their degree and career goals" (n.p.). The clarification of aspirations and identification of potential majors and career possibilities transforms the process of selecting courses from a mechanical check list into a goal-oriented process.

Advising approaches and processes are another important consideration. Smith (2002), citing the research of Saving and Keim (1998), cautions that the popularity of the developmental approach obscures the fact that "little empirical evidence is available to demonstrate that advisors consistently use developmental approaches in practice" (p. 4). This highlights the importance of formative assessments that focus on advisor-student interactions. Assessment of individual advisors can also provide useful data (Creamer & Scotte, 2000). Advising processes should also be assessed with the objective of improving efficiency so as to better serve students. This could include tracking the volume of student appointments throughout the year and their distribution among the advising staff. The general nature of those appointments, recommendations to students, and student compliance also should be tracked. The duration of appointments and missed or rescheduled appointments can be monitored as well. Proprietary software packages such as AdvisorTrac, Appointment-Plus, and EZappt academic advising system, as well as campus enterprise systems, provide efficient ways to gather data to inform process assessment.

Outcomes assessment is critical for an initiative whose purpose is to help students achieve academic success. It should focus on stated program objectives but also be able to capture unanticipated outcomes. Multiple success measures might be used, including grade point average; number of credits earned; rates for drops, withdrawals, and incompletes and failures; success rates in gateway introductory courses; developmental education; and 100-level courses, which enroll substantial numbers of first-year students. Credits earned and probation rates also should be tracked and compared with historical data, as might rates for declarations of major and retention.

Satisfaction surveys could be distributed to first-year students and all advising stakeholders who work with that population, including advisors, faculty, and peer mentors. Program assessment might examine factors that promote or impede collaboration among professional advisors, faculty advisors, and other relevant offices, as well as on the overall effectiveness of all advising approaches that are used in assisting students. One particularly important aspect of process assessment is communication among the various individuals and offices engaged in the new program, since the timely flow of information is critical for effective practice. Focus groups could provide additional background and depth on specific areas of concern. Involving advising practitioners in research on program evaluation also merits consideration. One of the national instruments might prove appropriate for institutional outcomes. The NACADA CD, *Guide to the Assessment of Academic Advising*, is an especially valuable resource, and several studies have focused on assessing advising (Suskie, 2009; Troxel, 2008; Troxel & Campbell, 2010; Aiken-Wisniewski, 2010).

Faculty perspectives should be included. A survey focused on student behaviors, both positive and negative, that have an effect on success could be distributed to faculty and instructional staff who teach 100-level classes. Interviews or focus groups with various advising stakeholders might also prove useful in ascertaining whether the new program is seen positively and has produced ripple effects in other offices.

Benefit Analysis

The centrality of advising to student success suggests that effective advising will benefit students by assisting them in clarifying goals and making appropriate academic choices in terms of majors and course selection, which also should result in higher rates of student satisfaction, retention, and graduation and reduce time to degree. Fewer drops or adds, course repeats, and major changes increase an institution's capacity to provide services to its student population. For example, when fewer students repeat classes, seats open for other students which may reduce the number of sections that need to be offered. Moreover, low-achieving students often account for a disproportionate amount of staff and faculty time. The costs of failure fall most heavily on the students. Extended time to degree is in itself a measure of inefficiency, and assuming that students do persist and graduate, they will have paid more in tuition and fees. Having taken longer to graduate, they may be reluctant to consider additional education, especially since they are likely to have accumulated considerable debt. That decision would limit their occupational choices and future earning potential, which makes it more difficult to pay loans. This also has a negative effect on lenders.

Successful students improve institutional reputation, which can lead to enrollment gains and attract additional external support. Increased student success rates should result in higher satisfaction rates among staff and faculty satisfaction, which may promote a willingness to innovate in other areas. At the same time, the benefits from student success also reverberate in the workplace, likely increasing job satisfaction and a belief that the institution is making a positive difference.

Institutional Practices

University of Akron

Located in Akron, Ohio, the University of Akron is a comprehensive public university that serves more than twenty-eight thousand students. Classified by the Carnegie Foundation for the Advancement of Teaching as a high research university, the university, which is largely nonresidential, emphasizes community engagement. The average age for its first-time, full-time student population is nineteen, and its first- to second-year retention rate for 2011–2012 was 62.2 percent.

Newly admitted degree-seeking students who have fewer than thirty credits are admitted to University College, which developed a centralized advising system to replace the former practice in which advising occurred in multiple colleges. That change reflected concerns raised by the campus's review of data from the National Survey of Student Engagement, which prompted the provost to request assistance from NACADA. An academic advising audit team visited the campus in 2009 and identified concerns related to "Leadership for Academic Advising, Communication, Collaboration and Coordination; Professional Growth and Development; Assessment and Data-Driven Decision-Making, and Resources." The major leadership issue related to the decentralized approach was the absence of a single chief administrator and administrative home for advising, which impeded the development of a coherent, unified communication strategy. The organizational change also promised to address professional development needs in a more consistent fashion.

Organized in University College as the Center for Academic and Student Success, it reports to the university's assistant vice president for student success. The center's mission is "to educate, counsel, and empower students to make effective academic decisions as they work to fulfill their educational, career and life goals," and it has established eight learning outcomes for students, for example, knowledge, values, and abilities, which include setting goals and developing an academic plan. The center's website includes a values statement: "to educate, advocate, and empower students to make effective academic and career decisions."

An academic advising syllabus sets out the center's mission statement and philosophy and enumerates the responsibilities for advisors and advisees. It also provides a statement, "Student Learning and Expectations of Advising for Undergraduates,'' divided into sections by class standing, and the most extensive section addresses first-year students.

The academic advisement center and a first-year-experience subcommittee on academic advising have collaborated to promote a culture of assessment with annual assessments ''to gather, analyze, and use institutional data to identify target populations and focused initiatives for the purpose of supporting student success'' and to use those to inform ''revisions of the advising program, policy analysis and the allocation of resources.''

One of the organizational changes impelled by the NACADA visit was the creation of several new positions, including an assistant vice provost for student success and a director and associate director for the university's Center for Academic Advising and Student Success. Among the new practices are the use of EBI's MAP-Works, which facilitates the early identification of at-risk students during their first and second years and the use of a transition survey administered to all new and returning first-year students to identify issues that might impede their success.

Akron's academic advising center website includes a page, ''Academic Advising Data and Assessment,'' that provides information and recommen- dations from the NACADA visit, advising reports and data, and next steps and also includes the advising standards from the Committee for the Advance- ment of Academic Standards. A spreadsheet, Enhancing Academic Efficiencies and Promoting Student Success: Advising Committee Progress Report, provides both data and descriptive information for 2008–2010, which indicate a rise in retention from 68 percent in 2008 to 68.7 in 2010, though that rate declined slightly in 2011 to 68.4.

Sam Houston State University

Founded in 1879, and located in Huntsville, Texas, Sam Houston State University is classified by the Carnegie Commission on Higher education as a Doctoral Research Institution. It serves nearly eighteen thousand students, about 45 percent of whom are identified as minorities. The Student Advising and Mentoring Center (SAM Center), which provides services to all students, is the designated advising home for all undergraduate students, including first-year students and transfers. The center opened in 2002 with twelve faculty members and three advisors whose advising skills were highly regarded. They agreed to spend fifteen hours weekly in the center, for which they received an additional stipend. Over time, seven additional faculty advisors and three professional advisors joined the staff. The center's executive director is a professor of English. The center uses an intrusive advising model and requires students to be advised if their grade point average falls below 2.5, have not yet completed course work at the university, or have accumulated ninety or more hours toward graduation. The center, which received recognition from NACADA in 2006 and 2011, provides a robust mentoring program for student and assistance with time management and study skills. It sponsors a speaker and discussion series, Grassroots: Conversations on Leadership in a Diverse Community, and ELITE, which focuses on male students of color.

The center's programs also include First Alert, an early warning system. Faculty provide the center with the names of students who are at risk because of grades or absences. The SAM Center initiates the contact and provides a supportive program, often through a mentor. Many of these students participate in the center's study-skills program, which consists of six one-hour seminars that deal with student success issues and strategies. Many other students voluntarily participate in the program. Over the past ten years, success rates for First Alert students have been about 73 percent. In 2002, the year of the center's founding, the university's four-year graduation rate was 17 percent, and the five-year rate was 35.1 percent. In 2010, those rates, respectively, had risen to 30 percent and 52.4 percent (Texas Tribune, 2012).

University of Central Florida

Located in Orlando, the University of Central Florida enrolls over fifty-eight thousand students and is classified by the Carnegie Commission on Higher Education as a Research-Intensive ("very high research") institution; it is largely nonresidential. All full-time incoming students are assigned to one of three first-year advising offices, but the vast majority, about 85 percent, is served by First Year Advising and Exploration. That includes students entering from one of the university's two summer bridge program, Pegasus Success Students, which is coordinated by the Student Academic Resource Center, and SOAR, a program of the Multicultural Academic Support Services Office. New students who enter with at least thirty college credits receive advising from the Sophomore and Second Year Center. Academic Services for Student Athletes serves all Division I scholarship students. The Office of Pre-Professional Advising, along with the Career Services Office, serves students who intend to pursue advanced degrees, and another advising offices works with students enrolled at the university's regional campuses. Further suggesting the complexity of this model, students who have not declared a major by the end of their first year work with the Sophomore and Second Year Center until they select a major, which then refers them to the appropriate college advising office. Some departments provide students with a faculty advisor.

UCF's approach also includes a well-developed advising network. The communication and development node for this highly distributed model is the Academic Advising Council (AAC), a university-wide body open to all advisors. It provides opportunities to network, exchange ideas and concerns, and engage in professional development activities. These include presentations, workshops, and focused discussions at monthly meetings that occur throughout the semester. Working with the university's Academic Enhancement Program, the AAC provides additional programming, including presentations and discussions of NACADA webcasts. Through its programs, the AAC promotes collegial relations among advisors, which stimulates exchanges of ideas and discussions of challenges and successes.

Chapter Five

First-Year Seminars

Originally introduced in the 1880s, first-year seminars are far from a recent innovation in postsecondary education (Gordon, 1989). After waxing and waning in popularity, first-year seminars have gained a strong foothold in American higher education over the past three decades and are now a commonly used tool in the transition and learning experience of new college students. While the term *first-year seminar* is often interpreted to mean an extended orientation course (i.e., a college survival and success course), data from national surveys suggest that the seminar is defined in a number of ways on American college campuses and that many institutions offer more than one type of seminar (Padgett & Keup, 2011; Tobolowsky & Associates, 2008). A significant body of research shows that these courses contribute to students' educational, personal, and interpersonal outcomes in a number of areas (summarized in Koch, 2001; Koch, Foote, Hinkle, Keup, & Pistilli, 2007; Padgett & Keup, 2011; Pascarella & Terenzini, 2005):

- Persistence to the second year
- Grade point average
- Satisfaction with faculty, peers, and the institution
- Use of campus services
- Interaction with faculty
- Development of academic, interpersonal, and communication skills

Thus, the first-year seminar is an important vehicle for achieving the learning and developmental objectives of undergraduate education in the United States.

In work initially conducted for her dissertation and then through the National Resource Center for The First-Year Experience and Students in Transition, Barefoot conducted the first comprehensive national survey of first-year seminars in 1988. The results of this survey provided a working definition for first-year seminars that still persists today: "The freshman seminar is a course intended to enhance the academic and/or social integration of first-year students by introducing them (a) to a variety of specific topics, which vary by seminar type, (b) to essential skills for college success, and (c) to selected processes, the most common of which is the creation of a peer support group" (Barefoot, 1992, p. 49).

The structure provided by this empirically driven definition allowed the proliferation of these courses at institutions across the country. Recent national data indicate that approximately 85 to 95 percent of institutions report offering a first-year seminar to at least some of their entering first-year students (Barefoot, Griffin, & Koch, 2012; Padgett & Keup, 2011). Although there is a great deal of variation among first-year seminars across and even within institutions, these courses tend to share some general structural elements. For example, the majority are offered for academic credit toward graduation, are evaluated on a letter-grade scale, are comparatively smaller in size (sixteen to twenty-four students) than other first-year classes, and tend to last for one term (Hunter & Linder, 2005; Padgett & Keup, 2011; Tobolowsky & Associates, 2008). Fewer than half of institutions require all first-year students to take the course, although it is common to require specific subsets of students to take a first-year seminar such as academically underprepared and provisionally admitted students, student athletes, honors students, or students in specific residence halls or majors (Barefoot et al., 2012; Padgett & Keup, 2011).

First-year seminars also tend to have similar outcomes, which include developing academic skills among students, fostering a connection with the institution, and providing an orientation to campus resources (Padgett & Keup, 2011). Other common domains for first-year-seminar learning outcomes are persistence, mastery of disciplinary knowledge, interpersonal skills, personal development, and civic engagement and democratic citizenship (Keup & Petschauer, 2011). In pursuit of these outcomes, first-year seminars also share some common characteristics with respect to what happens in the classroom. For instance, an overview of campus resources is a frequent topic in these classes, as well as study skills, academic planning and advising, critical thinking, and time management (Padgett & Keup, 2011). The small size and seminar structure of these courses foster greater instructor-to-student interaction and use of engaging pedagogies such as a variety of teaching methods, meaningful discussion and homework activities, challenging assignments, productive use of class time, encouragement for students to speak in class, and support for students to work together (Swing, 2002). The conditions of first-year seminars are so conducive to positive pedagogies that they often become a learning lab for faculty to develop, test, and integrate innovative and engaging teaching techniques that are then generalized across other courses (Cuseo, 2009).

Given its long history and the rate at which first-year seminars have been researched and assessed, it is possible to chart trends in their development and delivery. For example, while once almost solely aligned in content and administration with student affairs, the course has begun to move to a more central position within the academic side of undergraduate operations. Indicators of this shift include a move toward "more traditional academic content" in first-year seminars to complement or replace life-skills topics, offering the course for academic credit, use of letter grading, and involvement of tenured and tenure-track faculty in the administration and instruction of the course (Hunter & Linder, 2005, p. 281). In addition, the flexibility of these courses as a first-year intervention is being more readily accepted. For example, institutions frequently use them for specific student subpopulations and create seminars that draw on a number of different seminar types in order to be responsive to institutional culture, goals, and the student body. There have been advancements in instructor preparation programs for first-year seminars, which often serve as a model for faculty development initiatives throughout the institution (Hunter & Linder, 2005). Finally, the institutionalization and success of first-year seminars allows them to be an anchor for other high-impact practices for first-year students, including academic advising, service-learning, learning communities, peer mentoring, and summer reading programs (Keup & Petschauer, 2011;

Padgett & Keup, 2011). In fact, first-year seminars frequently serve as the cornerstone of an integrated, comprehensive, and intentional first-year experience (Barefoot et al., 2005; Padgett & Keup, 2011; Tobolowsky & Associates, 2008).

Although there are structural and instructional commonalities across first-year seminars, they also vary by institutional mission, control, and culture, as well as by student population. Barefoot's (1992) early research yielded a typology of first-year seminars that assists in the classification and discussion of these courses and is still widely used today:

- Extended orientation
- Academic with uniform content across all sections
- Academic with content that varies across sections
- Preprofessional, discipline-linked, or major-specific courses
- Focus on basic study skills

Extended Orientation

The earliest examples of first-year seminars would be classified within the contemporary typology as extended orientation, the iteration of the seminar that is most common even today. As the name implies, these courses generally extend the goals and content of new student orientation programs into the first year, with the primary emphasis on "student survival and success techniques" (Hunter & Linder, 2005, p. 279). Content of extended orientation courses often includes "introduction to campus resources, time management, academic and career planning, learning strategies, and an introduction to student development issues" (Padgett & Keup, 2011, p. 70). The three-credit Freshman Seminar course at Appalachian State University, the three-credit UNIV 101: Orientation to College and Beyond seminar at Northern Kentucky University, and the noncredit first-year seminar offered at the University of Wisconsin-Whitewater, are institutional examples of extended orientation first-year seminars dedicated to the successful transition of students into and through the first year and to their persistence to the second year and, ultimately, graduation (Griffin & Romm, 2008).

Although their reach is wide, extended orientation courses are more often represented at larger institutions, public colleges and universities, less selective campuses, and community colleges (Keup & Petschauer, 2011; Padgett & Keup, 2011; Tobolowsky & Associates, 2008). Despite widespread use, the majority of extended orientation courses are offered for only one credit, are taught by student affairs and other campus professionals more often than faculty, and are graded on a letter-grade scale at a lower rate than nearly all other types of first-year seminars (Keup & Petschauer, 2011; Padgett & Keup, 2011; Tobolowsky & Associates, 2008). These characteristics have the potential to marginalize the course and minimize its impact on student outcomes (Swing, 2002). Therefore, although extended orientation courses are broadly used, they share some commonalities that may limit the full potential of first-year seminars on the student experience.

Academic Seminars

Academic seminars are the second most common type of first-year seminars (Padgett & Keup, 2011; Tobolowsky & Associates, 2008). Academic first-year seminars "may be an interdisciplinary or theme-based course; . . . primary focus is on an academic theme/discipline, but will often include academic skills components such as critical thinking and expository writing" (Padgett & Keup, 2011, p. 70). This type of seminar is more often found at four-year institutions, private colleges and universities, and more highly selective institutions (Keup & Petschauer, 2011; Tobolowsky & Associates, 2008). Often used as a way to introduce students to college-level scholarship, model intellectual discourse, and facilitate academic engagement, "academic first-year seminars represent a valuable tool . . . to assist [students] in their adjustment to the life of the mind expected of them as college undergraduates" (Keup & Petschauer, 2011, p. 9). Academic first-year seminars may share common content across all sections or have content that varies by section or instructor. For example, Portland State University offers Freshman Inquiry, an academic course with variable content, as the foundation of its University Studies program, which is then connected to a senior capstone experience at the culmination of their experience in University Studies (Griffin & Romm, 2008). The University of Texas at El Paso also offers an academic seminar with variable content. Founded in 1999, the seminar is called UNIV 1301: Seminar in Critical Inquiry and is a three-credit course typically offered as part of a learning community.

Given their intellectual focus, academic first-year seminars are frequently modeled after other discipline-based courses. For example, academic seminars tend to be offered for academic credit toward graduation, carry three credit hours, and are taught by tenured and tenure-track faculty (Keup & Petschauer, 2011; Padgett & Keup, 2011). Academic seminars, especially those with uniform content, are required of all students at a higher rate than other types of first-year seminars. Both types of academic seminars often share a focus on critical thinking and writing skills, and those with variable content frequently include a service-learning component (Keup & Petschauer, 2011; Padgett & Keup, 2011).

Basic Study Skills

Basic study skills seminars typically focus on skills "such as grammar, note taking, and reading texts" and are often targeted toward academically underprepared, remedial, or provisionally admitted students (Padgett & Keup, 2011, p. 71). Common course topics for these types of seminars include study skills, time management, academic planning and advising, and an introduction to campus resources (Padgett & Keup, 2011).

Given national concerns about academic preparation, demands for remediation and developmental education, and high rates of student disengagement (Crissman Ishler, 2005; National Survey of Student Engagement, 2008; Pryor, Hurtado, DeAngelo, Blake, & Tran, 2009), it is not surprising that these types of seminars have grown substantially over the past few decades and are now offered on nearly 25 percent of colleges and universities across the country (Padgett & Keup, 2011; Tobolowsky & Associates, 2008). However, they are rarely the most prominent seminar type offered at four-year campuses and are disproportionately represented at two-year colleges and institutions with lower selectivity (Padgett & Keup, 2011). This type of first-year seminar tends to be taught by adjunct faculty rather than tenure-track faculty and student affairs professionals and is typically offered for elective credits rather than for general education units or requirements for the major (Padgett & Keup, 2011). In addition, basic study skills seminars are most often graded on a pass-fail standard, are overrepresented in online-only sections, and comparatively underuse other high-impact practices and pedagogies such as team teaching, service-learning, and learning communities (Keup & Petschauer, 2011). Examples of effective basic study skills first-year seminars can be found in the UNIV 101: University Experience elective offered at Northern Illinois University or The Student, the University and the Community seminars at California State University, San Marcos.

Preprofessional and Discipline-Linked Seminar

Preprofessional or discipline-linked seminars represent the final category in Barefoot's typology (1992). These courses are "designed to prepare students for the demands of the major/discipline and the profession" and usually reside within professional schools such as engineering, allied health, business, education, and criminal justice (Padgett & Keup, 2011, p. 71). These seminars typically serve as a vehicle to orient new students to a particular major, discipline, or profession, as well as providing a general introduction to the institution (Keup & Petschauer, 2011). Given their specific focus, only a minority of institutions offers this type of course, and campuses rarely use it as their primary first-year seminar (Padgett & Keup, 2011). Although preprofessional seminars are similar to other types of first-year seminars in many ways, they also share some unique elements. Most notably, they are rarely required of all students but instead are targeted toward students in specific majors. The targeted purpose and audience of this seminar type is also reflected in the common topics for these courses, which include career exploration and preparation, academic planning and advising, and specific disciplinary topics (Padgett & Keup, 2011). Finally, preprofessional first-year seminars tend to use service-learning, team-teaching strategies, undergraduate and graduate student instructors, and learning communities structures more frequently than other types of seminars (Keup & Petschauer, 2011; Tobolowsky & Associates, 2008).

Hybrid Seminars

While not a core component of Barefoot's (1992) initial typology, the emergence of a seminar type that represents a combination of two or more of these common iterations is worthy of note. Over the past five years, the number of institutions reporting that they offer this type of combined first-year seminar, often called a hybrid seminar, has grown (Padgett & Keup, 2011; Tobolowsky & Associates, 2008). It is therefore reasonable to assume that the first-year seminar has evolved to a point where institutions are able to draw from various types to create a course that is most aligned with the institutional mission and culture, as well as responsive to students needs.

Approaching the Work/Critical Partners

Trying to select the right type of first-year seminar and implement it effectively can seem to be a daunting task. However, much like many other first-year-student initiatives, a focus on student-centeredness provides both a foundation and a guide for decision making in the early stages of developing and administering an effective first-year seminar. More specifically, student-centered learning is an overall approach that focuses on the needs of the student as opposed to the priorities of faculty or staff. It is a recommended strategy because it illustrates the commitment of institutional leadership, faculty, and staff to placing first-year students' learning "at the forefront of the resources offered and the course material presented" (Keup & Petschauer, 2011, p. 16).

In order to be truly student centered and to be able to craft a first-year seminar that is relevant and responsive to student needs, it is critical to understand who the students are at the institution. Such an examination can be guided by a host of questions:

- What are the personal, familial, and educational backgrounds of our students?
- What is their level of academic preparation and engagement?

- What are their expectations of the collegiate experience?
- What is the distribution of declared or intended majors across the cohort of new students?

Full understanding is achieved when an institution looks to historic information, trends, and comparative data to understand another range of questions:

- What are historic challenges to new students at the institution that may be pitfalls for current and future cohorts of first year students?
- What are students' use and satisfaction rates for campus resources and services?
- How do empirical data on the needs and characteristics of the current students compare to previous cohorts and to the institutional representation of the student body?

Finally, it is advisable to disaggregate the data in the institutional self-study in order to explore the answers to these questions for key subpopulations of students whose voice might be hidden in the summary of data overall. "In sum, a current, accurate, and nuanced understanding of student needs is likely to suggest a fit between those issues and the purposes and common objectives of a specific seminar type, or different types, to address the needs of first-year undergraduates as well as different subpopulations of students" (Keup & Petschauer, 2011, p. 18).

Although highly related to student characteristics, it also is important to understand institutional culture and goals because of their influence on student centeredness and program development and delivery. Cultural cues and artifacts should be present in the campus mission statements, strategic plans, accreditation and self-study processes, program goals, and learning objectives. Understanding institutional culture requires a deep and honest look into institutional identity, what a campus does well, what it will choose not to do, what are the stated and implicit commitments to all constituencies, and how internal and external constituencies view the institution and its actions. An honest examination of institutional culture is vital since cultural congruence is essential to the success of any initiative offered within that cultural context, including a first-year seminar (Keup & Petschauer, 2011).

Beyond a focus on student centeredness, there are certain drivers of change that cause a college or university to consider developing a first-year seminar or change an existing program. One of the strongest of these forces is assessment, which illuminates strengths and highlights areas for improvement (Keup & Petschauer, 2011; Schuh & Upcraft, 2001; Upcraft, 2005). Another driver of change, both generally and with respect to a first-year seminar, is the arrival of new leaders. Given that first-year-experience programs, including first-year seminars, reach across many institutional boundaries, they are often highly affected by reorganization in any aspect of the campus, which is yet another driving force in the consideration of a new or current first-year seminar (Keeling, Underhile, & Wall, 2007). Economic realities and cost effectiveness represent another category of change factors that may motivate the creation or reexamination of a first-year seminar to maximize efficiencies and outcomes of the first-year experience (Keup & Petschauer, 2011; Upcraft, 2005). Strategic planning efforts, self-studies, and accreditation procedures also may inspire an examination of first-year seminars and other first-year interventions. These catalysts not only fuel change with respect to first-year seminars but also provide a foundation, chart a path, and help identify meaningful outcomes for the effort.

The success of the first-year-seminar initiative also depends on effective collaboration from multiple campus partners, so it is crucial to include representation from academic affairs, student affairs, and faculty at all stages of the process (Barefoot et al., 2005; Keup & Petschauer, 2011). Some common partners for a first-year-seminar effort are academic administrators; directors of the first-year experience, student transitions, or the student success center; housing and residential life staff (if the campus has a high proportion of residential first-year students); student affairs and campus life personnel; well-respected faculty; representatives from academic advising; assessment and institutional research staff members; and colleagues from admissions and orientation (Keup & Petschauer, 2011). Another excellent but often overlooked resource for the first-year-seminar effort is students, who bring a unique and highly relevant perspective to the seminar planning and implementation process. Effective collaboration among these critical partners can ensure that the change process with respect to first-year seminars progresses in a manner that is both student centered and consistent with the campus culture.

Organization/Implementation Process

Early efforts to develop or revamp a first-year seminar are often the vision of a single person or a small group at a college or university. However, while the charismatic energy of an early champion is a valuable resource in the process of corralling support and soliciting resources, "the heroic energy of a single person seldom leads to a sustainable course or program" (Keup & Petschauer, 2011, p. 23).

In the early days of launching a seminar or recommending significant programmatic change, support from high-level campus administrators, such as the president, provost, vice president for student affairs, or dean, is critical. It is helpful to quickly use this endorsement from high-level campus leaders and draw on the early work of the project champion to marshal a team of colleagues from a wide array of campus units to assist in the process. Given that first-year-student success is an issue of widespread ownership and interest across the campus, a planning and implementation team for a first-year-seminar effort can draw from a number of campus partners. The team should "represent the major stakeholders on campus while keeping the team small enough to manage the early stages of the work" (Keup & Petschauer, 2011, p. 23). Regardless of who is invited to join the team, there should be clear expectations for full participation in meetings as well as active engagement in planning and implementation activities. An estimation of the time investment for team involvement is a courtesy, and ongoing acknowledgment of service on the team to the participants' supervisors, personnel files, and campus community is a small yet often appreciated gesture.

Initial Tasks

Initial tasks of the planning and implementation team include conducting an institutional audit to help identify student needs, campus culture, and long-range goals of the first-year seminar. It also is important to identify resource parameters for the effort. A time line for implementation that includes both a pilot and a plan for scaling up the effort should be drafted. While most of the primary partners are likely to be a part of the leadership team, a review of other potential campus partners for the effort should also be considered. Once this planning and implementation team has been formed, a priority for it is to establish clear lines of communication, which may include the establishment of a listserv, e-mail list, Facebook group, website, or intranet site in addition to regularly scheduled conference calls or in-person meetings. While regular communication is essential, each message, call, or meeting should be purposeful, effective, and efficient. If the time demands on the team become too great and have minimal results, members will likely stop attending meetings and fulfilling their duties.

If the planning and implementation team is large, identification of subcommittees offers a valuable alternative to enhance the communication and work flow of the team. If subcommittees are used, there should be an established leader for each of these groups, clear expectations for the outcomes of each group, and regular reporting of committee activity to the larger group. Some tasks of organizing early first-year-seminar efforts and aspects of the implementation process easily lend themselves to such subcommittee work. Keup and Petschauer (2011) suggest a committee structure organized around six activities:

- Managing campus communication to facilitate information dissemination, internal public relations, and campuswide buy-in for the effort
- The development of a comprehensive curricular and cocurricular learning experience
- Identification of program and course outcomes, as well as the establishment of an assessment plan
- Oversight of the myriad logistics and administration processes necessary for the implementation of a new curricular initiative
- Creation and implementation of instructor recruitment and development efforts and student recruitment

Time Line

Regardless of whether these activities are addressed in the larger team or in subcommittees, a realistic time line is necessary for this work. Keup and Petschauer (2011) recommend a twelve-month cycle:

- Month 1: The focus is on establishing buy-in from campus leaders, creating the leadership team for the project, and establishing expectations and processes for communication among the team members.
- Months 2 and 3: The focus is on creating communication channels for messages from the team to the campus community and for idea sharing, discussions of program and course outcomes, initial brainstorming and early drafts of seminar content and curriculum, and identification of administrative processes necessary for implementation.
- Month 4: The leadership team "review[s] and approve[s] recommendations [for] curriculum development, administration and logistics, communications, and seminar assessment" (Keup & Petschauer, 2011, p. 22).
- Months 5 and 6: Planning shifts to student recruitment as well as instructor recruitment and training.
- Months 7 through 12: The tasks encompass implementation and assessment of a pilot first-year seminar, feedback to the leadership team and campus community, and a celebration of the process.

While the exact allocation of time may vary by institutional size, mission, and bureaucracy and may be affected by the size, support, and efficiency of the leadership team, this model provides a template that may be adapted. This task sheet, time line, and list of suggested partners also are appropriate resources for managing change in an existing first-year seminar as well as developing a new course.

Leadership Roles/Communication

While the planning and implementation team may take charge of the initial organization around the first-year-seminar effort, it is often necessary to reevaluate the composition of this team when the course moves from implementation to ongoing administration. When the initial efforts around the course are associated with a single person, the course may become vulnerable "or unsustainable if the early champion is reassigned to another campus unit, adopts another institutional change effort, or leaves the institution altogether" (Keup & Petschauer, 2011, pp. 43–44). In addition, the members of the planning and implementation team may need to reconsider their role once the seminar has been launched so as not to lose their institutional memory and investment in the course but to better meet the evolving needs of the seminar. Some possible examples for their ongoing engagement include serving as seminar advocates, members of an advisory board for the first-year seminar, or course instructors (Keup & Petschauer, 2011).

If it is deemed necessary to identify new administrative oversight for the course, it can be challenging to find the right home for the first-year seminar, particularly given the highly collaborative nature of course content and administration and the widespread ownership of this first-year-experience effort. Cross-campus collaboration and, more specifically, partnerships between student affairs and academic affairs are a hallmark of the course. However, actual oversight of first-year seminars typically resides in the academic domain, most notably in academic affairs, academic departments, or at the college or school level. This position within the institutional organization offers distinct benefits, such as "greater involvement from faculty, perception of greater academic rigor, the increased likelihood of course credit counting toward general education or the major, ... and budget allocation from student tuition and fees" (Keup & Petschauer, 2011, p. 44). However, the most important benefit of being situated in the academic domain is that the seminar maintains its centrality to the academic mission of the institution and thus is less likely to be marginalized. A much smaller proportion of first-year-seminar programs are administered by student affairs units or a dedicated first-year program office (Padgett & Keup, 2011). Other less common course management models for first-year seminars include oversight by enrollment management or residential life (Keup & Petschauer, 2011).

Regardless of where the seminar is housed, someone must take on a leadership role with the course in order for the seminar to have ongoing attention and advocacy. If administration and oversight are left to an unspecified group, members of the planning and implementation team in general, or the seminar's primary partners, the sustainability of the first-year-seminar effort will be compromised. Therefore, a dedicated leadership position for the course is most beneficial to its early implementation and helpful to its long-range sustainability. Unfortunately, national data indicate that only three-quarters of institutions assign a dean, director, or coordinator for the course (Padgett & Keup, 2011). Furthermore, the majority of institutions that do in fact have someone in this role report that the position is only part time and often combined with another role on campus, such as faculty member, student affairs administrator, or academic support personnel (Padgett & Keup, 2011). An even stronger model would include support staff among the first-year-seminar personnel in order to have customer service and clerical assistance in place for the director, dean, or coordinator.

Resource Needs/Personnel

Beyond the leadership role, the most essential personnel involved in the first-year seminar are the instructors for the course. As with any other class, the instructor is a pivotal role that is often the key to a successful educational experience. The skills, pedagogies, and facilitation of a first-year-seminar instructor are brought into even stronger relief when one considers the small size of the class and the fact that the content is highly process oriented. Consequently, instructors must showcase highly engaging pedagogy and empowering facilitation techniques as well as content mastery (Keup & Petschauer, 2011). However, "engaging pedagogies represent guidelines for practice rather than a prescription for teaching," thereby allowing instructors to adapt them to different seminar types, course goals, content areas, and personal teaching styles (Keup & Petschauer, 2011, p. 56).

Instructor Recruitment

When considering instructor recruitment, first-year-seminar leadership must start by consulting state employment law and institutional human resource practices (especially for unionized staff) to ensure that proper hiring and employment policies are followed. Even after this initial step, however, the institutional pool of potential instructors for first-year seminars is quite broad.

An obvious source for recruitment is the membership of the initial planning and implementation team. Student affairs professionals and academic advisors are another pool of talent to consider for first-year-seminar instructors. "Inviting the leadership and personnel from the other first-year-experience programs such as orientation, service-learning, residential life, Supplemental Instruction, and learning communities, is another way to strengthen the ties between programs in an intentional first-year experience and expand the instructor pool" (Keup & Petschauer, 2011, p. 57). Librarians, student health professionals (especially those in mental health services), admissions and enrollment management colleagues, and staff from auxiliary services are all underused but growing sources of instructor support for the first-year seminar.

Faculty members are another valuable resource for first-year-seminar instruction. Recent national data indicate that the majority of institutions are engaging tenure-track and full-time non-tenure-track faculty in this instruction and that campuses are starting to engage the growing number of emeritus faculty members as seminar instructors. Finally, both undergraduate and graduate student instructors for the seminar are used on 5 to 10 percent of campuses nationwide (Tobolowsky & Associates, 2008). Given recent data on the powerful outcomes of peer education for both the students receiving the instruction and those giving it, as well as the cost efficiency of this model, first-year-seminar peer leaders are likely to grow in popularity (Latino & Unite, 2012).

Funding Sources

As with any other initiative, resource needs are a critical consideration of first-year-seminar implementation, administration, and revision and are highly connected to leadership, staffing, organization, and collaboration. Funding models will be influenced by institutional type and governance (e.g., public versus private institutions, for-profit colleges, unionized staff) as well as budget models. Where the seminar is situated in the institutional structure also affects funding strategies and sources. For example, seminars that are housed on the academic side of the institution often draw from student fees or allocations from colleges and departments. Those administered by student affairs units draw from those budgets, and seminars managed by residential life or enrollment management most often use auxiliary funds collected from those programs (Keup & Petschauer, 2011).

Despite these differences in funding sources, many of the basic line items in a first-year-seminar budget are the same. Keup and Petschauer (2011) identify three primary areas of cost to administer a first-year seminar program. The first category includes central staff and office support in the form of salary, benefits, fringe, and professional development fees; course buyout for faculty leadership; and expenses for office operations such as facilities, utilities, and supplies.

The second category includes instructional expenses. The most significant cost in this category is instructor compensation, such as monetary remuneration, release time, graduate student support, professional development funds, or other payment strategies (Padgett & Keup, 2011). However, faculty recruitment, training, and ongoing development and support are hallmarks of high-quality first-year-seminar programs and require a steady funding stream to be successful. In addition, first-year seminars may engage guest lecturers or visiting speakers, conduct field trips and service-learning excursions, engage in outdoor adventure activities, and attend performing arts performances, which can all complement the instructor's input but also will need to be included in the budget for the course.

The third category of cost for a first-year seminar is related to instructional support: textbook costs; online instructional components, customizable social media packages, or educational technologies for the class; and expenses for copying and other general office supplies necessary for instruction.

Beyond knowing the types of expenses that comprise a budget, it is valuable to consider other elements in the funding of a first-year seminar (Keup & Petschauer, 2011). For example, during the development of a seminar budget, it is critical to distinguish between expenses in each of these categories that are recurring or represent one-time investments so that the leaders of the course can sustain appropriate levels of funding. In addition, given the horizontal nature of the course, the development or refinement of a first-year-seminar course may cut down on redundancy of programs across campus, the savings of which may be directed to the course. Since first-year seminars generally draw together partners from all sectors of campus, "involvement of multiple units on campus may introduce a number of different streams of support for the course" (Keup & Petschauer, 2011, p. 49). Finally, the leadership and staff of first-year seminars should be sure to think of resources as broadly as possible and not limit themselves to a financial model. Contributions of staff time, supplies, event tickets, classroom space, and other facilities are all components of a successful program.

Assessment

Demonstrating the effectiveness and impact of the first-year seminar is a key component of its sustainability and must be based on good assessment practices. Yet only about one-half to two-thirds of institutions that offer a seminar report that they engage in course assessment (Barefoot & Koch, 2011; Padgett & Keup, 2011). Whether addressing this gap or continuing an existing effort, any assessment of the course should be grounded in the learning outcomes and goals established at the outset. These help identify the best fit among the options for first-year-seminar assessment frameworks and determine course impact and effectiveness. Assessment frameworks may be used individually or in connection and include criterion-referenced assessment (assessment activities that are measured against an existing set of standards), benchmark comparisons against peer groups both within and outside the institution, trends analyses, and longitudinal (pretest and posttest) designs, as well as formative assessment for program improvement or summative assessment for program evaluation or accreditation (Friedman, 2012; Keup & Petschauer, 2011; Upcraft, Crissman Ishler, & Swing, 2005).

Beyond the notion of what to assess with respect to first-year seminars and the approach toward assessing them, it is necessary to think about how to collect assessment data. Most institutions rely on quantitative assessment strategies for first-year seminars, which is conducted with data collected from student course evaluations, analyses of institutional data (e.g., admissions data, registrar information, satisfaction and use statistics from campus services), locally developed institutional questionnaires, and national survey instruments (Padgett & Keup, 2011). The most commonly used national survey instruments for first-year-seminar assessment efforts are the National Survey of Student Engagement or Community College Survey of Student Engagement, the Cooperative Institutional Research Program Freshman Survey and Your First College Year Survey, and the First-Year Initiative Survey sponsored by Educational Benchmarking (Padgett & Keup, 2011). While quantitative assessment has been the norm historically, it appears that qualitative inquiry is growing in popularity for first-year-seminar outcomes, particularly with respect to interviews and focus groups conducted with seminar students. National research on assessment practices also shows that similar qualitative data collection strategies are used to gather information from seminar instructors (Padgett & Keup, 2011).

First-year-seminar staff and leadership must consider to what end the assessment is being conducted. Addressing the stated outcomes of the course is vital to the success and sustainability of the seminar. Common assessment outcomes include improved connections between students, stronger persistence and graduation rates, grades and levels of academic achievement, and satisfaction with the course (Padgett & Keup, 2011). Although these are noble goals, they are not always the best measures of the broader intellectual, personal, and interpersonal goals of these courses (Friedman, 2012). Keup and Kilgo (in press) summarize this disconnect: "Too often [first-year-seminar] objectives represent articulation of broad learning objectives but the assessment strategy relies upon transactional measures that do not adequately capture progress and achievement of student learning and program goals." As such, it is important to leverage all of the data and assessment resources on the course to strive to truly evaluate its impact on learning outcomes and program goals.

Benefit Analysis

Developing or redesigning first-year-seminar programs requires a substantial investment of time and fiscal and human resources. Redirecting the efforts, expertise, and time of the members of the planning and implementation team; hiring leadership and support staff for the course; investing in instructor recruitment, training, and compensation; facilities; and instructional resources each represent a significant allocation of capital. Yet any discussion of costs also deserves a critical analysis of benefits, and a first-year seminar is no exception.

Although first-year seminars can be a cost-intensive endeavor, the evidence is strong that these seminars are a worthy investment. In fact, this research has established the first-year seminar as one of the most important instructional vehicles for achieving the learning and developmental objectives of undergraduate education in the United States. The bulk of these studies have examined the impact of the course on retention, persistence to graduation, and academic performance (Barefoot, Warnock, Dickenson, Richardson, & Roberts, 1998; Bedford & Durkee, 1989; Cavote & Kopera-Frye, 2004; Cuseo, 1991; Fidler, 1991; Fidler & Moore, 1996; Schnell & Doetkott, 2002–2003; Tinto, 1988, 1993). Other studies have indicated the positive effects of first-year-seminar participation on a range of other outcomes, such as involvement in campus activities (Starke, Harth, & Sirianni, 2001), interaction with faculty (Keup & Barefoot, 2005; Hopkins, 1988; Maisto & Tammi, 1991), student engagement (Kuh, 2005), and improvement of students' skills in problem solving, critical reading, writing, and general study behaviors (Barefoot et al., 1998; Tobolowsky, Cox, and Wagner, 2005). Summing up this research, Pascarella and Terenzini (2005) suggest that "FYS [first-year-seminar] participation has statistically significant and substantial, positive effects on a student's successful transition to college and the likelihood of persistence into the second year as well as on academic performance while in college" (p. 403).

Institutional Practices

University of South Carolina

Long considered the birthplace of the modern renaissance of the first-year seminar, the University 101 Program at the University of South Carolina (USC), a large, public research university of nearly thirty thousand students, has enjoyed forty years of success. Born out of a need to address student protests of domestic political injustices and international military involvement in the early 1970s, the course was developed to help "build trust, understanding, and open lines of communication between students, faculty, staff, and administrators" (University of South Carolina, 2012, para. 3). The initial leaders of the course hoped to increase persistence and graduation rates, enhance "students' understanding of the purposes of higher education, and [facilitate] a faculty development initiative to enhance undergraduate teaching and learning" (Latino & Unite, 2012). Today the seminar "aims to foster a sense of belonging, promote engagement in the curricular and co-curricular life of the university, articulate to students the expectations of the University and its faculty, help students develop and apply critical thinking skills, and help students continue to clarify their purpose, meaning, and direction" (University of South Carolina, n.d., para. 1).

Structured primarily as an extended orientation seminar with a strong infusion of academic content, the course carries three academic credits, is assessed on a letter-grade scale, and uses both a common institution-specific textbook and an elective text or instructional resource identified for each section. Although the seminar is not required of all students, about 80 percent of all first-year students participate in approximately two hundred sections of nineteen to twenty-two students each.

Instructional teams of one student affairs professional, academic affairs administrator, or faculty member, coupled with one upper-division student peer leader or graduate student leader, facilitate each section of the seminar, although colleagues from various student support units across campus are frequently engaged as guest speakers. Content is informed by a set of thirteen learning outcomes focused on three primary areas: fostering academic success, helping students discover and connect with the university, and preparing students for responsible lives in a diverse, interconnected, and changing world. By design, "the broad nature of these outcomes signifies that no single approach may be appropriate for all sections or all students." Thus, the course is highly flexible and "the content, topics, and methods to achieve the outcomes should be tailored to the needs of the students in a given section and to the strengths and expertise of the instructor" (University of South Carolina, n.d., para. 3).

A hallmark of University 101 is its extensive faculty development program. New seminar instructors are required to attend an intense three-day faculty training called a "Teaching Experience Workshop." All instructors, both new and returning, are invited to attend a one-day on-campus professional development event, Building Connections Conference, in the spring before instructors are scheduled to teach. The conference presents and models in-class programs, engaging pedagogies, and instructional technologies. Training does not end at that point. Throughout the summer and into the fall semester, seminar instructors are invited to attend faculty meetings, and the University 101 Programs staff members coordinate faculty development sessions featuring successful pedagogical approaches, innovative classroom practices, and various student success programs. Finally, assessment data are collected, analyzed, and reported to seminar faculty in order to facilitate instructional improvement. This comprehensive approach to faculty training and support earned national recognition when it received the Gold Award in Excellence from NASPA, Student Affairs Administrators in Higher Education in 2011 for the category of "Administrative, Assessment, Information Technology, Fundraising, Professional Development and Related."

Assessment data indicate that University 101 has a strong, positive impact on student outcomes. More specifically, data show that seminar participants report better first-year grades, higher persistence rates to the second year of college, and higher five-year graduation rates than nonparticipants. When these data are disaggregated, they yield an inverse relationship with students' expected performance. In other words, the course results in even greater positive outcomes for students who have lower expected rates of success at college entry.

Concordia University

Founded in 1893, Concordia University is a small, private, religiously affiliated (Lutheran) four-year college in St. Paul, Minnesota, that serves a diverse student body of nearly twelve hundred traditional undergraduates. Not only is their institutional setting vastly different from that of the University of South Carolina, but the first-year seminar is a relatively new institutional endeavor.

Developed by a group of twelve faculty members and piloted in 2005, the one-credit first-year seminar falls into the category of an academic seminar with variable content. Learning outcomes identified by these faculty members for the seminar include "(a) to explore the academic community and develop new mentoring relationships with faculty, staff, and peers; (b) to experience the academic world through the community, intellectual inquiry, and relationships; (c) to evaluate sources of information, seeking answers to personal and intellectual questions; and (d) to express ideas by clearly articulating thoughts in written and oral forms of communication" (Troxel & Cutright, 2008, pp. 99–100).

Given these learning outcomes, Concordia's first-year seminar focuses heavily on student engagement and mentorship. Students are given the opportunity to select their seminar with the notion that the elective nature of the course sets the expectation for a high level of student engagement at the outset. However, students entering the university with fewer than twenty college credits are required to take the course (Troxel & Cutright, 2008). Each section has an instruction team: a faculty member who also serves as the academic advisor for the students in the course and a peer leader. The course and faculty development are supported by grant funding and the Office of Student Services.

Another key element of the program is its tight connection to assessment practices. Assessment data are collected from students and instructors on both the process and outcomes of the seminar experience. These data are then merged with institution-wide data sets to integrate the seminar activity into the broader assessment agenda and strategic goals of the institution.

At the early stage of seminar development, assessment data focused on student interaction with faculty and staff, development of academic skills, and student success and retention. These data continue to be collected, analyzed, and used to improve and refine the course. For example, based on faculty and student feedback, the focus on general academic skill enhancement has been narrowed to an examination of information literacy (Troxel & Cutright, 2008). This change allows the instructor to respond to student needs and advance an academic skill in a one-credit course.

Miami Dade College

Miami Dade College (MDC) has eight campuses throughout Miami-Dade County in Florida and serves a highly diverse student population of more than 174,000 students. It is a public, open-access college that awards both two- and four-year degrees. Given its open access, MDC enrolls a high number of first-generation college students (56 percent of credit students) and students in need of developmental or English-as-a-second language course work (about 75 percent of new students). All students testing into remedial courses are required to take one of two first-year seminars. Students testing into one remedial course must take a one-credit course, College Survival Skills, and students placing into two or more developmental courses are required to take a three-unit first-year seminar, Preparing for College Success. These courses carry transferable, elective credit, and students receive letter grades as a final evaluation of their performance. The primary goals of this course emphasize "supporting the student in transition, shaping success strategies and attitudes, forming lifelong learning skills, . . . developing personal awareness and emotional intelligence," providing career skills, and developing "information literacy and technology skills" (Griffin & Romm, 2008, pp. 49–50).

Approximately two-thirds of first-year students enroll in MDC's first-year seminars. Each section enrolls approximately twenty-seven students, who are taught by part-time and full-time student life skills faculty as well as "student services personnel known as Intervention Specialists" (Griffin & Romm, 2008). All faculty members hold advanced degrees in a specific discipline. These instructors lead class sessions on topics such as managing stress; developing good study skills; selecting a major; exploring careers; balancing school, work, and family; learning leadership; and increasing personal effectiveness. These seminar instructors also "serve as mentors and advisors, providing a critical connection between the students and the College" (Griffin & Romm, 2008, p. 50). They use engaging pedagogies and high-impact practices such as service-learning, online learning management systems, global learning, online assessments, and learning communities (Griffin & Romm, 2008). The faculty members teaching these courses meet regularly to review student needs and issues, as well as to share innovative approaches and ideas for classroom activities and instruction.

Assessment data indicate that this basic study skills first-year seminar has helped students achieve the desired outcomes at a statistically and practically significant rate. Specifically, assessment studies have shown that successful completion of the seminar has resulted in higher pass rates in remedial courses and higher rates of reenrollment for the spring term among participants when compared to their peers who did not take the seminar. A five-year longitudinal study of remedial students who enrolled in these courses showed that the positive impact of first-year seminar participation continued past the first year: five years after students took the course, they had either "graduated, [were] still enrolled with a satisfactory GPA, or transferred to a state university" at a higher rate than students who did not take the course. Furthermore, they had higher rates of overall academic success than those students who did not take the course: 58 percent versus 41 percent, respectively (Griffin & Romm, 2008, p. 50).

Chapter Six

Learning Communities

Learning communities, generally defined as "clusters of courses organized around a curricular theme that students take as a group," have deep historical roots in higher education (Laufgraben, 2005, p. 371). Evidence of such communities can be found from the late nineteenth and early twentieth centuries (Henscheid, 2004). Several movements in higher education that converged in the late 1970s and early 1980s allowed learning communities to gain prominence as an intervention and success strategy for first-year students. First, undergraduate education experienced a shift from an emphasis on teaching, which kept the professor at the center of the instructional model, to a focus on learning and a far more student-centered approach (Barr & Tagg, 1995). At about the same time, educators began to embrace a social constructionist view of knowledge acquisition that brought the notion of collaborative learning to the fore in discussions of educational processes and pedagogies (Love, 1999).

These shifts in higher education philosophies were coupled with a concern about retention and an increased interest in the roles of peers in the undergraduate experience (Astin, 1993b; Newton & Ender, 2010) and occurred within the larger context of a growing first-year-experience movement (Dwyer, 1989). More specifically, the first-year-experience movement was gaining momentum on a national and international scale, providing a rationale and foundation for the administration of student learning and support programs for first-year students. Together these forces created the perfect environment for learning communities to gain a strong foothold in the higher education landscape.

Learning communities continue in undergraduate education as a widely used and effective student success initiative. Recent national data show that 90 percent of institutions offer them for first-year students and that campuses are experimenting with them in the sophomore, junior, and senior years as well as for transfer students (Barefoot, Griffin, & Koch, 2012). In addition, the Association of American Colleges and Universities (2011) has identified learning communities as a high-impact practice, which further solidifies their position in the ongoing discussion of best practice and the research agenda related to student success and college outcomes (Brownell & Swaner, 2010; Kuh, 2008). It states that the primary purpose of learning communities is "to encourage integration of learning across courses and to involve students with 'big questions' that matter beyond the classroom" (Association of American Colleges and Universities, 2011, p. 18).

In support of this broad purpose, successful learning communities share several structural and instructional characteristics (Brower & Dettinger, 1998; Laufgraben, 2005; Love & Tokuno, 1999):

- Small class size
- A high degree of student collaboration inside and outside the classroom
- Many opportunities for interaction with faculty
- Interactive pedagogy
- Group identity
- Seamless integration of social and academic experiences
- Some degree of curricular coordination

Learning communities may also have common readings that are often addressed through the lens of different disciplinary perspectives, take place in shared learning spaces, and may be linked to first-year seminars or service-learning initiatives (Henscheid, 2004; Inkelas & Longerbeam, 2008; Kuh, 2008; Love & Tokuno, 1999). Furthermore, learning communities should "provide a context for developing complex thinking skills, . . . social cognition, creativity, and metacognition . . . so that students interact with the material at a much deeper level than simply receiving information"

(Brower & Dettinger, 1998, pp. 20–21). Ultimately the conditions of first-year learning communities should create a setting to introduce students to the rigors and processes of college-level work, forge academic and social support connections with faculty and fellow students, and orient students to the values and habits necessary to be successful in college (Laufgraben, 2005).

A Model for Learning Communities

Brower and Dettinger (1998) propose a model of learning communities that seeks to capture their multidimensional nature, provide guidance for educators to develop new programs, and offer a framework to examine and refine existing learning community structures. Their model is built on two assumptions. First, learning communities should have clear parameters that delineate membership without being exclusive or elitist. It is from this clear message about membership that a true sense of community can emerge. The second assumption is related to the size of the learning community: a learning community must be large enough to represent the critical mass necessary to achieve its purpose and allow anyone who wants to join it to participate. However, it must be small enough so that it does not lose its core purpose of creating a sense of community and an effective learning space.

Beyond these two structural principles, Brower and Dettinger (1998) posit that certain educational components are necessary "to create a community effectively and enhance learning" (p. 17). More specifically, an effective learning community should integrate academic elements in the form of curricular content; social components in the form of interactions between students, faculty, and staff; and the physical aspect of learning space. The effective balance of these three components creates a solid base for the learning community on which to build a curricular and cocurricular program that develops students' professional, civic, and ethical skills and responsibilities. Efforts to foster students' learning and development in these areas will of course overlap. In fact, "what sets learning communities apart is their explicit and intentional focus on all three responsibilities" in one learning experience (Brower & Dettinger, 1998, p. 18).

General Typology for Learning Communities

Although Brower and Dettinger (1998) provide a general model for learning communities, they can vary by academic content, class size, linkages between courses, and degree and format of interactions between faculty and students (Gabelnick, MacGregor, Matthews, & Smith, 1990; Laufgraben, 2005). Thus, it is difficult to discuss learning communities in the aggregate. To address this challenge, a general typology has evolved. It identifies four primary models: paired or clustered courses, student cohorts in larger classes, team-taught programs, and living-learning communities. These structures resulted from a two-dimensional scheme that represents the intersection of integration across courses and the complexity of collaboration involved (Inkelas & Longerbeam, 2008; Love & Tokuno, 1999).

The first model, paired or clustered courses, represents the simplest form of a learning community. Paired or clustered courses are a coenrollment model that link two classes for a small group of students (usually around twenty to thirty). This learning community model usually maintains linkages between courses that are based on "logistical curricular connections and skill areas" rather than sophisticated thematic ties, typically connects courses with large concentrations of first-year students, and often includes a basic composition course or first-year seminar as part of the pairing (Laufgraben, 2005, p. 378).

Wright State University, an urban, comprehensive, open-admission, public, four-year institution that serves just over thirteen thousand undergraduates, offers this type of learning community. Wright State administers learning communities as part of an integrated first-year-experience program that is housed in its University College. Each learning community has twenty to twenty-five students who are enrolled in two or more classes together, and most include at least one general education course and a first-year seminar course. Although the learning program is elective, it serves nearly 80 percent of its first-year students.

The next type of learning community is an intentionally structured cohort drawn from students in larger classes and has come to be called freshman interest groups (FIGs). Similar to the paired courses model, FIGs are small groups of students who are coenrolled in two or more classes. However, they represent a subset of the total student population in these courses. They are typically combined with a designated discussion or recitation section solely for the FIG cohort and often focus on the interdisciplinarity of the two larger courses. This model is especially useful at large institutions to help mediate the potentially negative impact of large lecture-based classes on the social and academic integration of first-year students.

The FIG program at the University of Oregon, housed in the Division of Undergraduate Studies, represents one of the longest-running learning community programs of this type in the country. FIG students are connected as small cohorts in two general education classes and linked through a first-year seminar course, College Connections, taught by one of the faculty from the two larger general education courses. The FIG section of College Connections explores the disciplinary connections and differences represented in the two general education courses, gives projects and assignments specific to the FIG, and often engages students in out-of-class activities that complement the in-class learning.

Team-taught programs represent the third type of learning communities. As the name implies, these programs are highly integrated for the faculty teaching the course. However, they also maintain strong linkages for the students in the community, who take all of their course work together (Love & Tokuno, 1999). This learning community model is thematically oriented, and the theme, typically one that spans several disciplinary areas, becomes the foundation for group identity in the learning community. In addition, this type allows "a variety of perspectives on a topic to be brought forward, providing students with an idea of how an issue can be understood and evaluated from different points of view," thereby creating an opportunity to explore interdisciplinarity and understand academic and civil discourse (Love & Tokuno, 1999, p. 11).

The Freshman Clusters program at UCLA is an example of this type of learning community. Housed in the Division of Undergraduate Education, freshman clusters are "year-long, collaboratively-taught, interdisciplinary courses that are focused on a topic of timely importance" (UCLA College of Letters and Science, 2011). These lecture courses are taught by prominent faculty and are coupled with small discussion sections or labs. They also fulfill both general education and writing requirements. Examples of cluster themes include the global environment, interracial dynamics in American society and culture, the history of modern thought, and evolution of the cosmos and life.

The fourth model, living-learning communities, represent the newest addition to the typology and add a residential component to the model toward the "integration of students' living and academic environments" (Laufgraben, 2005, p. 380). Living-learning communities not only use the model of coenrollment in courses but also draw on the residential space as part of the learning experience by placing students from the learning community in the same hall, wing, or floor of the residential environment. Living-learning communities may even meet in residentially located classroom spaces, arrange corollary programming in the residence halls, and are highly thematic in focus (Inkelas & Longerbeam, 2008; Laufgraben, 2005). In addition to the examples covered in chapter 7, the Collins Living-Learning Center at Indiana University provides an example of this model of learning communities.

Learning Community Populations

Despite the specificity that these models provide, they do not prescribe the student population for the learning communities. Learning communities may be, and often are, offered for the general first-year student population but also can target certain groups of students, such as honors; developmental, remedial, and provisionally admitted students; and students in specific majors such as science, technology, engineering, and math (Barefoot et al., 2012). Students may be recruited for learning communities through other first-year programs such as orientation, advising, and summer bridge programs. In addition, students may be automatically eligible for these programs due to their placement in a specific residence hall, selection of major, or participation in a first-year seminar that is connected to a learning community. Finally, many first-year students elect to participate in learning communities based on their general academic interests, desire to mediate a large learning environment, pursuit of a particular major or career, or curiosity about the nexus between two disciplinary areas.

Approaching the Work/Critical Partners

Like any other first-year initiative, efforts to create or refine learning communities are most successful when they are structured in a way that is consistent with campus culture, are fully integrated into the institution, and effectively serve the college or university by addressing student needs (Laufgraben, 2005). Thus, it is essential to identify what the learning community seeks to accomplish and what institutional "problem" it will attempt to cure. By recognizing a campus issue that needs to be improved, it is possible to create an opportunity for change. Laufgraben (2005) identifies valuable resources in this initial examination of need and recognition of the opportunity for transformation through the addition of a learning community, including "the institutional mission statement, strategic plans or annual reports, department or program reviews, existing examples of collaboration between departments, programs and units, and external reviews or reports on trends in higher education" (pp. 382–383). Some common goals of learning communities are the same as many other first-year initiatives: ease the transition to college, foster academic performance, encourage cognitive and affective development, forge interpersonal relationships, and facilitate persistence to the second year and beyond. However, learning communities are unique in their ability to address some other needs of first-year students (Pascarella & Terenzini, 2005; Zhao & Kuh, 2004):

- Increasing interaction between faculty and peers
- Integrating the curricular and cocurricular aspects of student life
- Making academic content more relevant
- Increasing students' academic engagement and cocurricular involvement
- Helping students navigate and create a sense of belonging at a larger institution
- Making the campus environment feel more welcoming and accessible

Deciding on a set of outcomes that the learning community is intended to address is an excellent starting point for any effort to develop or refine this first-year intervention.

Another step in the process of developing or revamping learning communities is to survey which programs that currently exist on campus may reasonably connect with it. Learning communities often integrate first-year seminars, information literacy modules, service-learning initiatives, remedial courses, introductory composition classes, gateway classes to the major, or honors programs. If one or several of these initiatives are already in place on campus, they can provide some momentum toward launching learning communities. The existence of separate first-year support programs may even provide a rationale for a learning community structure, which may integrate and enhance existing first-year initiatives. Finally, the leadership of these other first-year programs offers potential partnerships and advocates in the effort toward the creation of learning communities, such as first-year-seminar coordinators, librarians, faculty, writing center staff, and colleagues in the honors program. Given the consistent element of coenrollment across all types of learning communities, registrar's office staff represent a critical partner in any learning community effort. It is important as well to generate buy-in among colleagues in orientation and advising because they are the primary staff who promote the effort among new students and guide them into the appropriate learning community.

Faculty members teaching courses with a high concentration of first-year students are also valuable colleagues in a learning community effort, as are members of undergraduate councils, participants in general education committees, and representatives from academic departments. Not only are these individuals able to provide valuable pedagogical and developmental input for the creation of learning communities, they are also likely to be among the campus personnel who review and approve the application of credit for learning communities toward general education, requirements toward the major, or elective units.

Other key collaborators are likely to emerge as the type of learning community is identified. For example, housing and residential life staff members are valuable colleagues in the development and delivery of living-learning communities. Similarly, learning communities associated with service-learning initiatives rely heavily on community partners, and preprofessional learning communities will draw support from the associated college, department, or major as well as from career services. Because of this rich potential for cross-campus collaboration, learning communities span traditional boundaries in higher education and are horizontal in structure, which makes them especially powerful as an educational reform effort (Elliot & Decker, 1999; Keeling, Underhile, & Wall, 2007).

Organization/Implementation Process

After recognizing the opportunity for change, Laufgraben (2005) identifies the creation of structures to support learning communities as the next step in program implementation. These structures can be loosely placed into two categories: organizational and instructional.

Organizational Elements

The organizational elements of the implementation process include decisions about place and purpose. It is important for any educators who lead a learning community effort to address a number of issues and questions at an early phase of the development and implementation process.

The administrative home of the program may be predetermined and thus inform the answers to the following questions, or it may emerge as the result of addressing these issues:

- What type of learning community is most appropriate for the goals that have been determined and institutional issues that must be addressed?
- How many classes and credits will comprise the learning community?
- How integrated will the course work be, and to what level will faculty collaborate across the courses that comprise the learning community?
- What capacity and resources does the institution have to address these expectations?
- Will the program take place in one term, or will it span the entire first year?
- Will all students be eligible, or are specific subpopulations going to be the target of the learning community effort?

- If all students are eligible, what will be the selection process for the program?
- How will the learning community be intentionally connected to other high-impact practices such as service-learning, developmental education, writing-intensive instruction, common reading, and residential life?

There are no single answers to these queries. However, all of the answers must remain firmly rooted in the institutional culture, purpose of the initiative, a clear understanding of resource parameters, and buy-in from campus leadership and critical campus partners.

Instructional Elements

Instructional elements are also important to the program and must address who will teach the courses in the learning communities. Faculty members from the disciplines are the most likely candidates. However, academic staff, student affairs administrators, other campus personnel (e.g., librarians, academic advisors, counselors, residence life personnel), graduate students, and undergraduate peer educators are also potential instructors for learning communities. Establishing an instructional team made up of colleagues from several of these sources is another promising practice in the administration of learning communities (Brownell & Swaner, 2010).

Regardless of the source of learning community instructors, expectations must be established in the recruitment and selection processes for collaborative teaching, engaging pedagogies, interdisciplinarity, comfort in teaching small classes, and a high degree of student contact both in and outside the classroom. Thereafter, these principles must be supported in initial and ongoing faculty development that can be coordinated by the learning community office or take place in collaboration with offices of faculty development; centers for teaching excellence; or state, regional, or national conferences and workshops. Again, it is necessary to keep the faculty recruitment, selection, and training processes closely connected to campus culture, institutional strategic plans, student needs, program goals, and student learning outcomes.

Ensuring Program Visibility

Throughout the process of determining these structural and instructional aspects of the learning community, the program must remain visible. This can take place through regular campus reporting channels, the student newspaper, social media outlets, websites, campus and community presentations, and invitations for faculty, staff, students, and campus partners to visit the learning communities. Not only will such visibility keep the campus community informed, it will serve as a source for marketing the program to faculty and, especially, prospective learning community participants.

Two other valuable partners in the promotion of the program to students are colleagues in orientation and advising. Favorably positioning the learning community on the orientation program and gaining support among academic advisors to assist students with their enrollment in these programs leverage collaborations with staff who are gatekeepers for learning community participation.

Leadership Roles/Communication

One of the most important categories of resources in the organization and implementation of learning communities is the network of people to steer the ongoing effort after initial implementation. The composition of this group will draw from partners across campus but also must maintain some degree of centralized oversight for the learning community program.

A key component of this group is a dedicated program coordinator or director. Often drawn from the faculty or the ranks of academic administrators, this individual serves as the unit administrator, is the primary advocate for the learning community, and maintains budgetary oversight and supervisory control for the program (Elliott & Decker, 1999; Laufgraben, 2005). Typically this person serves as the most connected node in the network of academic and student affairs professionals that is needed to support a learning community initiative. Depending on the size of the program, the learning community coordinator or director may be supported by professional staff, administrative and clerical staff, and student paraprofessionals.

In addition to a central staff, it is advisable that a learning community engage a coordinating committee or an advisory board. This committee should include representation from key campus partners such as the registrar, housing and residential life, advising, orientation, departmental support staff, and faculty who teach in the learning communities as well as faculty from outside the program. It should include student members to ensure that the viewpoint of the program's primary beneficiaries is adequately represented in decisions about the learning community. Although the units represented on this committee are likely to remain fairly constant, it is advisable that the committee members serve staggered multiyear terms to create a balance between institutional memory and fresh ideas and perspectives.

The program coordinator ultimately will be in charge of and accountable for all decisions for the learning community. Existing campuswide policies regarding course approval and credit application will likely dictate many of the processes related to the program. However, the coordinating committee or advisory board helps retain the sense of collective ownership and maintains the boundary-crossing nature of learning communities by creating a sense of shared program governance. Regular communication between the program leadership and the advisory committee facilitates discussions about program policies, dilemmas, strategic directions, and assessment outcomes. In-person meetings of the learning committee leadership, staff, and advisory committee should occur at least once a term. Asynchronous reporting channels may be established as a complement to meetings, including regular written or electronic reports, a listserv, or a dedicated website for the learning committee leadership and advisory committee.

Resource Needs/Personnel

Laufgraben (2005) proposes that the general categories of costs for learning communities include one-time start-up costs, administrative and operating expenses for a learning community to function as an integrated part of the campus infrastructure, and dedicated funds for faculty development and rewards. An early examination of available fiscal, human, space, and other resources will allow a learning community initiative to start successfully and ensure long-term sustainability.

Start-Up Costs

From a process perspective, starting a learning community may seem daunting. Yet from a resource perspective, start-up costs are often the most manageable. Resource needs at this early point include those that are truly one-time expenses as opposed to recurring budgetary items: funds to recruit staff, faculty, and peer leaders; administrative and instructional space allocations; initial costs to develop a faculty training module; purchase of training and resource materials; and development of communication and marketing materials for the program.

One common way to address one-time start-up costs for a learning community is through an external grant or gift, as well as an institutional program development award (Laufgraben, 2005). Another option is to do an internal audit of programs that may become part of the learning community, such as first-year seminars, service-learning, residential life, developmental education, and honors colleges, in order to negotiate budgetary reallocation of funds for the start-up phase of the program (Elliott & Decker, 1999). By working across campus lines, the proposed learning community may be able to identify economies of scale among units and savings from integrating programs more effectively, which then may be passed on to the learning community budget (Keup & Petschauer, 2011). The most crucial aspect of resource development at the start-up phase is to realize that these expenses will disappear or change after the initial launch of the program and to plan the program budget accordingly.

Administrative and Operating Expenses

The second category of learning community costs, administrative and operating expenses, includes the salary, fringe, and professional development costs for the program coordinator or director, as well as any ongoing expenses to support the coordinating committee or advisory board. The learning community coordinator usually engages a small professional support staff, which is instrumental in the administration, communication, and customer service for the program and needs to be considered in the program budget. Some learning communities engage more experienced undergraduates in peer leader, educator, advisor, and mentor roles, which may represent another expense category. Whether they serve as coinstructors in the classes for the learning community, resident assistants or mentors in the residence halls for living-learning communities, or administrative support in the coordination of the program, student paraprofessionals are an accessible, effective, and cost-efficient way to fulfill the resource needs of learning communities and other first-year initiatives (Cuseo, 2010c; Keup, 2012; Newton & Ender, 2010).

Ongoing funding is necessary for standard operational expenses such as office space, equipment, supplies, and technology. A key consideration in planning for this category of expenses is the issue of scalability. Administrative and operational resource allocations are pivotal to the effective transition of a pilot program to an institutionalized learning community initiative, so they must grow with the program.

Faculty Development and Rewards

The third category of learning community costs relates to faculty development and rewards. These resource allocations are often overlooked but are arguably the most important component of the program (Brownell & Swaner, 2010; Laufgraben, 2005).

Learning communities certainly draw on the basic tenets of good teaching but also require skills that are not always at the fore of courses taught in a more traditional format. For instance, a smaller number of students in a course, as is often the case in learning community classes, requires faculty to become more informed, aware, and effective at teaching processes. The more intimate environment of a seminar associated with a learning community will require certain interpersonal interactions and learning strategies. Furthermore, learning communities carry expectations for experiential learning, engaging pedagogies, and out-of-class learning, which may represent new territory for many faculty members. Finally, the degree of faculty integration present in learning communities is often at odds with the typical teaching autonomy of a college course. The ability to appreciate and integrate the points of a different discipline, engage in critical discourse across areas of expertise, and participate in a true team-teaching model (not just a "divide-and-conquer" approach) are all skills that require training and practice. As such, investment of resources in training materials, modules, and workshops as well as mentorship for faculty and ongoing professional development support "should be considered long-term investments in teaching and learning" (Laufgraben, 2005, p. 384; Brownell & Swaner, 2010). Thus, allocating resources to not only engage in these opportunities for faculty development but also providing rewards for participation is a significant resource consideration for any learning community program.

Assessment

Assessment of learning communities should incorporate general principles of good assessment practice. These include starting the process with an established set of student or program outcomes, identifying where to get the data (including an audit of existing data), drawing on quantitative and qualitative methodologies for a richer picture of the student experience and program effectiveness, using high-quality instruments and protocols, leveraging existing data, and committing to a full program of data analysis and dissemination to internal and external audiences (Upcraft, Crissman Ishler, & Swing, 2005; Ketcheson & Levine, 1999). It is also valuable to engage in assessment processes for both the purposes of proving learning community effectiveness (summative) and improving program processes and outcomes (formative) (Ketcheson & Levine, 1999).

It is important as well to include issues that are more specific to learning communities when charting a plan for their assessment and evaluation. The first of these is to connect the assessment process to the institutional issues or problems that the learning community sought to address in the initial phase of approaching the work. This commitment to providing feedback on those specific outcomes of interest will ensure that the learning community program remains relevant to the institution. In addition, these reporting activities will serve as ongoing promotion for the program and identify the leaders of the initiative as good stewards of the institution's resources and worthy of ongoing administrative buy-in for the program.

The second issue to consider when assessing learning communities is the challenge of identifying outcomes that are appropriate to the effort. Retention and grades are certainly valuable indexes of student success. However, they are not always the most appropriate and direct measures of learning, disciplinary integration, collaboration, faculty interaction, and academic and social engagement, which are common reasons for starting learning community programs and outcomes of these initiatives (Barefoot et al., 2012). "Assessment of learning communities...requires a more creative approach which acknowledges that teaching and learning occur in a dynamic environment" (Ketcheson & Levine, 1999, pp. 97–98). Therefore, assessments must identify student learning outcomes that are a good match to the program, operationalize them effectively, and strive to establish direct measures of learning. Existing national survey tools, pedagogical and learning theories, and predetermined rubrics for assessment of learning outcomes can help this process.

A third key factor regarding the assessment of learning communities is to address the issue of self-selection in these programs. As mentioned previously, learning communities are highly flexible programs. Therefore, there are many different iterations of this student success initiative even within the same institution. Some may be targeted to specific student subgroups such as developmental, STEM, or honors students, while others are primarily intended for students living on campus. In any assessment plan, it is essential to account for the impact of different preexisting student characteristics on the outcome so that effectiveness (or even ineffectiveness) is not ascribed to the program when it is truly the result of the type of students who elect to participate in that program. This issue can be addressed in the form of value-added assessment models (pretest-posttest comparisons), engaging control groups in the assessment studies, or the use of statistical controls in more sophisticated analyses.

As a fourth issue, learning community assessment plans must consider the appropriate time line for evaluation. The type of changes that these programs seek to create (e.g., academic performance, deep learning, skill development, interdisciplinary appreciation and fluency) are ones that may not see their fulfillment during the first year of college. Therefore, the most effective assessment plans follow learning community participants beyond the first year. Only then will it be possible to capture the full range of effects of this important initiative on student learning and success throughout college.

There are several common methods to assess learning communities. Due to their ease of administration and breadth of analysis, quantitative survey instruments are a common tool in the assessment plan of an institution. Several national surveys include items that inquire about students' participation in high-impact practices such as learning communities, as well as collect data on a host of first-year student outcomes, including retention, learning, academic performance, adjustment, interpersonal communication, development of social networks, and academic and personal skill development. Locally developed instruments may either replace or complement these national surveys and allow for more specialized questions about the specific model of the learning community, the content and pedagogy included in it, and the institutional context and goals that affect the learning community experience. Data drawn from both of these types of surveys provide the opportunity to conduct descriptive and multivariate analyses to identify relationships between participation in learning communities and key student outcomes.

Qualitative assessment strategies are also valuable to an assessment plan for learning communities. Given their emphasis on community development and peer support, focus groups may be a valuable way to examine the interpersonal aspects and group dynamics of a learning community. In addition, individual interviews and reflective journaling provide a forum in which narrative data can be drawn to assess social and psychological experiences and outcomes of the learning community experience. Finally, student portfolios of work, either electronic or print, may provide another source of assessment data for learning community effectiveness.

Not all learning community assessment strategies require collecting new data. Existing data in the form of admissions information, attendance records, course grades, and utilization statistics for campus services may provide valuable information about learning community experiences and outcomes. Also, course evaluations are widely administered in all classes, including those associated with learning communities. The data collected from these evaluations are woefully underused as a source of feedback on the intellectual and interpersonal encounters in the learning community and may even provide control data from similar classes that are not connected to a learning community. Effective use of these existing data sources can lead to a manageable and cost-efficient assessment plan for learning communities.

Benefit Analysis

Learning communities require funds for their initial development and implementation, ongoing operational expenses, and resources for faculty development and instructional transformation. However, "learning communities are not inherently costly or time-consuming, but [instead] require a reorganization of standard operating procedures within most colleges and universities" (Elliott & Decker, 1999, p. 19). Ultimately several models of learning communities are generally a low-cost means of gaining large-scale benefits (MacGregor & Smith, 2005).

The primary beneficiaries of the learning community model are, of course, the students participating in them, and the literature on higher education scholarship and practice provides ample evidence of their positive effect. Taylor, Moore, MacGregor, and Lindblad (2003) summarized the impact of learning communities with data gathered for the National Learning Communities Project. Most notably, evidence from this research showed greater retention rates and higher levels of academic achievement due to learning community participation, a finding validated in a host of other studies (Baily & Alfonso, 2005; Commander, Valeri-Gold, & Darnell, 2004; Johnson, 2000–2001; Tinto, 2000). However, research indicates that too often the discussion of return on investment for learning communities ends with these two measures and does not adequately address direct measures of student learning (Elliott & Decker, 1999; Taylor et al., 2003). Other research shows that students' experiences in learning communities have a positive impact on corollaries of persistence:

- Greater cognitive development (Walker, 2003)
- Increased engagement (Zhao & Kuh, 2004)

- Enhanced interaction with faculty (Blackhurst, Akey, & Bobilya, 2003; Dillon, 2003; Logan, Salisbury-Glennon, & Spence, 2000)
- Stronger peer connections (Hoffman, Richmond, Morrow, and Salomone, 2002–2003)
- Better health decisions and habits (Dillon, 2003)
- A smoother transition to college (Blackhurst et al., 2003)

Studies also show that students in these programs recognize the integrated nature of learning community structures, which helps them appreciate multiple disciplinary perspectives, connect the content from several courses, and yields positive outcomes (Franklin, 2000; Luafgraben, 2005).

The powerful impact of learning communities extends beyond the students in these programs. Faculty members who participate in learning communities, and especially those who take advantage of the professional development associated with these initiatives, tend to have "greater attention to pedagogy and enhanced collegiality across disciplines" (Lafgraben, 2005, p. 374). These faculty members also learn and apply more active pedagogies in learning community classrooms, including group work and collaborative learning techniques. They more effectively engage the cocurriculum in the learning experience, which leads to increased rates out-of-class contact with students and a more holistic understanding of student learning and development (Laufgraben, 2005; Love, 1999; MacGregor & Smith, 2005). Even more important is that these teaching techniques and perspectives do not end when the professor leaves the learning community experience. Instead, the learning community becomes a pedagogical laboratory, and these instructional skills are generalized to other classes.

Ultimately when the student-level and faculty-level benefits are aggregated, institutional impact is inevitable. Increased student learning, engagement, and persistence, coupled with more effective teaching and learning and faculty development, result in a more successful college or university. Learning communities can provide the framework for a more integrated approach to learning and teaching, foster a collaborative environment in the classroom and across units and departments, offer a cost-effective and proven way to address success for new students, and help expand an institution's understanding of student outcomes of the first-year beyond grade point average and persistence (Laufgraben, 2005; MacGregor & Smith, 2005). The flexibility of learning community structures and the myriad institutional benefits have made them an effective tool on campuses nationwide and, most recently, as a first-year student success initiative at community colleges (Jedele & Tinto, 2011).

Institutional Practices

Elgin Community College

Elgin Community College (ECC) is a two-year community college located just outside Chicago and serves over twelve thousand students. As part of a full complement of academic programs, ECC offers paired learning communities based on coenrollment in usually two, but sometimes three, connected courses in the same term. Learning communities are open to all students, although the course pairings most frequently include first-year classes, and enrollment in the learning community classes may include fewer students than regular sections.

The content of the courses is integrated and may focus on a single discipline or be interdisciplinary in nature. Each learning community program may be visualized as a series of intersecting circles, each representing a linked course, whereby instructors agree to use at least two integrated assignments. Each learning community receives administrative support during development and implementation, and participating instructors engage in ongoing professional development as they are expected to collaborate with one another before, during, and after the semester. In addition, instructors integrate student support services into their classroom and connect their students to the necessary resources on campus, such as counselors, librarians, tutors, and other student services departments. The primary goal of integrating the services into the learning community is to require students to engage with resources that will promote their success, as well as to better connect the services as learning collaborators.

There are several learning community options from which to choose based on student interests and needs. Examples include a collection of developmental course work in the Emerging Scholars Program, a coupling of a college success seminar paired with high-enrolled first-year courses, and communities for honors students. In most learning community models, the institution's first-year seminar, College Success, is also included. This one-credit-hour course provides information and skills important for transition to and success in college. All scheduling is based on student needs and is organized in a block in order to provide the consistency and structure students require.

Institutional assessment results show that ECC students who participate in learning communities are more connected with classmates and instructors than the overall student population is. Participants recognize important interpersonal and community benefits such as building stronger connections with students and faculty and feeling a deeper sense of community at the institution. In addition, they self-report engaging at a greater rate in successful student behaviors, such as asking questions, participating in discussions, and working with others outside class. Moreover, learning community students are more likely to return the following fall semester, and they earn higher grades than their non–learning community peers.

ECC's learning community program is equally focused on helping instructors improve teaching and learning. Learning communities provide faculty with a forum to collaborate and engage with others in meaningful conversation about disciplines and pedagogy through a sustained and collective effort. Instructors report that the learning community has allowed them to explore new ideas and to be more deliberate in directing students to apply the concepts to other courses rather than just implying the connections. They are also more aware of and actively engaged in resolving student issues and concerns than before.

Wagner College

Wagner College is a small (fewer than two thousand undergraduates), private, primarily residential, liberal arts campus located on Staten Island in New York City. Since 1998, Wagner has institutionalized learning communities as part of its Wagner Plan, a curriculum model that draws on the foundation of a liberal arts education and is dedicated to the integration of deep learning and practical application. Under the Wagner Plan, students are required to enroll in three learning communities, totaling six to seven courses, as part of their undergraduate education: one as a first-year student, one as a senior, and one during their intermediate years. A dean of integrated learning oversees the coordination of these learning communities.

All learning communities at Wagner are thematically linked and enroll a common cohort of students. The First Year Program (FYP) learning community is a three-course learning community that includes two courses from different disciplines and a one-unit Reflective Tutorial course, "which includes the experiential learning and writing intensive components" (Troxel & Cutright, 2008). The goal of the program is to advance liberal learning outcomes through "(a) critical analysis; (b) improvements of reading, observational, and writing skills; (c) recognition of cultural diversity; and (d) service to the community" (Troxel & Cutright, 2008, p. 72). The FYP serves as the cornerstone learning community experience that is continued by the Intermediate Learning Community, and culminates in the capstone experience of the Senior Learning Community. All three FYP learning community classes, and especially the Reflective Tutorial, focus heavily on reading, writing, and experiential education in the form of internships, fieldwork, and service-learning experiences that draw on community partnerships in New York City. Full-time faculty members teach in the FYP learning community and also serve as the advisors to the first-year students. These learning communities also engage peer leaders; a writing-intensive tutor and a research-intensive tutor are assigned to each learning community (Troxel & Cutright, 2008). The dean of integrated learning coordinates a yearly retreat and monthly meetings for all faculty teaching in the learning communities to identify program goals and standards, conduct training and faculty development workshops, communicate about ongoing issues, and disseminate assessment data (Troxel & Cutright, 2008).

Wagner College also illustrates its commitment to the success of learning communities by investing in an extensive assessment plan for each learning community and for students' experiences across all three during their college career. Moreover, they have maintained longitudinal assessment data to evaluate the ongoing effectiveness of the program from year to year. The primary focuses of the assessment plan for FYP are awareness and appreciation of the nexus between liberal arts learning and practical experiences, provision of writing-intensive instruction, closer engagement with the institution and the surrounding area, increased student-faculty interaction, facilitation of the transition to college, and increased retention to the second year. Assessment findings yield consistent positive results with respect to these outcomes, as well as student satisfaction with the program and increases in retention rates.

University of Michigan

Since 2000, the University of Michigan in Ann Arbor has offered the Michigan Community Scholars Program (MCSP), a residential learning community in which 125 first-year students participate and 35 additional students serve as peer advisors, peer mentors, course facilitators, and resident advisors. The goals of this learning community are fourfold: deep learning, engaged community, meaningful civic engagement and community service-learning, and diverse democracy and intercultural understanding and dialogue (Troxel & Cutright, 2008). Although the title of the program bears the name "scholars," it is not an honors program, and any of the over six thousand first-year students, primarily representative of a traditional college student profile, are eligible for the learning community. Participants are selected through a competitive application process.

MCSP is highly focused on the issue of diversity, and learning community participants are equally divided between white students and representation from the students of color and international students in the first-year class. This notion of boundary crossing goes beyond the students in the class and carries over into the administration of the program, which "engages academic and student affairs, academic disciplines, faculty and student divisions, as well as . . . the community" (Troxel & Cutright, 2008, p. 66). It is actively funded and supported by the College of Literature, Science, and the Arts, as well as University Housing. Students are expected to enroll in three MCSP courses during the fall and winter semesters in their first year of college. These courses include a small number of students, are taught by research faculty, and integrate a number of high-impact practices such as collaborative projects, interaction with faculty, service-learning, diversity, and writing-intensive instruction.

Although it has many goals, this learning community is dedicated to its emphasis on issues of diversity. The return rate for the second year of college among MCSP is higher than nonparticipants and the persistence rate for students of color has been especially impressive (as much as 100 percent in previous years). MCSP students also outperform their non–learning community peers at the university on a number of measures of intercultural development such as participation and leadership rates for multicultural organizations, engagement in other academic experiences focused on diversity, and commitment to service work with diverse populations. MCSP students also go on to serve in campuswide student leadership positions. In addition, many university faculty members have an interest in teaching in the program, and faculty retention rates for the program are high. This learning community has brought national attention to the university in the form of grants, media, and scholarship.

Chapter Seven

Residential Learning Programs

Residential learning programs, also known as living-learning programs, promote interactions among students, residence hall professionals, and faculty in both formal and informal settings, which helps to build a sense of community among all participants. Student learning benefits by engaging in an academic or cocurricular program designed around a specific area of study or common interest (Smith, MacGregor, & Gabelnick, 2004). The National Study of Living Learning Programs (NSLLP) defined residential learning programs as ones in which "undergraduate students live together in a discrete portion of a residence hall (or the entire hall) and participate in academic and/or extra-curricular programming designed especially for them" (Inkelas & Brower, 2007, pp. 1–2). The Residential Learning Communities International Clearinghouse at Bowling Green State University provides a complementary definition: "a residential education unit in a college or university that is organized on the basis of an academic theme or approach and is intended to integrate academic learning and community living. The unit may or may not be degree granting and may involve collaboration with formal academic departments outside the unit. It provides formal and/or informal, credit and/or noncredit learning opportunities (courses, seminars, tutorials, firesides)" (Bowling Green State University, 2013).

Coresidence is a critical distinction between learning communities—a high-impact practice (Association of American Colleges and Universities, 2011) that is common throughout higher education, especially for first-year students (Barefoot & Koch, 2011)—and living-learning programs. Schein (2005, p. 87) suggests that residential learning communities allow large universities to "approximate the setting of a small, liberal arts college," which enables students to "get a level of intellectual interest in their everyday lives, both in and out of the classroom that integrates their academic and personal development." Identified by Shapiro and Levine (1999) as one of the four major types of learning communities, these residential programs bring significant educational benefits to students through the mix of in- and out-of-classroom activities that facilitate academic connections among students (Pascarella & Terenzini, 1991, 2005). They build on a long tradition of residence hall programming for students, and the documented positive outcomes, both intellectual and affective, that result from participation in learning communities (Gabelnick, MacGregor, Matthews, & Smith, 1990; Cross, 1998).

Characteristics of Residential Learning Communities

The focus of residential learning communities varies widely and may include specific academic or societal interests and lifestyle preferences. The NSLLP 2003 pilot study examined thirty-four institutions, with a combined total of 297 individual programs. Having examined some six hundred programs, the 2007 NSLLP created a thematic typology that identified eighteen broad categories (with forty-one specific program types):

- Civic and social leadership programs
- Disciplinary programs
- Fine and creative arts programs
- General academic programs
- Honors programs
- Cultural programs
- Leisure programs
- Umbrella programs (multiple communities but not officially distinguished thematically)
- Political interest programs
- Distinct living-learning communities not disaggregated by theme
- Residential colleges

- Research programs
- ROTC programs
- Sophomore programs
- Transition programs
- Upper-division programs
- Wellness programs
- Women's programs

Since almost all of the general categories included multiple specific programs, it is clear that residential learning communities can serve a broad variety of student interests and class standings. However, first-year students formed the largest cohort in all programs, and "only five programs—environmental, culinary, language, research, and upper division—had more than 20 percent of participants with junior or senior standing" (Inkelas & Brower, 2007, p. III–9).

The academic mission of residence halls is embedded in the Council for the Advancement of Standards in Higher Education (CAS, 2006, p. 203), which states: "What distinguishes group living in campus residence from most other forms of housing is the involvement of both professional and paraprofessional staff members in providing intentional, as opposed to random, educational experiences for students." Those standards also stress that programs should promote "learning and development in the broadest sense, with an emphasis on academic success." Residential learning programs are designed "to bridge students' academic experiences with other aspects of their lives" so as to produce an integrated learning experience (Inkelas, Vogt, Longerbeam, Owen, & Johnson. 2006, p. 40). A wide range of students, including nontraditional and at-risk student populations (Pasque & Murphy, 2005), first-year students who have not declared a major (Heiss-Arms, Cabrera, & Brower, 2008), and first-year students, regardless of their level of college readiness, benefit from participating in residential learning communities (Stassen, 2003).

Brower and Inkelas (2010) suggest that three features distinguish the most robust programs: "strong partnerships between student and academic affairs, . . . well conceptualized, academically oriented learning objectives," and "took full advantage of their community setting to promote learning whatever and whenever it occurred" (p. 42). Nonetheless, only half of the programs in the 2007 NSLLP survey provided a specific academic component, and academic aspects of programs were not robust. Moreover, approximately 25 percent had no faculty involvement (Brower & Inkelas, 2010). To an extent, that reflected the fact that residence life, whose approach was informed by student development theory, drove these innovations. The NSLLP survey found that 85 percent of living-learning communities included student affairs professionals, and their guiding purpose was to enhance the residential experience of students by building specific skills, including leadership and communication, and promoting a sense of community among students and with the institution. Despite the absence of a robust academic component, the NSLLP survey found that participants in living-learning programs showed gains with regard to learning outcomes and goals established by the Association of American Colleges and Universities' (AAC&U) initiative, Liberal Education and America's Promise. Skills in the category of personal and social responsibility and such practical skills as oral communication and teamwork are likely to be fostered in residential learning communities, which reflect the positive impacts of community, and the interactional skills and behaviors promoted through participation in student affairs programs (Kuh, Kinzie, Schuh, Whitt, & Associates, 2005).

Some programs have designed activities around the goal of collaborating to promote student learning. For example, learning communities at California Polytechnic University are based on a partnership between housing professionals and academic affairs, including faculty, and a key program goal is to "link the curricular and housing experiences in ways that create opportunities for deeper understanding and integration of classroom material" (California Polytechnic State University, 2013). The motto for Washington and Jefferson University's living-learning communities is Bridging Academics and the Residential Community, and they all are tied to a first-year seminar or a specific theme, for example, leadership and service, and civics. In some programs, participating faculty live in campus residence halls, and many others promote social activities that include faculty.

In both residence halls and classrooms, the configuration of space merits attention in that it can either facilitate or impede the interactions that contribute to community and learning (Bickford, 2002; Chism & Bickford, 2002; Oblinger, 2006; Scott-Weber, 2004). This is especially critical for living-learning communities, given that they may be located in residence halls that do not provide appropriate gathering or instructional spaces. Similarly, positive meaningful interactions among diverse students, pedagogical or social, are less likely to occur if activities are not intentionally designed to achieve that result (Nieto, 1999).

The electronic infrastructure of residential learning communities becomes an important consideration given that contemporary technology "distinguishes digital content as not just content accessed by students but as content around which they engage and construct knowledge in a social manner" (Brill & Park, 2008, p. 70). While students' ability to engage in productive face-to-face relationships remains important, integrating social media into the teaching-learning environment creates an additional means of communication and an opportunity to discuss appropriate social discourse (Aragon, 2003). Georgia State University has provided iPads and flip phones to students in a first-year learning community, which enables them to engage in and document out-of-class learning experiences and share those with all community members.

The Students

Residential learning communities generally require formal applications that require students to address the reasons for their interest, and some are open only by invitation. These typically include honors, which set grade point minimums, and discipline-based programs, for example, business or music. Others are limited to students interested in specific societal or lifestyle issues or areas of interest, such as foreign language and global affairs. Residential learning communities for first- and second-year students also are common, and institutions with well-established programs often allow students to develop a theme for a new learning community. Students typically take one or more classes in common, and some of them may be a section open only to those in a specific residential community. In many cases, one or more of those classes are taught in the residence hall. The Academic Village, which includes two residence halls, is home to the first-year honors program at Colorado State University. The complex includes high-tech classrooms.

Approaching the Work/Critical Partners

In terms of oversight, the NSLLP 2007 survey found that 46 percent of programs were organized and administered exclusively through residence life and only 15 percent by academic affairs, which also included some department-based programs. Collaborative leadership by student and academic affairs characterized only 31 percent of the programs (Brower & Inkelas, 2010).

Programs resulting from academic and student affairs partnerships are more likely to include academic programming as part of the residence experience, but even those do not necessarily ensure that "meaningful informal interaction between faculty and students will occur" (Wawrzynski, Jessup-Anger, Stolz, Helman, & Beaulieu, 2009, p. 139). Alderman (2008, pp. ii–iv) identified several kinds of interactions between students and faculty: "course-related activities; traveling for conferences or study abroad; casual interactions around campus; career and graduate school focused interaction; visiting faculty in their offices (most common); and participating together in campus clubs or athletic activities." She suggested that "the most powerful element of high-quality faculty-student out-of-classroom interaction is that of relationship." Given that such interactions "are essential to high-quality learning experiences" (Kuh et al., 2005, p. 207), they should be built into the program design.

Brower and Inkelas (2010) affirmed that the "strongest LLPs were those that produced the strongest learning outcomes in students" and identified three defining characteristics of those programs: "a strong student affairs–academic affairs presence and partnership; clear learning objectives with strong academic focus throughout the program," and they "capitalize on community settings to create opportunities for learning wherever it occurs" (p. 42). Program goals for students should include both academic and personal/interpersonal development. In operationalizing the partnership, it is important to think broadly about the collective expertise that is relevant to supporting students, including, for example, advising, counseling, tutoring, developmental education, peer mentoring, student activities, and the broad array of campus events, all of which can provide opportunities for learning and building a sense of community. They suggested that "outcomes are also strongest when the LLP provides ample opportunities for faculty, staff, and students to collaborate in ways that allow for practice in working with others and . . . are able to take on a variety of roles together" (Brower & Inkelas, 2010, p. 42). As such, crafting a coherent integrated program should inform the overall approach.

A focus on that goal suggests a number of critical partners whose perspectives are likely to contribute to program design. Students, especially those already living on campus, can provide valuable perspectives regarding activities within and outside the residence halls. Planning and budget offices can ground discussions dealing with reconfiguring spaces and developing off-campus activities. It also is important to identify potential community partners and bring them into the conversation. Student activities may take place off campus, and local organizations, professionals, and practitioners can help identify, and in some cases provide access to, appropriate venues. Active participation by those professionals can enrich the learning experience.

Senior administrators in academic and student affairs should engage in strategic discussions regarding the number, focus, and outcomes of programs, as well as potential student populations. The institution's mission, strategic goals, and campus culture should inform and guide those conversations. For example, a residential honors program might be seen as a way to recruit and retain high-performing students in specific disciplines that are regarded as mission critical, and a civic honors program might smooth town-gown relations. The current strengths of academic programs and critical student affairs offices, as well as the capacity of campus housing, should be surveyed and evaluated. Political and fiscal considerations also merit discussion. Candid conversations should provide a rationale for determining the nature and number of programs to be initiated. Discussions also should propose a preliminary implementation schedule that includes some general time lines and cost estimates.

Another critical planning element is an evaluation of the existing configuration of space within the residence halls to determine a rough cost estimate for any modifications needed to provide an appropriate environment for the initiative.

Organization/Implementation Process

Organization and implementation of a living-learning program should be the responsibility of a collaborative leadership group that represents key campus constituencies, and many of its members will have participated in the initial campus discussions.

The Leadership Group

The leadership group should have codirectors from student and academic affairs who are of similar rank and are respected by both constituencies. It is important as well to balance the leadership group's membership in terms of representation from academic and student affairs. Assuming that program mission and outcomes were drafted during the earlier discussions of approaching the work, the leadership group might begin by reviewing those documents. This is likely to result in some changes, which can contribute to the group's sense of ownership. Once formally adopted by the leadership group, those should guide its subsequent work. Meeting minutes should be posted on a dedicated living-learning community site.

The initial number and focus on living-learning communities will reflect institutional mission, size, complexity, core strengths, and capacity. Numerous practical issues are likely to surface, including, for example, the configuration of space, occupancy limits of campus residence halls, classroom and meeting space, technology infrastructure, and provision of food services. Campus planning offices can provide critical intelligence, especially with regard to the possibilities for reconfiguring existing spaces. Campus budget and facilities planning officers can develop general cost estimates and suggest realistic time lines for that work. Assuming that costs and space set limits on the initial size and number of living-learning programs, identification of the specific number and their focus should reflect broader campus conversations and relevant external reviews, for example, accreditation reports and community or stakeholder surveys. Campus development and fundraising offices can provide suggestions and leadership for identifying donors to underwrite remodeling of existing space and expand the existing capacity of campus housing.

Other critical partners are faculty and staff from participating academic departments or programs and all residence staff who will share responsibility for the program's success. The campus police, who have a primary role with regard to on-campus security, as well as parking, should provide their perspectives, since it is likely that these programs will involve bringing speakers from community organizations into the residence halls. Once the number, nature, and sequencing of programs have been identified, each of them should have codirectors—one from academic affairs, preferably a faculty member, and one from residence life. This communicates a positive message regarding the collaborative nature of the program. In terms of both symbolism and functionality, they should report to the codirectors of the leadership group. A focus on joint responsibility and collaboration promises to benefit the ongoing development and sustainability of a living-learning program.

Other critical issues include the design and delivery of academic and cocurricular activities for the learning community. This could be tasked to a group that includes both faculty and residence life professionals. As noted, since the physical configuration of space plays an important role in facilitating formal and informal learning, campus planning and facilities management also need to be engaged in the process. Representatives from campus technology can provide suggestions regarding platforms for student interaction. The group is likely to be sizable, but it is best to begin with a broadly collaborative effort (Kezar, 2005).

Smaller cross-functional work groups could form around specific issues. From a practical perspective, it is easier for smaller groups to arrange meetings. Those groups might decide to include people who are not members of the leadership group but bring needed expertise. Depending on the nature of their specific tasks, the work of these groups might be completed at different times, but all target completion dates should form part of an iterative calendar. When small groups work independently, they often become invested in a particular point of view. A schedule specifying dates for presentations by these groups at meetings of the full planning team should minimize that issue and help move the work ahead in a positive, collaborative fashion. While the general concept of developing a residential learning program for first-year students may have support, moving from that to identifying specific program themes can prove problematic, especially if plans call for only one or two programs. Given their academic nature, it is important to engage academic deans and chairs and identify areas of strength and the potential for interdisciplinary collaboration. At the same time, outcomes from a student affairs perspective should be incorporated into the design. With the program identified and costs and time frame for housing issues in place, institutions are likely to need a marketing campaign to publicize the new program and begin recruiting students. They also might begin a development campaign to support the program.

Time Line

The leadership group should develop an implementation time line that includes program planning milestones and a target start date for the initial living-learning programs that reflects the complexities inherent in any new program's development, including the campus's program and course approval process, which may require approvals from multiple committees.

The collaborative nature of the program, which is likely to include both on- and off-campus activities and partners, introduces further complexities in terms of program design and required approvals. Reconfiguring or adding space to existing campus housing can be a lengthy process, requiring preliminary plans, a design charrette to promote broader campus awareness and input, a working budget, and a process for bidding the work. Depending on the nature of the institution and the scale of the project, in addition to on-campus endorsement, it may require approvals from governing boards, state and local government agencies, or central system officials. If private funding is critical to success, campus development offices need lead time to identify potential donors. Lead times for printing new materials and recruiting students also must be considered.

Leadership Roles/Communication

Since residential learning communities involve both student and academic affairs, senior administrators in those areas must provide ongoing leadership and support. Champions at other levels of student and academic affairs, especially those already engaged in campus or community collaborations, also can play important leadership roles by educating their colleagues with regard to how these programs benefit students and the institution as a whole. Student voices are especially valuable, given that a primary purpose of the program is to promote student development and academic success. Above all, members of the leadership group must support the initiative publicly and in meetings within their functional areas.

The process of fleshing out the specific contours of the new program may suggest a role for other offices related to the enhancement of teaching and learning that did not directly participate in the earlier discussions. As that occurs, the leadership group should provide structured opportunities to elicit information and advice from the broader campus community. The configuration of space can facilitate or impede learning, and that is especially important for programs that seek to facilitate ongoing interactions among students, residence life personnel, and faculty. Campus planners should be able to provide examples of such spaces at other institutions, identify potential fit with current residence hall space, and develop a preliminary budget for potential changes.

Closed meetings, especially those that involve senior administrators, often create suspicions, especially in fiscally challenging times. At the same time, fully disclosing unresolved sensitive issues can harden positions and impede their resolution. It becomes important, therefore, to find a viable middle ground. Ongoing communications, both formal and informal, need to navigate that difficult terrain, and the ability to find what is appropriate is likely to be critical to a successful initiative. An effective communication strategy should help the campus community focus on the positive outcomes of residential learning communities as related to institutional mission and student needs (Weick, Sutcliffe, & Obstfeld, 2005). Communications also should include cost estimates. It is unlikely that many institutions have the capacity to establish a comprehensive array of residential learning programs in the short run, and in a democratic setting, a program seen as providing benefits to a select few often provokes negative reactions. A plan that provides a rationale for the initial implementation and a vision and potential time line for adding more programs help address such concerns, as might discussions of spillover effects that will likely benefit the entire campus community.

Many institutions have long-standing residential learning communities, and the student success data and broader intuitional benefits resulting from those programs should be researched and shared with the campus community. Potential examples may be found in the NSLLP study and the Residential Learning International Clearinghouse at Bowling Green State University. Examples of successful programs at peer institutions can help overcome concerns that this initiative is not appropriate for your campus. Inviting speakers to campus from one of or more of those institutions can prove effective in resolving doubts about both the viability of your campus efforts and the positive outcomes associated with these programs. If resources permit, sending a small team to visit a peer or aspirational institution that has successful residential learning programs should prove helpful, especially with regard to implementation processes, outcomes, and sustainability issues. National conferences, residence life associations, and proprietary organizations also sponsor programs that focus on living-learning programs, some of them webinars. Sending teams to conferences and workshops and having on-campus presentations that include speakers from cognate institutions can build community among members of the campus leadership group, add to their expertise, and build knowledge of and support for the program across the institution. Couched in terms of benefits to students and the campus and its community, the rationale for establishing a living-learning program should drive the communication process.

The campus area most dramatically affected in terms of physical changes is the residence hall that will house the community. These might include reconfiguring space to accommodate classrooms, meetings, and offices for advisors, mentors, and faculty. Other changes are likely to prove unsettling and difficult to negotiate, especially those that relate to ownership issues. Academic affairs tends to see itself as the epicenter of the educational process, while student affairs regards the affective domain and cocurricular activities as its preserve. Residence life personnel naturally see themselves as owning their domain and having specialized knowledge of and experience with residential students.

Change is invigorating, but also unsettling and at times threatening, especially when it involves ownership issues, which magnifies the importance of open communications and visible positive leadership within residence life. Planning and implementation activities should honor residence life's deep knowledge of students. Faculty champions, especially those engaged in community-based learning, service-learning, practicums, and internships, also can play important leadership roles. The varied claims and concerns of campus stakeholders make it especially important that senior administrators and academic and student affairs leaders emphasize the benefits the program will likely bring to students in terms of building their academic and affective abilities and providing them with a sense of self-efficacy. The broader institutional benefits of student engagement with the local community provide an additional rationale for these programs.

Resource Needs/Personnel

Responses to the 2007 NSLLP indicated $21,000 as the average program cost, but 25 percent reported budgets of under $1,000 and 10 percent had no budget. These figures reflect the fact that in many cases, personnel who participated in these programs did so as part of their normal duties. For example, a regularly scheduled and budgeted course may have formed part of the learning community experience. Participation of residence life staff may have been budgeted in a similar fashion, and that may also have been the case for student activities budgets. Costs would increase if a residence life professional and a faculty member codirected a community, which is a best practice. Expenses also would rise if one or more of the courses were open only to students in the residential community, and therefore enrolled a smaller number of students, and if it included a variety of community activities.

Remodeling residence halls to create dedicated space for meetings, offices, and perhaps classrooms might also be required. Other costs are likely to include hiring additional personnel, including some at the director level, and providing release time and stipends for participating faculty and staff. The number of programs, their nature, and the total numbers of students served are major cost variables. For example, programs with a strong community focus may entail significant transportation costs. Although it is likely that many community members will volunteer their time, there might also be costs for honoraria. Smaller class sizes in residence halls also increase instructional costs, though greater student-faculty interaction is likely to result in higher levels of student attainment and fewer drops and incompletes.

Faculty members leading a community would need release time and, depending on campus traditions, a stipend. The faculty release could increase expenses for adjunct instructors. If the faculty member's commitment is likely to extend over several years, it might be best to think in terms of other ways to deal with ongoing class coverage. Program faculty living in the residence hall would likely receive a housing supplement.

Residence life professionals also would confront challenging workload issues, and an ongoing, sustainable program might necessitate hiring more people to assume those responsibilities. Professional development activities and stipends for peer leaders are another potential cost. Creating the kinds of formal and informal spaces that facilitate interactions among the community's participants and encourage learning forms another cost category (Bickford & Wright, 2006), as does the provision of an advanced technology infrastructure. In addition, students and staff displaced by the remodeling need to be accommodated. New residential programming may create additional workload for campus police, and there are likely to be increased expenditures for food and off-campus learning activities.

Assessment

Assessment is a central mission of the NSLLP, and it provides institutions with an online instrument for submitting data on campus programs. Its national reports enable institutions to view their own data in a broader comparative context. NSSLLP also notes that it includes institutional variables, such as mission, culture, policies, and program offerings. A robust approach should include perspectives from all participating staff, faculty, and students and use those data to inform ongoing program development. It also might assess the perspectives of nonparticipants. Depending on the nature of the program, community impact might be an important consideration. This could include questionnaires or focus groups for community partners, an analysis of news media coverage, and perhaps members of foundation or governing boards.

A growing body of assessment literature focusing on specific groups as well as more generalized impacts promises to facilitate that process. For example, Inkelas, Daver, Vogt, and Leonard (2007) examine the impact of learning communities on first-generation students. Brower (2008) investigated examined patterns of alcohol abuse among students and found a positive impact attributable to participating in a living-learning community.

In addition, a variety of standard student success measures can be used to compare residential learning community students to the general student population. Assessment also should focus on institutional goals associated with the program, for example, increasing student satisfaction, attracting larger numbers of high-achieving high school students, increasing rates of admission to graduate and professional schools, and achieving institutional reputation in its major service area and, perhaps more broadly, within higher education, which might increase the institution's donor base and help in recruiting of applicants. Some goals will have greater importance than others. Ideally, assessment would include all institutional goals.

Impacts on student academic success can be assessed using standard academic measures such as grade point average, retention, and graduation and, if relevant, admission to graduate and professional programs. These can be compared with prior institutional data and with the performance of students who did not participate in the residential communities. For communities that focus on a specific student cohort, for example, first-year or first-generation college goers, success rates within those communities could be compared to nonparticipating students within the institution and nationally. The results of satisfaction and attitudinal surveys could be compared for participants and nonparticipants. That could include outcomes for faculty and staff and specific impacts on the university, for example, fostering a more collaborative campus culture (Banta & Kuh, 1998).

Many of these assessments could be compared with national data available through NSLLP. Assessment should be implemented in a way that enables it to capture unanticipated program outcomes, both positive and negative, whether on campus or in the community. Formative assessment of the effectiveness of program components should help identify program changes that merit study. Satisfaction surveys and focus groups can help document and assess the experiences of students, residence life and student affairs professionals, and faculty. Since the residential component distinguishes residential learning communities from other learning communities, it becomes especially important to focus on that, which should include both formal and informal learning experiences and relevant student development goals. It is important as well to capture the perspectives of community partners. Those can benefit both the process and outcomes and communicate that the institution values their participation.

Benefit Analysis

Benefits can be assessed at several levels, but the primary focus should be on tracking impacts related to student academic success and student development, especially those that were built into the design as program outcomes. Those might have included various academic and student development measures such as grade point average, identification and declaration of majors, progress toward degree completion, sense of self-efficacy, feeling part of a community, stronger leadership and interactional skills, and higher overall rates of student satisfaction with regard to both their residential and academic experience. Moreover, the NSLLP identified positive spillover effects for students living in the residence hall who were not part of a living-learning community. According to Stassen (2003), "The consistent positive effects of LC participation across a variety of outcome and experience measures provides compelling evidence that even relatively modest LCs, in residential environments, can provide a number of benefits to participants" (p. 581).

Residential learning communities also bring benefits to faculty participants who live in the residence halls, including "a self-reported positive change in both their professional paradigm as educators and their personal lives," which also increased their overall job performance (Siriam, Shushock, Perkins, & Scales, 2011, p. 50). The development of more positive relations between residential life personnel and faculty participants is another poten-tial benefit, which likely will contribute to program sustainability and encourage other cooperative initiatives.

An assessment of first-year students carried out towards the end of the first semester at the University of Massachusetts, Amherst, found that students in living-learning communities had higher levels of peer contact, academic commitment, commitment to the institution, and informal interactions with faculty, and also reported greater satisfaction with their learning environment as compared to other first-year students (University of Massachusetts, Amherst, 2001). Successful programs can contribute positively to recruiting and retaining students, faculty, and staff and to raising an intuition's reputation. Since many living-learning programs emphasize engagement with the surrounding community, positive interactions with the students and staff in those programs is likely to contribute to the institutional image. In turn, that may ameliorate town-gown frictions, which is likely to facilitate other collaborations and an increase in the institution's donor base.

Institutional Practices

Boise State University

Located in Idaho, Boise State University enrolls about nineteen thousand students. Classified by the Carnegie Foundation as a Master's/L, Boise State has multiple colleges and offers a wide range of master's degrees. Its living-learning program has a clearly articulated mission that stresses the positive impacts on student learning produced by ongoing interactions with faculty "who bridge academic and personal life," and it suggests that participating faculty become more reflective practitioners. A set of overarching values and outcomes guide these programs: "Self-Assurance, Community Engagement, Intellectual Curiosity, Love of Learning, Openness and Inclusion." Other explicit program outcomes include positive impacts on student learning, retention, and faculty development (Boise State University, 2012).

Boise State informs students that the residential colleges consciously model the approach to learning at Oxford and Cambridge universities, where professors in residences focus on student learning both within and outside the classroom. Admission to all these programs is competitive, and applications include an essay in which students explain why they are interested in the specific living-learning community to which they are applying. They also provide a résumé listing prior activities that relate to the program's focus.

Some residential learning communities are open to all students, and first-year-student participants often return for one or more additional years. Others target only first-year students, and one is designed for returning sophomores. Five living-learning programs, identified as residential colleges, have a faculty member who lives in a residence hall along with the students and engages in numerous formal and informal activities and interactions with them. Four of the programs are associated with specific colleges: Arts and Humanities, Business and Economics, Engineering, and Health Professions.

The program also has two interest communities—living-learning programs that share the overarching goals, objectives, and outcomes of the residential college but whose faculty advisor does not live in the residence hall. One of those, Lifetime Recreation, cosponsored by campus recreation and university housing, is designed for first-year students interested in participating in recreational activities, for example, club sports, fitness, and a variety of outdoors programs. An administrator associated with health and recreation services serves as the faculty advisor, and a Boise student is the resident assistant. Another community, First Year Focus, automatically coenrolls students in eight credits of core classes, including University 101, First Year College Transitions, which is taught by the assistant director of residential education, whose office is in the residence hall. The course syllabus lists specific relationships between class content and activities and the two other core courses.

Faculty in residence participate in recruiting students by making presentations to internal and external audiences. They also communicate regularly with the assistant director for residential education and the resident director of the facility in which the program is located. Both tenured and tenure-track faculty can participate, and the university prefers a two-year commitment. The formal application must discuss educational strategies designed to achieve the program's outcomes, and the process includes an interview with housing department staff, the vice president for undergraduate education, the dean of the relevant college, and a residence hall student. The selection is made jointly by the vice president for student affairs and the vice president for academic affairs, and the faculty member receives an official letter of appointment.

Survey data from students in the engineering residential college focused on four dimensions—"Development of Communication Network; Confidence in Communication; Sense of Community and Belonging; [and] 'I Can Do Spirit' " — and resulted in an overall rating of good on a four-point scale. Areas of strength included that students "highly valued" the program and "felt a strong sense of community and support." They also reported improved leadership skills (Rist & Allen, 2011, pp. 1–2). Additional program assessment is ongoing and reflects the interests and expertise of an assistant director of residence life at Boise State, which centers on living-learning communities and their impact on program assessment and student learning.

Illinois State University

Classified as a doctoral research university, Illinois State University is located in Bloomington-Normal and serves some twenty thousand students. It offers forty-seven undergraduate majors and a high concentration of professional doctorates. University housing services offers twenty-nine themed learning communities. Some focus on specific academic disciplines, for example, math, music, and curriculum and instruction. Others focus on general academic areas such as fine arts, co-sciences, and information technology. Several communities support lifestyle preferences, for example, substance free, quiet, wellness, and restricted visitation. Other learning communities serve transfer students and returning sophomores. Depending on the cohort size, one or more floors of a residence hall are reserved for each of the programs. The Department of Residence has an office that focuses on academic services.

The communities sponsor a variety of activities designed to promote students' academic development and social adjustment to the university. The university participated in the National Study of Living-Learning Programs, and its website includes student comments on their participation in learning communities. These communities serve different student populations, and their admission requirements vary. For example, programs that focus on a specific major are open only to students who have declared a major or minor. The honors community admits students who have been accepted into one of several university honors programs. Communities focused on lifestyle preferences require students to affirm their commitment to a specific set of behaviors consonant with that lifestyle and also require a formal application.

The themed learning communities all have one or more faculty directors and a designated student mentor. Residence hall programs provide academic support, career exploration, and volunteer and social activities. Programs create opportunities for informal interactions between students and members of the faculty. All students participate in a designated first-year seminar and must register for several courses specific to the theme they have chosen. For example, the first-year seminar for students in the Living Green community is Contemporary Green Living: Life Choices for Sustainability. Those students also engage in on- and off-campus activities. For example, in a learning-by-doing approach, students become familiar with and practice green consumerism and encourage one another to minimize energy consumption.

The university participated in the 2010 NSSLP survey and received a customized institutional report that indicated positive results reported by students in the themed learning communities. These included, among others, "Higher course-related faculty interaction; Higher rates of faculty mentorship; Higher use of co-curricular residence hall resources; Higher interactions with professors; Higher attendance at seminars and lecturers; Higher agreement that the residence hall is academically and socially supportive; Higher positive peer diversity interactions," easier transition to college, and a greater sense of belonging (Reeland & Jaeger, 2011, p. 10).

Southern Arkansas University

Established in 1909 and located in Magnolia, Southern Arkansas is a comprehensive liberal arts university with a total enrollment of about thirty-five hundred students. University Housing features residential interest groups (RIGs), which are available to all residential students. The program encourages student involvement in campus activities and provides academic support. Peer and professional mentors work with each of the communities and encourage student involvement and academic success. Students share a common floor in one of the university's residence halls, and that approach provides space for a broad program array.

Two of the RIGs, Honors College and Residential College, serve high-achieving incoming students, with admission based on ACT scores. The Residential College emphasizes service-learning and requires students to participate in one community project during the academic year and log fifteen hours of community service. The Leadership College is open to first- and second-year students; through participation in a program known as MULE.org (Meaningful Undergraduate Living/Learning Experience-Orientation, Retention, Graduation) they plan and initiate a variety of campus activities. MULE also focuses on opportunities for students to interact with faculty in both their classes and within the residence hall. The Residential College and MULE require participation in learning communities; residents coenroll in two or three classes every semester. MULE participants consistently have higher retention rates than students who have not been part of a learning community.

The first-year experience RIG focuses on student engagement with campus activities and leadership development. Other RIGs emphasize specific career areas, for example, nursing, agriculture and business, and performing arts. Greek Groups and Sports and Fitness are also available, and it is possible for students to custom-design a RIG. Several of the RIGs are gender specific. Bussey Hall is reserved for women and includes five living-learning programs: Health and Wellness, First Year Experience, Education, Greek women, and upper-class women interest groups. Both Residential College and Honors Hall include a classroom.

Chapter Eight

Developmental Education

The higher education boom of the later 1960s and 1970s witnessed a significant expansion in the number of four-year and two-year campuses that dramatically changed the socioeconomic profile and academic preparedness level of incoming students (Cox, 2009; Nuss, 2003). In response, colleges and universities established or expanded learning services that focused on providing entering students with courses designed to enable them to develop college-level skills in reading, writing, and mathematics. In contrast to remedial education, which viewed such students in terms of deficits, both learning assistance and developmental education emphasize that almost all college students require some assistance during their college years, whether formal or informal, and all education focuses on developing knowledge, skills, and abilities (Arendale, 2005).

At a 1996 conference of the National Association of Developmental Education (NADE), which had been founded in 1976, several groups joined together to establish the American Council of Developmental Education Associations, which then served as a clearinghouse for information sharing and collaboration among professional associations in the field (Boylan, 2007, p. 34). Six years later, it adopted a broader mission and formed the Council of Learning Assistance and Developmental Education Associations. Its members include the Association for the Tutoring Profession; the College Reading and Learning Association; NADE; the National Center for Developmental Education, which had been established at Appalachian State University in 1977; and the National College Learning Center Association. This reflected the tradition of collaborative relationships among practitioners and organizations engaged in various aspects of developmental education.

NADE (2011) defines the nature and scope of its work as "a field of practice and research within higher education with a theoretical foundation in developmental psychology and learning theory. It promotes the cognitive and affective growth of all postsecondary learners, at all levels of the learning continuum." Emphasizing that broad mission, Casazza (1999) pointed to a 1998 NADE executive board resolution affirming that developmental education includes the "intellectual, social and emotional growth and development of all learners."

Chickering's 1969 classic, *Education and Identity*, updated with Reisser in 1993, established a theoretical basis for academically focused developmental education, while adopting a holistic view of students that included the affective domain. Although universities provide support programs to address affective, attitudinal, and life circumstance issues that can have a negative effect on student success, those issues generally are not seen as relevant to course placement.

Writing about community colleges, Zachary and Schneider (2010) suggested a typology of interventions for developmental education: "(1) strategies that help students avoid developmental education and move directly into college-level work; (2) interventions that accelerate students' progress through developmental education; (3) contextualized instructional models that connect students with workforce training and college-level courses; [and] (4) supplemental supports aimed at improving students' success" (p. iii).

The major diagnostic tools measuring the core skills of reading, English, and math include standardized tests such as ACT's Compass and the College Board's Accuplacer, which have a dominant share of the market (Gerlaugh, Thompson, Boylan, & Davis, 2007). At a 2012 forum sponsored by the New England Board of Higher Education, the president of the Community College of Vermont expressed concerns regarding the degree to which Accuplacer is sufficiently nuanced in its identification of students' strengths and weaknesses and noted that "the college is asking developmental English students to do a self-assessment, not of their skills, but of their practices, asking for example, if they read newspapers and magazines regularly" (Harney, 2012).

Institutions may also use customized ACT reports to place students or, as in the case of Texas, statewide exams. Mandatory placement appears to promote student success at four-year institutions but not at two-year institutions (Roueche & Roueche, 1999). Institutions use different cut scores for placement, and Bailey (2009) asserts that "there is no national consensus about what level of skills is needed to be college ready or about how to assess that level" (p. 14). He also suggests that placement tests do not capture the broad array of factors that contribute to students' readiness for college-level work. Boylan (2009) proposed an approach known as targeted intervention that would be informed by a broader array of student and course data rather than focusing on only data from placement tests.

Boylan, Bliss, and Bonham (1997) emphasized the benefits of clustering services in a single unit, and that has become a common best practice in larger institutions, though the specific services included often vary. For example, some centers focus exclusively on developmental course work in English, reading, and math, though both the number and sequencing of those courses differ. Other programs may include study skills, critical thinking, or test taking. Services that all students use, for example, advising, typically are not housed in developmental education departments.

The math and English departments at some colleges and universities offer developmental courses. The University of Minnesota's Jandriss Center for innovative education, for example, pioneered an approach that "embedded" developmental education in college classes, and "while this approach cannot overcome severe academic under preparation in mathematics, reading, or writing, it does permit more students to be admitted and be academically successful" (University of Minnesota College of Education and Human Development, 2012). Another model is to include developmental education in their cognate academic departments, For example, math and English faculty at Delgado Community College in New Orleans teach both precollege and college-level courses.

All developmental education programs include courses in math, reading, and English whose purpose is to prepare students for college-level work. Students enter these sequences based on standardized tests—some national, others state or institution specific. Those courses typically are identified with a "0" prefix and do not count as credits toward graduation, but they often are included in calculating students' grade point averages. Moreover, even when students successfully complete required developmental work, their time to degree will likely be longer, which in itself has a negative effect on their rates of success.

Course sequences vary considerably in terms of number and credits. Among thirty-eight community colleges participating in a National Center for Academic Transformation (NCAT) project course sequences in developmental math ranged from a high of six to a low of two, with three as the most common pattern (Twigg, 2010). Many developmental education programs focus either solely or mostly on bringing students to the point where they are able to register for college-level math and English. Students may choose whether to use other campus support services. Since the causes of poor classroom performance often involve a wide range of issues, contemporary best practice emphasizes the need for communication and collaboration among the various services that support student success. This facilitates a coordinated approach and more comprehensive monitoring of student challenges and progress. University colleges often provide these opportunities. For example, the University College at Wright State University has a Student Academic Success Center that includes developmental education and supplemental instruction, as well as a math learning center, tutoring services, and a university writing center. In addition to providing a seamless experience for students, this model facilitates collaboration among staff.

Concerns regarding student success rates at community colleges spurred "Achieving the Dream," a Lumina Foundation project that provided funding for projects to develop and improve programs that supported student success. Lumina required all proposed projects to have a data-rich research design. One of its partners, MDRC (formerly the Manpower Demonstration Research Project), worked extensively with community colleges on research and evaluation design. Building on that initiative, the Gates Foundation launched a developmental education initiative that included fifteen community colleges. NCAT also has engaged with community colleges, sponsoring an ongoing series of workshops focused on course redesign. Based on the results of those workshops, NCAT (Twigg, 2010) identified six characteristics of an effective approach to developmental education: whole course redesign, active learning, computer-based learning resources, instructional software packages, mastery learning, and on-demand help. It also suggested different staffing models and modularizing courses.

Both projects in part reflected the growing movement among various state governments to make developmental education the purview of community colleges. The contemporary political and fiscal landscape has engendered considerable discussion regarding the inappropriateness of providing developmental education at four-year state colleges and universities. Greene (2008) observes that "policymakers . . . have a hard time getting past the belief that the state should not have to pay twice to get students ready for college, while image-conscious college leaders and faculty, fearing they will be seen primarily as 'remedial' institutions, have too often relegated developmental education to the periphery of their missions" (p. 1). In Florida, state colleges must contract with community colleges to provide developmental courses. In 2008, the Indiana Commission for Higher Education issued a set of strategic initiatives, one of whose goals was to "substantially eliminate all remedial courses in public four-year colleges and universities" (Fulton, 2008).

The push to move this "remedial" education to community colleges has also brought to the forefront such questions as why high schools graduates are not adequately prepared for college work and why four-year colleges and universities admit them. The California State University board of trustees issued an executive order in 2010 stating that as of summer 2012, students identified as deficient in math or English would be required to "begin remediation" during the summer prior to their initial enrollment and "had to demonstrate proficiency in English and Math on or before the end of their first year of enrollment at a CSU campus." Complete College America, an alliance that includes thirty state governments and has funding from major corporations, issued a report in 2012 with the title, *Remediation: Higher Education's Bridge to Nowhere*. Clearly developmental education's current practices and role in higher education confront an environment that emphasizes the importance of research-based practices and accountability.

Approaching the Work/Critical Partners

In the 1990s, the College Reading and Learning Association (CRLA) and the National Association for Developmental Education (NADE) partnered with the Council for the Advancement of Standards in Higher Education (CAS) to establish standards for the field; they were revised in 2007. These cover critical program aspects, including mission, learning outcomes, assessment, leadership, human and fiscal resources, organization and management, and other topics critical to establishing a strong, comprehensive program. The standards' initial section affirms: "The primary mission of Learning Assistance Programs . . . must be to provide students with resources and opportunities to improve their ability to learn and to achieve academic success" (CAS, 2009). Those goals, operationalized in terms of specific outcomes for students, should inform institutional approaches to developmental education. CAS standards also note that programs should address "the cognitive, affective, and socio-cultural dimensions of learning" (CAS, 2009).

The breadth of these goals suggests that a broad array of partners should engage with this initiative, including faculty members in English and math and the directors and staff of relevant student support offices. Establishing good lines of communication between developmental educators and members of the English and math departments can help inform the work of both, thereby easing student transitions to college-level courses in those disciplines. However, since developmental education students also are registered for college-level classes, it is important to engage faculty who teach those classes. Ghere (2000) discusses how that might affect an introductory course in US history. The leadership and staff of advising, student success, and first-year centers also can play a role in supporting the need for and positive impact of developmental education. Both academic and student services professionals work with students taking developmental education courses, as do other offices that provide support services for students. Senior administrators, directors, and staff from those areas should participate in discussions that focus on establishing or strengthening a developmental education program. Academic vice presidents and deans can play an important role in fostering cooperation by emphasizing the importance of developmental education to student achievement. Other partners include committees related to academic policies, teaching and learning, and the first year, as well as directors of admissions, testing, and tutoring. Whatever their organizational homes, a collaborative and collegial relationship between the heads of those areas becomes an important factor for building a successful developmental education program or strengthening an existing one.

Organization/Implementation

Inventorying existing services, including where they are housed, and creating a leadership team or task force, are good initial steps for developing or enhancing a developmental education program. For example, a student success center or university college may offer services that are important to an effective program. Governance issues also should be considered, since colocating individuals and offices with different report lines can prove problematic. If the campus already provides some developmental courses, it makes sense to identify the informal and formal partnerships they already have with other areas. If those seem to include the relevant offices and personnel, trying to create a new organizational model might prove disruptive and unproductive. Instead, consider the possibility of formalizing some of the existing informal links. This could include revising department mission statements and job descriptions to include developmental education. A learning community approach linking one or more of the developmental classes with a first-year seminar appears to have a positive impact for developmental education students in terms of accelerating their progress through the courses (Weiss, Visher, & Weissman, 2011).

The leadership team or task force should include representatives from the developmental education program and from advising, counseling, tutoring, and other offices that provide services important to student success. A mechanism for providing student input, particularly from successful students who tested into one or more developmental education classes, promises to add valuable perspectives. Program outcomes should drive the proposed change and be reflected in both the organization and implementation of a new or revised program. Outcomes might be defined minimally as preparing students to succeed in college-level math, reading, and English with a grade of at least "C" in the next-level class. A more ambitious agenda might include accelerating student progress through these developmental sequences and identifying college level courses in which developmental students have a reasonable chance for success. For example, courses that employ alternative teaching-learning and evaluation strategies, such as community-based learning, may provide better opportunities for developmental students to succeed. A review of developmental students' success rates in college-level courses should identify courses in which they have a reasonable opportunity to succeed.

Organizational Options

Multiple organizational options exist, moving from highly clustered to distributed but coordinated programs. That raises questions regarding the specific programs or offices to include. Research suggests that "distributive" models, that is, a range of services housed in different offices, can work effectively if they are "highly coordinated" (Boylan, Bliss, & Bonham, 1997), though centralized models facilitate communication and enable students' needs to be assessed and addressed in a single location. A minimally clustered program might include all developmental education courses and some allied courses, for example, study skills. A more densely clustered approach could include tutoring, testing, counseling, and advising, all of which contribute to program success (Boylan et al., 1997). Integrated models place developmental courses in broader learning assistance or developmental education departments or centers, which also include other academic support services. For example, Learning Assistance at University of Wisconsin-Parkside houses developmental courses in mathematics and English, which it designates as academic skills courses, and also has a writing center and an academic resource center that provide tutoring in a wide variety of subject areas to all students. It offers a college-credit critical thinking course as well. Mt. San Antonio College's Learning Assistance Center offers both developmental reading classes and a 100-level college reading course, along with developmental writing and developmental math and a study skills class. Students can elect to take any or all of their developmental courses on a pass/fail basis. The center's services also include tutoring and a learning laboratory.

As these examples suggest, integrated models do not necessarily provide the same array of services or include all services that are needed to meet the needs of students. Adding voices from all relevant student support offices can help create a more seamless student experience. The question becomes one of balance in terms of identifying the core components for the integrated model while also creating structured links among other campus offices and departments, many of which might be in student services. This should provide the basis for a more cohesive system of support for student success throughout the campus. And no matter how densely or minimally clustered, links to other areas are likely to be important, so whatever the model, it makes sense to think broadly and identify other offices and programs that need to be engaged to some degree. Whether directly integrated into a center for developmental education or colocated within a larger home, students should see access as seamless.

Alternative Approaches

Exploring alternative approaches to developing entering students' skill levels can reduce the demands on developmental education. Many of these focus on mathematics. In part, because once high school students meet the required units for graduation, many of them take no additional math classes, and when they take a placement examination, they have forgotten much of what they once knew. Providing a brief refresher course prior to the start of the semester can enable some of those students to test into college-level math. For example, Utah State University allows students to take the math placement exam, and if their scores fall below the level for entry into a 100-level math class, they can register for a four-day refresher course and then repeat the exam. Arizona State University allows students to take the math placement exam two times during the twelve months prior to enrolling. An online math refresher is available to assist students who want to improve their score. A math "boot camp" organized as a summer program or embedded in a bridge program can also prove effective. Great Basin College in Nevada, which participates in both the National Complete College America and National Governors' of America Complete to Compete Programs, offers two-week math refresher courses that cover three levels of developmental education prior to the start of both the fall and spring semesters.

Selecting appropriate college courses for students taking developmental English also can prove challenging because their low reading rates and limited vocabularies make it difficult for them to succeed in reading-extensive classes. Similarly, the content and approach of many 100-level classes in the social and behavioral sciences are likely to prove overly challenging to students who lack mathematical reasoning skills.

Under the umbrella of learning assistance, a program known as structured learning assistance (SLA), which has proven successful in assisting students in introductory classes, was developed at Ferris State University. It provides course-specific assistance by attaching an SLA section to courses that have proven challenging to first-year students. Ferris State offers a wide range of courses with SLA sections, including 100-level math, bioscience, and chemistry. Austin Peay University eliminated developmental courses in math, reading, and English, and replaced them with SLA sections attached to the college-level courses. Supplemental Instruction (SI), developed at the University of Missouri, Kansas City, is similar to SLA in targeting specific courses rather than a specific student cohort. The focus on challenging courses instead of challenged students minimizes stigma (Stone & Jacobs, 2008). Both SI and SLA have shown positive impacts on student success (Ogden, Thompson, Russell, & Simons, 2003).

Boylan (2004) expressed concerns about the appropriateness of the standard semester-long developmental education course and noted other possibilities. Among those were more robust assessment of entering students, creating alternatives to course-based remediation, and promoting broader and more effective collaborations. Providing structured opportunities for interactions among developmental educators and high school teachers might well benefit the students, schools, and college. This could prove especially effective at institutions whose area high schools provide a large percentage of the institution's first-year students. The Texas Higher Education Coordinating Board has funded several developmental education demonstration projects initiatives that "are designed to boost completion rates among at-risk students by improving remediation programs" (Texas Higher Education Coordinating Board, 2012). One initiative seeks to accelerate students' progress by enabling them to complete courses in remedial and college-level math in the same semester.

Staffing

Sharing staff between developmental math and math departments can prove valuable in terms of facilitating student transitions from the developmental sequence to the initial college-level course and for creating positive relationships, one of which might be exchanging some teaching assignments. Developmental educators teaching the initial college algebra class would gain a more accurate sense of the expectations and pace of that course, and math department faculty members would gain similar insights through teaching the final developmental math course. Those experiences might lead to productive conversations about course alignment, resulting in smoother transitions for students. Zachary and Schneider (2008) underscored the importance of designing a repertoire of pedagogical approaches to address student needs, given the variability of skill levels among developmental students and the fact that students with similar composite scores on placement exams may have differing needs.

As noted, at four-year colleges and universities, developmental courses overwhelmingly are taught by academic staff members and adjunct faculty rather than by professors. At many regional colleges, it is not uncommon to find former or current high school math and English teachers instructing developmental classes that include students who performed poorly in their high school classes. This can predispose both instructors and students to have negative feelings about the possibilities for success, which suggests the utility of establishing a required orientation workshop for all new instructors, whether full or part time, that would also include the other members of the program. The orientation could provide an overview of the area and include discussions of policies, pedagogy, and student success strategies.

An orientation program for new full-time and adjunct instructors creates an opportunity to discuss program mission and objectives and effective ways to approach students. It also might include discussions of best practices, which could include presentations from developmental educators and members of the English and math departments. Active participation and sponsorship by a senior administrator would convey the importance of the program.

Leadership Roles/Communication

Whatever the organizational models, it is likely that cooperation among offices in student affairs and academic affairs will be needed to establish an effective developmental education program, and collegial leadership by their chief administrative officers will greatly facilitate that process. Academic deans also can play a positive leadership role by providing opportunities for discussions about developmental education at collegewide and departmental meetings. That is especially important for faculty in math and English, who often are frustrated by low levels of student performance in their classes and see that as reflecting a lack of rigor in developmental classes. Department chairs, given their role as academic leaders and their responsibilities for developing course schedules and making teaching assignments, also should become familiar with the campus's developmental education classes and the appropriate teaching and learning strategies for students served by the program. Student and academic affairs leaders in such areas as advising, counseling, and testing can add important perspectives to this work. Staff involved with TRIO programs, summer bridges, and Upward Bound work with populations that are heavily represented in developmental education classes and can offer valuable insights.

Broad-based, candid campus conversations which are receptive to differing points of view and focus on the shared responsibilities for improving student success rates, are most likely to produce positive results. These "stakeholder" meetings, which might be sponsored by the institution's chief academic officer, should boost transparency and encourage productive dialogue. Meetings could include a variety of formats and subjects, for example, brown bag luncheons, presentations on barriers to student success, joint teaching-learning improvement projects, and discussions of pedagogical strategies. Bringing people together from diverse areas also helps build positive personal relationships that can dispel damaging stereotypes about developmental students, developmental educators, and faculty. Faculty who teach large introductory sections could offer their classroom-based experience as to what English and math skills, including mathematical reasoning, are important to success in their courses, and developmental educators could dispel concerns regarding both the rigor and effectiveness of their classes. Those perspectives should help ground discussions of student readiness.

A study by McCabe (2000) pointed to the overrepresentation of ethnic minorities in developmental education programs, especially in the cohort testing into the lowest level of remediation. Reyes and Nora (2012), citing the work of Bettinger and Long (2005), pointed to data from Ohio indicating that 75 percent of African American and Latino students were placed into developmental education in math, as opposed to 55 percent of white students. Moreover, they noted a study by Nora & Crisp (2012) indicating "that Black students are more likely to enroll in developmental coursework when compared to White students with the same academic skills, preparation and social background." However, a study of Latino students found that successful completion of developmental English correlated positively with college success (Swail, 2004).

Stein (2005) suggested that instructors of developmental classes that include large numbers of Latinos should receive professional development to heighten their sensitivity to this population and promote inclusion of culturally relevant content. That general approach might prove successful with other student populations. Given the disproportionate numbers of Latinos and African American students who test into developmental education classes, connections with successful students of color and participation in campus events sponsored by various multicultural organizations could prove beneficial.

Resource Needs/Personnel

Institutional costs vary widely depending on admissions standards, the size of the student population that needs to be served, the length of required course sequences, and the adequacy of instructional staff. For example, setting lower enrollment caps, creating learning communities, and implementing ongoing assessment of student learning would have budgetary implications. Similarly, a new organizational model also might require additional administrative costs. Funding for campus-based professional development and for sending teams to regional and national conferences should be considered, along with costs of having programs certified. Policies regarding class size, cut scores, and course sequences have implications for staffing, as do the characteristics of the student population served and the campuses' approach to program implementation. For example, a lower cap on enrollment in developmental classes would increase the number of sections. High priority should be given to identifying strategies to improve the effectiveness of developmental education to accelerate and facilitate students' success in both their developmental and college-level courses.

Given fiscal pressures throughout the academy, most colleges and universities have unmet staffing needs. Efficiencies might be identified, but it is unlikely that significant new responsibilities can be carried out by existing staff. As well, there may be needed expertise not present on the campus, so positions that do come open should be evaluated in terms of their potential for enhancing developmental education.

Providing professional development for key staff and faculty should also help to address that issue. As has been noted, multiple national organizations are engaged with developmental education issues. Sending leadership teams to state, regional, or national conferences and workshops can address expertise needs and foster productive working relationships. Providing subsequent campus-based professional development opportunities confirms that message.

In sum, launching a new program or ramping up an existing one will likely require significant expenditures for both on- and off-campus professional development, as well as for personnel.

Assessment

A 2004–2005 NADE study examined rates of developmental education course completion and student success in the subsequent college-level class. Persistence rates in developmental classes were 80 percent for math and 83 percent for both reading and writing. Defined as a grade of C or higher, success rates for that group were 68 percent in math, 73 percent for writing, and 76 percent for reading. The study also examined student success rates in the next college-level class and found that 69 percent of the students achieved at least a grade of C in reading, 64 percent in writing, and 58 percent in math (Gerlaugh et al., 2007).

Identifying a set of key outcomes for students while they are enrolled in developmental courses can yield data to help revise courses and course sequences. Grades in those developmental classes can be tracked, as can performance in college-level classes for which they were registered. That analysis might identify classes in which such students achieve greater or lesser success rates compared to students who tested into college-level work in math and English. Overall credit load as related to grades can be tracked, and that analysis might suggest the need to set credit limits for students taking two developmental classes. Monitoring their subsequent performance in college-level math and English will also provide evidence on program effectiveness.

Standard success markers such as probation rates, grade point average, credit completion, and retention and graduation rates can be used to compare the success rates of developmental students over time as compared with nondevelopmental students. A campus might focus on reducing the time it takes students to achieve college-ready proficiency in English, reading, and math, while also reducing drop, withdrawal, and failure (DWF) rates in their college-level classes. In addition, it is important to assess students' perceptions of the program. A study focused on community colleges concluded that to entering students, the developmental education program "must appear confusing, intimidating, and boring" (Bailey, Wook Jeong, & Cho, 2008, p. 28).

Assessment should include program components and personnel. Seeking national certification could both advance and help institutionalize assessment. Boylan and Saxon (2009) list five such associations: "The Association for the Tutoring Profession (ATP), the College Reading and Learning Association (CRLA), the National Association for Developmental Education (NADE), the National College Learning Center Association (NCLCA), and the National Tutoring Association (NTA)" (p. 5). All of these certifications require self-study and reflection that includes broader campus-based discussions, which should facilitate the development of rubrics for ongoing assessment.

In 1994, Boylan et al. placed the rate of ongoing evaluation of developmental education programs for community colleges at 14 percent and at 25 percent for four-year institutions. A 2007 study of community colleges found that assessment had become a common practice at 64 percent of those institutions (Gerlaugh et al., 2007). Lesik (2008) emphasized the power of a "regression discontinuity model that researchers can use to establish a causal link between participation in a developmental program and student retention" (p. 1).

Developmental education programs may be assessed across multiple dimensions, one of which might include an institution's process for course placement. Bailey (2009) suggests that while placement tests assess a student's mastery level, a more productive approach might be one that "tries to determine what skills a student will need to succeed in college" (p. 24). Failure to ensure a seamless transition to college-level work topped Hunter Boylan's list of the top ten mistakes in developmental education programs. He defined this operationally as failing to recognize that the "transition in developmental and college level courses requires that the exit standards of one level course are consistent with the entry standards of the next" (Boylan, 2009, pp. 1–2). Though writing with regard to community colleges, Boylan's observation applies to developmental education programs at all campuses, since that transition has a powerful impact on student persistence. Assessment of student success rates in the next college course in a sense closes the loop.

A 1988 NELS study found that completion rates for a three-course remedial sequence were at best 20 percent. Ten years later, an analysis of developmental education at community colleges (Bailey, Wook Jeong, & Cho, 2010) found that approximately 30 to 40 percent of students completed the recommended sequence, but that dropped to 20 percent when the recommended sequence was three courses. The study also reported lower completion rates for several student cohorts, including students pursuing occupational programs or enrolled part-time, men, and African Americans.

Benefit Analysis

Student success, operationally defined by the goals and outcomes established for developmental education, drives the analysis of benefits. For example, fewer repeats in developmental courses translate into additional seats for new students, which may reduce the number of sections needed, thereby lowering instructional costs. Lower DWF rates in college-level classes should reduce instructional costs by reducing the number of sections needed. When students develop the skills, attitudes, and behaviors that promote success in college, retention and graduation rates typically rise, which translates into lower tuition costs and debt burden to students and overall tuition gains for the institution. Higher rates of student success should contribute to the institution's reputation within its service area, which also might make it more attractive to students. Benefits analysis might also include the positive impacts for staff, faculty and student morale, and overall workplace satisfaction. The inclusion of ongoing, robust assessment should not only enhance program effectiveness but also suggest ways to increase program efficiency. In sum, although establishing or ramping up a developmental education program will require new expenditures, the human and fiscal benefits to students, their families, and the institution are likely to be substantial.

Institutional Practices

Jacksonville State University

Located in Jacksonville, Alabama, and classified by the Carnegie Foundation as a Master's L (larger programs), Jacksonville State University (JSU) is characterized as "liberally selective" and enrolls about ninety-five hundred students. Its Department of Learning Services received Distinguished NADE certification for its Developmental Quantification and Developmental English courses in 2007. Organized as the Center for Individualized Instruction in 1977 as part of a Title III grant, it initially focused on basic and advanced academic skills. Since that time, the center has developed into an academic and service department that is fully funded by the university. As an intentional strategy to decrease a sense of stigma for those who use its services, the center provides assistance to a broad range of students. Peer mentors and student workers support its professional staff. Its teaching-learning strategies include precision teaching, direct instruction, and a "flipped classroom" approach, in which class time centers on active, engaged learning and content is delivered electronically to students before class. Rather than only measuring the percentage of correct responses, the courses within the department measure student performance and focus on increasing correct responses across time to train fluent performance (Binder, 2005).

Housed in the College of Arts and Sciences, Learning Services is unusual in that it offers developmental courses at both the "0" and 100 level which collectively provide an orientation to college life, while also developing students' skills, and three 300-level courses focused on performance management. Institutional credit-only offerings include Reinforcing Communication Skills, a three-credit course focused on grammar and college-level writing, and a one-credit Writing Competency Skills class. Of the fall 2010 cohort that passed Reinforcing Communication Skills, the writing skills class, and the 100-level college English class, 82 percent achieved passing grades in English Composition II, a prerequisite for taking the university-wide English competency exam. A three-credit refresher course, Basic Algebra Skills, focuses on arithmetic and basic algebra. Data for the fall 2010 cohort indicate that 82 percent of students who passed that class and the intervening math classes passed the college-level math course required for their major. The 100-level curriculum has three classes: a three-credit course focused on reading skills; Academic Success Skills, a three-credit course required for all conditionally admitted first-year students that concentrates on academic and coping skills and provides an orientation to college life; and a three-credit course that focuses on critical thinking. The integration of 100-level classes enables students to accumulate degree credits in a supportive environment.

Students who fail the English competency exam (ECE) are required to take ECE remediation, an optional one-credit or noncredit course or one-on-one learning assistance before they take the exam again. Both options require the students to write six passing essays to be certified to retake the exam. From 2002 to 2012, Learning Services served over nineteen hundred students, and

75 percent of those passed the ECE on their next attempt. Learning Services also oversees ExSEL (Experiencing Success in Education and Life), a summer bridge program required of all students with ACT scores between 14 and 17 or a combined SAT between 650 and 820 for critical reading and math. The two-year retention rate for the 2010 ExSEL class was 78 percent, and 62 percent of those were enrolled for the following year. These success rates are among the highest retention rates at the university.

Northern Kentucky University

A metropolitan university about seven miles from Cincinnati, Northern Kentucky University (NKU) has an enrollment of 15,700 undergraduates and 1,600 graduate students, and also offers a JD and a doctorate in education. Learning Assistance at NKU espouses the mission of the National Association for Developmental Education (NADE, 2013): "Help the underprepared [student] to prepare, the prepared student to advance, and the advanced to excel!"

In 2009, Kentucky's General Assembly approved a bill that set goals for reducing developmental education in math and English by 50 percent over four years. As part of enabling legislation, the state established the Kentucky Online Testing Program (Kyote). Out-of state student placement is based on ACT, SAT, or COMPASS scores.

The Learning Assistance Program at NKU includes centers for math, writing, and tutoring and offers programs in supplemental instruction and developmental education. Students who test into developmental education must enroll in all required developmental education courses during their initial college year. Those are not included in calculating their grade point average and do not count as credits toward a degree. Writing Lab (ENGI 080) supports the two-course developmental English sequence, which is graded on a pass-fail basis. The department also provides writing workshops and reading workshops, with sections designed for native and nonnative speakers of English. An additional course, Critical Reading (RDG 110), focuses on reading strategies for general education. The department has developed a detailed course information sheet for instructors, an important practice given the use of adjunct instructors in some sections. That document includes learning outcomes, suggestions regarding the organization of individual class sessions, and strategies to engage students.

All developmental education courses in mathematics and English have specific learning outcomes. The math sequence begins with elementary geometry, a prealgebra course that promotes skill development in inductive and deductive reasoning. Essential Algebra and Intermediate Algebra develop competencies needed for success in College Algebra. Pretests administered during the initial week of class are compared with posttests, which form part of the final exam and provide a basis for assessment. Approximately 75 to 85 percent of students score at least 60 percent on the posttest for algebra, and more than 90 percent of students achieve that score in geometry. Student achievement levels exceed the pretest benchmarks in all courses. Faculty also review the questions associated with each learning outcome to identify outcomes that are not being met. The tutoring center, staffed by upper-division mathematics students, provides course specific assistance, and the online site, MY MATH LAB, is another resource.

Writing assignments form the basis for assessing student performance in developmental literacy, and classes may also include a posttest. A rubric based on student learning outcomes is used to grade those assignments. Student success rates vary significantly from course to course and across semesters, ranging from a low of 52 percent to a high of 96 percent. Faculty use these results to suggest changes to improve student learning. ENGD 090, "Writing Workshop," a three-credit course, is a prerequisite for college English that focuses on preparing students to write at the college level. Satisfactory completion of Reading 091, a three-credit course, enables students to register for English 101. Mean student scores on the Degrees of Reading Power test, used in RDG 091 as a pretest and posttest, have always increased from the pretest to the posttest, and data also suggest that students who successfully complete the developmental sequences in math and English achieve pass rates similar to those of students who tested directly into college-level English and math, including students who placed directly into College Algebra. However, in some semesters, pass rates for students who took developmental courses are significantly lower than students who placed directly into the general education mathematics courses. Nonetheless, since the inception of the new developmental mathematics curriculum in fall 2009, at least 76 percent of the students who completed the required sequence achieved passing grades in their first college-level mathematics class on their first attempt.

Los Medanos Community College

Located in Pittsburg, California, Los Medanos is part of the Contra Costa Community College District and enrolls over twenty-one thousand students. It offers approximately forty associate degrees and fifty certificate programs to a majority minority student population. Los Medanos established a decentralized but coordinated developmental education program that reflects the work of the campus Developmental Education Committee (DEC). Both the dean of liberal arts and sciences and the dean of student development serve on the committee. A half-time administrative release is often split between an English and a math faculty member. They coordinate professional development, curriculum development, institutional reporting and documentation, and assessment activities.

This broadly representative committee includes faculty and staff members from math, English, and English as a Second Language, the coordinator of the Reading and Writing Center, and the tutor coordinators for the departments of English and math, along with a representative from the Counseling Department, the coordinator of the Developmental Education Program, and the senior dean of instruction and senior dean of student services. Their work responds to a state initiative, Accountability Reporting for the Community Colleges, which requires reports on student performance to be sent to the legislature.

The committee's purview includes assessment, oversight of course placements, curriculum development, and professional development. The college's math department provides additional support for developmental math through its developmental math committee, which meets weekly to develop and coordinate assessment, professional development, and other services for the developmental math program. Further modeling the distributed but highly coordinated approach, the program coordinator's duties include a liaison role with academic support services. The program also works closely with institutional research and engages in ongoing formative and summative evaluation.

The Developmental Education Committee (DEC) coordinates ongoing assessment of student progress based on a set of institution-level student learning outcomes. The assessment reviews direct measures of student learning, including, for example, final examinations in the capstone English and math courses. It also partners with the Office of Institutional Research to develop and implement indirect measures of student achievement and surveys students to get a better of sense of their experience in and satisfaction with the program.

The DEC also engages in curriculum development and coordination of professional development, and it works to ensure the fit between the needs of students and the college's developmental education program, which informs the development of new approaches and courses—for example, Acceleration Flex, a pilot designed to move students through developmental math more quickly. Data from spring 2012 indicated the students in Math 910, which was equivalent to completing a two-course developmental sequence (Math 25 and 30), had a success rate of 84 percent, which generally exceeded the pass rate in those courses in four of the five previous semesters. An ongoing assessment of credit completion, using thirty credits as a target, which tracked and compared data from academic year 2003–2004 to 2010–2011, indicated an ongoing positive trend. Persistence rates for students who earned at least six credits in their initial semester rose from 65.6 percent in 2007–2008 to 71.1 in 2008–2009, then dropped slightly to 70.3 percent in 2009–2010 (Los Medanos College, 2013). These and many other ongoing assessments provide a data-rich environment for ongoing program development and program improvement.

Chapter Nine

Early Alert Warning Systems

According to 2010 data for all four-year institutions from the Integrated Postsecondary Education Data System (IPEDS), 30 percent of first-year students failed to return for a second year. Responses to a Noel-Levitz midyear retention report indicated that, depending on institutional type, anywhere from 9 to 19 percent of first-year students did not return for the second semester (Noel-Levitz, 2011). Not surprisingly, students who do not experience academic success during their initial semester of attendance are the least likely to be retained (Ishitani & DesJardins, 2002). These statistics suggest the importance of identifying and providing early assistance to first-year students who are experiencing difficulties in their transition to college. To address that need, colleges have established early alert warning systems (EAWS), also known as early warning systems (EWS).

Cuseo (2003a, n.p.) defines *early alert* as "a formal, proactive, feedback system through which students and student-support agents are alerted to early manifestations of poor academic performance." The oldest practice, which still remains common in higher education, is requiring midterm grades for all first-year students. Data for 2004–2005 on policies at four-year master's-granting and research universities indicate that approximately 58 percent had a midterm grade policy, and the rate for baccalaureate institutions was close to 70 percent. A substantial number of institutions required that report at the end of the sixth week of classes (College Board Advocacy, 2009).

EAWS programs are an institutional response to concerns about retention and to the fact that student disengagement is likely to begin during the initial weeks of the academic year, as indicated by habitual lateness, poor attendance, and failure to participate in class activities and complete assignments in a timely fashion. In fact, surveys report high levels of academic disengagement among first-year students, as evidenced by "boredom, absenteeism, and cheating" (Strayhorn, 2011). Kuh (2003) suggests the existence of an unseemly bargain—the "disengagement compact": "'I'll leave you alone if you leave me alone.' That is, I won't make you work too hard (read a lot, write a lot) so that I won't have to grade as many papers or explain why you are not performing well" (p. 28). Harward (2008) points to data regarding high rates of depression among millennial students and their perception that the problem goes unnoticed by faculty. He also notes the prevalence of binge drinking and drug use.

Whatever the factors that have a negative impact on student performance, initial identification of unsuccessful students toward the midpoint of the first trimester or semester reduces the probability that students will be able to succeed, and many of them may see a negative report at those points as confirmation that they do not truly belong in college. Notification at those points may also make it difficult or impossible to add a new course. Moreover, depending on total credit load, dropping a course might shift a student's status to part time, resulting in a loss of financial aid. Given the critical nature of the initial weeks of the academic year, especially for first-year students, early identification of students who are experiencing a difficult transition provides opportunities for effective interventions.

Simons (2011) found that approximately 68 percent of EAWS programs had been in existence for "five or fewer years" (p. ii). As such, a formalized typology does not yet exist. However, critical distinctions among EAWS programs include program goals, target populations, timing of the alert, the degree of student and faculty participation, the nature and number of interventions, and the range of campus offices and personnel associated with the program. All programs, however, center on the goal of student success. Elgin Community College in Illinois listed five specific objectives for their program: "Increase retention in class enrollment; Increase success rate ("C" or better); Formalize the partnership between ECC student services and faculty to impact student success; Increase an awareness of institutional and community resources; [and] Increase student success and create positive student development" (Elgin Community College, 2012). At the University of Cincinnati, goals included "student satisfaction, engagement, learning/development, and implementation of a new comprehensive academic plan" (Donnelly, 2011, p. 40).

EAWS programs also vary in terms of target student populations, which may include entering students who are considered at risk, all first-year students, both first- and second-year students, or all students on probation. In some instances, the early alert is for all students regardless of class standing. Similar variation marks the timing of alerts. Some are implemented only during the first semester or trimester, while others occur in both fall and spring or throughout the academic year. Variability also occurs with regard to the nature and number of interventions, the involvement of classroom instructors, and relevant academic and student services offices. That also characterizes follow-up activities with students who have been identified as experiencing difficulty and the role of professional advisors and other academic and student support services. Policies regarding compliance by students and faculty and instructional staff are an additional and highly critical distinction.

Institutions commonly implement alerts in the fall semester, usually during the fourth through sixth week, or early in the first trimester, though some, for example, Marietta College, focus on the first two weeks of the semester. Despite the term *early alert*, many campuses accept alerts throughout the entire academic year. The target population most frequently is first-year students, or a specific first-year cohort, such as students who have been preidentified as belonging to one or more at-risk categories. The basis for making these assessments varies. At some institutions, admission profiles are used to preidentify at-risk students, and psychological factors also can serve as predictors (Allens, Robbins, & Sawyer, 2009). Beck and Davidson (2001) suggest that results from the Surveys of Academic Orientation have strong predictive value in identifying first-year students who are at risk of failure. Some campuses track performance in a specific set of gateway classes seen as critical to student progress, such as math, English, and introductory surveys (Hossler, Kuh, & Olsen, 2001), while others include all students' first-semester classes.

The nature of interventions and policies regarding student compliance varies across institutions and is influenced by campus culture and the characteristics of the student populations. In the majority of cases, both student and faculty compliance tend to be voluntary, and available interventions range from conversations with advisors, counselors, and professors to participation in collaborative programs of involved support offices. Similarly, student participation in programs and activities designed to contribute to their academic success may be either encouraged or required. For example, students may be directed to look at information on the institution's website to see the services available to them and encouraged to speak with their advisor.

In her survey of EAWS, Simons (2011) found that "45.6% of the respondents reported to an academic affairs division as compared to only 26.4 percent who reported to student affairs units" (pp. 50–51), and most of the rest had dual report lines. Nearly 60 percent used a centralized model in which the alert was "coordinated by person, team, or unit" (p. 105).

A quality of institutions identified as exemplars of good practice in the Demonstrating Effective Educational Practices project was the presence of "redundant early-warning systems that identify and respond to students whose academic performance or other behaviors put them at risk of failure or dropping out" (Kuh, Kinsie, Whitt, & Associates, 2005, p. 260). The use of multiple data points and processes to identify and intervene with students who are experiencing difficulties, along with ongoing collaboration among student and academic support services as part of the follow-up, creates a more robust system. At most institutions, classroom performance remains the critical indicator for early alerts, so instructional staff and faculty are the main sources for referrals; at other institutions, student life personnel, including mentors and advisors, also submit alerts. Many EAWS reporting forms may include specific categories, such as low levels of student engagement as indicated by attendance patterns, including late arrival and early departure, participation in class activities, and grades on quizzes, papers, and presentations.

A seamless system for initial reporting and subsequent follow-up that facilitates participation by classroom faculty and staff, student and academic affairs offices, and institutions frequently uses existing software for the initial report. For example, University of Texas at Austin's EAWS integrates with Blackboard Grade Center and can be used as soon as any grade has been entered. Those grades could be for any classroom behaviors or activities, including quizzes, assignments, or attendance, and concerns can be submitted as early as the third week of classes.

Approaching the Work/Critical Partners

Reflecting on the development of an early alert program at the University of Cincinnati, Donnelly (2011) presents a set of questions regarding participants, delivery mechanisms, and measures that will be used: "Which students, faculty, staff? What mechanisms and measures to use including the timing of the alert? When to alert and intervene? With whom should the alert be initiated? How: online, in person?" (p. 40). He also stresses the importance of identifying outcomes. Clearly the mechanics of the EAWS program are important, but more critical are the anticipated outcomes for student, faculty, and staff participants and the university as a whole. Responses to the last question can inform the overall approach, identification of partners, and a variety of decisions regarding organization and implementation.

Since classroom faculty and instructors are best positioned to observe and evaluate students' academic performance, their active participation is vital to successful early alerts. At many institutions, part-time instructors are assigned to introductory classes. Many of them also teach classes at another college and may have little familiarity with the institution or its students. Many community colleges provide development programs for adjunct faculty and instructors, and this practice might prove beneficial at other institutions.

Consistent attendance is critical for student success, but institution-wide mandatory attendance policies are uncommon in higher education, although the California State University System has raised this issue with faculty (Rae, 2011). Many instructors believe students are adults and should assume both responsibility for and the consequences of their own decisions. First-year students in large introductory courses where attendance is not taken and does not "count" toward a grade may assume that the professor has no way of knowing they are not in class unless they miss a scheduled quiz or fail to turn in an assignment. They also may assume that if attendance is not taken, it must not be important, since their experience to that point is that teachers grade what they value.

Orientation programs for students and faculty could include discussions of behaviors that promote success. Campus teaching and learning centers, first-year programs, and campus committees that focus on teaching and learning partner to develop programs on discussing alternative ways to track student attendance. These could include incorporating activities to track attendance and identify students who might benefit from early interventions. For example, short in-class papers, brief quizzes, and structured class discussions can be used to monitor attendance and student progress. Faculty and staff development workshops also might include discussions of pedagogical strategies that engage students and challenge them to become active learners.

Although institutions vary in terms of size, organizational complexity, and their array of academic and student support services, critical partners for early alert warning systems are likely to include advisors, counselors, developmental educators, peer mentors, tutors, and financial aid officers. Decisions regarding which offices should send and receive the alert, or additional offices that are likely to participate in providing support services for students identified by the alert, will suggest other critical partners. At institutions with significant residential populations, student or residence life professionals can contribute to the identification and support of students who are at risk, especially since multiple developmental and affective factors may play a role in students' classroom behaviors. Campus security may also provide helpful information and advice regarding student behaviors.

An efficient, effective, and user-friendly platform for both the initial alert and ongoing communications with students, classroom instructors, and the full array of offices and professional staff participating in the program promotes both initial and ongoing use, and therefore program reach and effectiveness. As has been noted, an institution's existing student information system may have that capability. However, commercial vendors also provide dedicated early alert systems, including, for example, DropGuard, Early Alert Retention Software, GradesFirst, Starfish Student Early

Alert System, and Pharos 360 (Early Alert Systems, NACADA Clearinghouse). Whatever the software used, a EAWS program should be designed to take full advantage of their capacity, and for this reason, campus technology services becomes another critical partner in identifying an appropriate proprietary software package or developing a home-grown campus-specific program, and providing ongoing technical support in terms of facilitating its use, and responding to user queries and technical problems.

Faculty and instructional staff who teach classes included in the alert can provide insights regarding the organization of course syllabi and the management of instructional challenges that arise during the first weeks of class, for example, significant numbers of drops, adds, and late registrations. Senior academic administrators, deans, and department chairs also need to engage with the EAWS. As academic leaders, they could promote collegial discussions of the program's importance for students and for the institution.

Students' social and emotional adjustment to college is an important factor in their academic success (Tinto, 1993; Lotkowski, Robbins, & Noeth, 2004). Contemporary students lead complicated lives, and that is especially the case for first-generation students, academically underprepared students, returning adults, students from lower socioeconomic status, and students of color. Therefore, multiple campus areas and offices, including, for example, academic support areas, student success centers, counseling and student health offices, and residence life professionals, can play a role in identifying and supporting students who appear to be experiencing difficulties (Allens et al., 2009). The configurations of offices and specific campus cultures and working relationships vary widely, but critical partners are those offices and individuals whose participation in the EAWS are important to the initiative's success.

Organization/Implementation Process

Donnelly's questions—the who, what, when, where, how, and why—can guide the organization and implementation of an EAWS program, and it is especially important to think in terms of desired outcomes that are measurable, relevant to student success, and reflect the institution's mission, culture, and characteristics of its student population. Student success data for both the institution and its peer or aspirational institutions can help ground these discussions. Identifying a home office and point person for the initiative is one of the most critical decisions for successful organization, implementation, and ongoing development of the EAWS.

Advancing the Development of EAWS

Given the broad array of campus stakeholders who engage with students, it makes sense to begin development of a program with an environmental scan to identify the administrative, faculty, and staff leaders in both student and academic affairs whose participation would advance the initiative. Campus culture should guide decisions regarding the appropriate balance in terms of academic affairs and student affairs, which can become a divisive political issue. Campus culture should also help identify the appropriate individual or office to issue the call for the initial meeting, but ideally it should come from the senior administrators of student affairs and academic affairs.

The meeting could begin with a brief overview of EAWS at peer or aspirational institutions and focus on their goals, processes, and assessment data. Depending on the size and composition of that group, it might assume responsibility for developing a proposal or assign that to a smaller EAWS task force. That task force should include faculty, academic staff, and student services and an administrator from both student and academic affairs. The EAWS task force's charge would include carrying out a campus environmental scan to identify assets and deficits, and also become familiar with programs at other peer or aspirational institutions. This information should help to flesh out the experience of implementation, monitoring, and follow-up.

Relevant assessment data from those institutions would be especially helpful in structuring a proposal. It is important to set target dates for completing these tasks and sharing updates with the campus community. There also should be date for producing a final draft proposal that addresses key EAWS elements, including target student population, specific goals, timing of the alert, compliance, organizational structure, including where the program will be housed, a time line for implementation, an overview of assessment strategy, and a budget. That might then be circulated to institutional leadership, critical campus partners (as identified in the preceding section), or even the entire campus community with a request for comments. While that vetting process is time-consuming on the front end, it likely will promote broad campus buy-in and a less problematic implementation.

Among the list of critical decisions, identifying a home for the EAWS is particularly important since transforming a plan into a program requires effective implementation and oversight. While EAWS programs are largely academic in terms of stated outcomes and rely heavily on reports from classroom instructors, their administrative home typically is in student affairs. For example, at Tidewater Community College's Chesapeake Campus, the point person for early alert is the dean of student services, and academic support coordinates the program on its other campuses. The Student Success Center at the University of Alabama in Huntsville is the home for Project Success, an early alert program that takes ongoing referrals during the first ten weeks of the semester and provides one-on-one interventions. Collaborative collegial relations can ease workload issues. For example, at the University of Southern Maine, the Office of Academic Assessment sends out the report, and the Division of Student Success oversees interventions. Focusing on the practical tasks and anticipated student outcomes associated with implementing and managing an EAWS should facilitate the identification of offices and personnel best equipped to provide follow-up services to students. Moreover, no matter where the initiative is housed, ongoing communication with students, course instructors, and academic and student support offices remains central to an effective EAWS.

The specific courses for an EAWS also vary. Some institutions include all developmental and 100-level classes, while others target a specific set of classes seen as critical to student success. Student success data indicate that first-year seminar grades correlate strongly with student success (Cuseo, 2003b), which might provide an efficient cost-effective way to pilot an early alert. As has been noted, the timing of graded experiences in courses becomes a critical factor for an early warning. Especially in large classes where exams include some writing, even when administered early in the term, it may prove challenging for instructors to provide feedback to students the following week. Institutions often are reluctant to take up this issue because it might be seen as impinging on academic freedom. An official policy at the University of North Carolina, Asheville, states that students should receive at least one graded piece of work in each of their courses by the end of the fifth week of the semester. That language provides wide latitude for what that piece of work might be.

Implementation

Concerns about academic freedom and a belief that students need to take responsibility for their actions also contribute to the relative absence of institution-wide mandatory attendance polices, yet class attendance is critical to the success of most students, especially first-year students. Guidelines at many colleges and universities emphasize the importance of students getting off to a good start, and they encourage—but do not require—early reports on students who are not attending regularly. Given that culture, the effectiveness of an EAWS implementation is likely to be promoted by positive collaborative relations with academic departments whose introductory courses typically attract large numbers of first-year students. Frank discussions with academic deans or department chairs regarding the importance of establishing attendance and grading policies to facilitate the early identification of underperforming students might prove productive, given that erratic attendance patterns and students entering late or leaving early cause problems for both classroom instructors and other students in the class (Deering, 2011).

Given the primacy of the classroom in identifying nonattending and underperforming students, effective implementation must engage faculty and focus on strategies to identify those students early in the semester (Thompson & Geren, 2002). Classroom faculty and instructors who continue to monitor and meet with their students are likely to communicate that they care about them and want them to succeed, a positive factor in promoting better performance and persistence (Kuh, Kinzie, Schuh, Whitt, & Associates, 2011). Fresno City College's early alert site lists seven benefits to faculty from participating in the program, including that it "establishes a communication loop between faculty, counselors, support service personnel, and students" and provides "opportunity for counseling and special programs to follow up with a student's progress" (Fresno City College, May 2012). Couching the value of the program in these terms might increase faculty participation and also be important to collaborative relationships across campus.

Providing feedback to all personnel who submit reports is another critical implementation factor, and this should go beyond the initial e-mail acknowledging that their report has been received. While adhering to privacy regulations, advisors and student services professionals working with referred students should remain in communication with one another and with those who made the referral. At the Community College of Allegheny County, student support professionals monitor referrals, then communicate with students and connect them to the appropriate services. They also communicate with the person who made the referral, using an early intervention feedback form.

Depending on campus size, culture, and the nature of its student population, implementation might be phased in over several semesters. Piloting, assessing, and revising provide an opportunity to identify unforeseen issues and challenges while also yielding data that support generalizing the initiative to the entire first-year population. Repeating the initiative in the second semester can produce benefits in terms of student retention and identifying or testing modifications to capture an often overlooked population—students whose first-time entry is in the spring. Moreover, the so-called second-semester slump, marked by a decline in student grades, also suggests that a second-semester alert is a worthwhile practice (Grove & Wasserman, 2004).

The scope of the intervention could be scaled in various fashions. For example, a course focus might identify a set of 100-level classes that have proved challenging for first-year students, as evidenced by high rates of drops, withdrawals, and incompletes, as well as grades below C. Alternatively, it might include all students who have been identified as at risk. The early warning could include other student cohorts, for example, students on probation or students who left but have reentered the institution. However, identification without effective follow-up is not productive, so the total size of the student population relative to program capacity merits consideration.

The alert may serve as a wake-up call for some students, and they will commit to changing their behaviors. For example, if they have been missing classes, they will begin to attend regularly. However, most students will require some supportive interventions to help identify and address behaviors and skill levels that are barriers to their success. Students may be taking notes, but not in a fashion that can help them achieve good grades. First-year students may anticipate that the professor will provide a study guide, since that may have been a common high school practice. Appropriate interventions might include meetings with advisors and counselors to address specific issues related to their academic performance, participation in study groups led by upper-class students, and, perhaps, a decision to participate in Supplemental Instruction or structured learning assistance. Whatever the nature of follow-up activities, it is important to share that information with all relevant campus offices.

Deadlines embedded in campus policies, for example, dates for drops, adds, withdrawals, and tuition refunds, should align with the implementation dates for receiving early warning reports. In some cases, students may be in classes that require skill levels they do not yet possess, or they may be taking too many credits. Minimizing or eliminating onerous penalties for late drops enables students to maximize their chances to succeed. An allied implementation issue comes to the fore when it is best for a student to drop a class, but that would result in their falling below the full-time load and therefore lose eligibility for financial aid. Providing alternatives, for example, a set of second eight-week classes, can address this problem, and many institutions provide that option. Community colleges typically include eight-week sessions as an option, as do some four-year colleges and universities. College summer session programs typically offer four-, six-, and eight-week classes, and these might serve as models for developing syllabi for courses to offer during the second half of the semester. Some evidence suggests that students succeed at a higher rate in eight-week courses (Austin & Gustafson, 2006), and success data from 100-level courses taught in those formats could inform the development of such options within the regular academic year.

Leadership Roles/Communication

Moving from conception to initial implementation requires the cooperation of multiple offices and campus actors. As those conversations move ahead, staff and faculty participants should initiate discussions with their colleagues. It becomes especially important to be sensitive to how those areas are likely to be affected in terms of budgetary and human resources. Given challenging fiscal and workload issues, realistic discussions about incorporating the work related to the initiative are especially important. If critical resource needs surface, these must be acknowledged and incorporated into the planning and implementation process. Creating an atmosphere of trust facilitates candid discussions of perceived obstacles, including the capacity, interest, and willingness of other relevant offices and actors to participate fully and effectively. Faculty buy-in often surfaces as an issue, but relationships among other offices critical to the initiative may also prove problematic.

Given the array of personnel and tasks required to organize and implement an EAWS, numerous leadership roles exist. Whatever the origins of the initiative, senior administrators in academic and student affairs should play a leadership role. The heads of offices and committees whose purviews relate to student success and academic departments whose courses serve significant numbers of first-year students also provide good venues for discussing an EAWS program. Conversations are likely to become more productive if they provide opportunities for faculty and staff to identify and discuss challenges common to the early portion of the semester or trimester. For example, once the program has been launched, discussions might center on issues related to implementation and feedback. Unanticipated fiscal and staffing issues also may surface. Campus assessment specialists have particular importance because data-based evaluations of these interventions can substantiate their positive impact and provide information and suggestions to increase their effectiveness.

Establishing a provisional advisory group or steering committee to support the person or office in charge of the EAWS should facilitate both the launching and successful development of the EAWS. Consider as well mechanisms to elicit ongoing student input, such as a student advisory group. Scheduling meetings of broadly representative groups often is challenging. Breaking that larger body into smaller work groups to focus on specific issues may prove effective, but it is important to provide opportunities for all stakeholders to receive information, ask questions, and air concerns. In addition to discovering synergies and sharing strategies, this communication strategy helps to maintain partici- pants' focus on the entire program. Each of the groups should have a specific charge and a set of iterative deadlines for pro- ducing its report, which might include potential time lines for concluding discussion and moving to implementation. The report then could be posted on the campus website, referred to in other campus communications, and discussed at a series of informational meetings.

Resource Needs/Personnel

Essential elements for initiating and maintaining an early warning system include the development of a web-based reporting system accessible to all instructors whose classes have students included in the alert and to personnel in other campus offices that will be making referrals or carrying out interventions. An immediate resource-related decision is whether to purchase an EAWS software package or customize software available in the existing campus information system. Either might create additional demands on campus personnel. Whether software is purchased, gathering and processing EAWS data may exceed the capacity of personnel already in these roles. A specific point person or office must be designated to receive the data and follow up by communicating with students and arranging appointments with advisors. That information should be shared with the classroom instructors and other personnel who referred that student.

Multiple factors determine the volume of referrals, including the number of students included in the alert, whether participa- tion by students and faculty is mandatory or voluntary, and the nature of follow-up procedures for missing reports. Moreover, both the volume and timing of referrals will reflect the behaviors and achievement criteria for them. For example, if attendance is tracked, referrals might begin at the end of the second week of classes, but they could arise throughout the semester. Class participation, graded work, and behavioral issues might also vary. The number of courses included in the EAWS affects the volume of referrals, as does whether the alert is administered multiple times during the academic year. In addition to the number of referrals, tracking compliance among personnel involved in the initiative and maintaining frequent communication among all participants may exceed the capacity of existing personnel and thereby become a resource issue.

Follow-up protocols also bear on workload. Students identified as at risk of failing will need to meet with advisors or other academic counselors at least once, and probably more often. And if the system operates effectively, it likely will result in increased student traffic at other offices that provide academic resources and support for students, such as advising and counseling. It might also suggest the need to develop additional ways to provide support, for example, linking with a campus probation program or with developmental education. Maintaining ongoing communication and accurate records also creates demands on staff resources. If the information in these records is not confidential, student paraprofessionals and peer mentors might absorb some of the additional work, and universities with relevant graduate programs might be able to provide interns.

An EAWS is likely to increase the number of students seeking assistance from academic and student support offices, which might exceed the capacity of current staff and therefore require additional resources. Supporting the critical role of faculty and instructional staff may require expenditures for professional development given the predominance of the lecture format in gateway classes, an approach that reduces levels of student engagement (Cuseo, 2007). Professional development could also include workshops on effective practices for monitoring student attendance and performance by embedding graded classroom experiences and assignments in the syllabus that occur during the first few weeks of the semester and discussing student behaviors that likely indicate disengagement. Those teaching large gateway classes may require assistance to keep accurate records related to student behaviors and performance.

If participation in the alert is voluntary, incentives for faculty and instructional staff participation could be another cost. Institutions might also need to reconsider their use of part-time adjunct faculty to teach large introductory surveys and developmental education classes. Enrollment caps for first-year classes might also make sense pedagogically and in terms of practicality. Reduced teaching loads could provide participating faculty with additional time, thereby enabling them to become more effective in teaching, advising, and supporting student learning. It also could require the expense of adding faculty or full-time lecturers.

Assessment

Based on the experience of the University of Cincinnati, Donnelly (2011) suggests that "notification of student progress by classroom instructors throughout the academic term is a simple way to go beyond traditional measures of college preparation to predict student success" (p. 42). The effectiveness of EAWS programs rests on early and ongoing assessment of underperforming students, effective supportive interventions, and ongoing communication among individuals and offices that initiate referrals and with students. An assessment plan should focus on both process and outcomes. For example, assessment of the implementation process might analyze student response rates to referrals from faculty and instructional staff, as well as those submitted by other offices. It also might include tracking initial and ongoing student compliance with suggested activities and then comparing success rates as related to student participation in those activities. Addressing the student experience through focus groups with students who participated in prescribed activities should provide qualitative insights that could strengthen the program. Discussions with students who decided not to participate also might provide useful perspectives. That approach could be replicated with academic and student services personnel and with faculty.

Analysis of participation rates among faculty and instructional staff in terms of submission rates for initial referrals and follow-up reports would provide important process insights. Tracking faculty and instructor response rates both within and across departments could suggest the need for follow-up conversations with specific departments or individual instructors to identify the causes for their disengagement. That might also focus on both initial and ongoing faculty and staff engagement with the program and provide data regarding implementation issues, including, for example, unanticipated course or process-specific challenges.

Baseline data for offices engaged in advising, mentoring, tutoring, and skill building could indicate if and where the early alert system increases student traffic, and analysis of referrals could identify both initial and ongoing compliance rates for students. Since a number of aspects of the program can be tracked, assessment should target the process and compliance issues that are most relevant to program goals and outcomes. In terms of compliance, at some institutions, faculty and instructional staff participation may be a given, while at others, faculty buy-in may prove challenging. Unanticipated problems associated with the implementation dates, size of the target student population, and the reporting software may also surface in the assessment data.

Analysis of process issues and student success data provides an empirical framework for assessing the early warning system's effectiveness. Simons (2011) reports that the outcomes of many program were "too general and hard to measure," noting, for example, that while 40 percent of them stated improved retention as a goal, "most did not clarify a specific program outcome that precipitated retention" (p. 116). Assessment approaches and results at other institutions can provide guidance and insights. For example, a study at California's Irvine Valley College noted significant student success and retention rates for students participating in the program as compared with their peers and also assessed the predictive value of the College Student Inventory (Rudman, 1992), a Noel-Levitz student survey instrument. At the University of North Texas, data for 2008–2009, the initial year of its early warning system, indicated a positive impact on student persistence from fall to spring. Students who had direct contacts with faculty or advisors fared better than those limited to e-mail interactions (Temple, 2010).

Institutions considering this intervention might begin with a review of their first-year student success data, for example, number of credits completed, grade point average, probation and dropout rates, persistence from first to second semester, and retention to the second year. Group-specific satisfaction surveys can be distributed to classroom instructors, professionals in relevant support offices, and students. These could assess overall satisfaction from the perspectives of process and results, identify both problems and unanticipated positive outcomes, and elicit suggestions for improving the initiative. A recent study by the John N. Gardner Institute for Excellence in Undergraduate Education found that "only 40% of all respondents [reported] finding improved retention and/or graduation rates that correlated with their early warning/academic alert efforts," even though 90 percent of those institutions had identified that as a goal (Barefoot, Griffin, & Koch, 2012, p. 33).

In assessing the initial years of an EAWS, a bottom-line measure is student performance in the courses for which they were referred:

- Did the performance of students in the early alert program improve over the course of the semester?
- How do the grades of early alert students compare with those of other first-year students?
- What impact did it have on drops, adds, and incomplete grades?
- Do participants in the EAWS have lower rates of probation?
- What percentage of early alert students wind up on probation, and how does that compare with past rates?
- What impact does it have on registration for the second semester, and how does that compare with data prior to implantation of the system?

Formative assessments could focus on student, staff, and instructor satisfaction with the program and elicit suggestions for improving the program. These data, both positive and negative, should be shared with the campus community and used to modify the system. If the alert occurs in the second semester, results can be compared with those from the first semester. Multiple items could be of interest, including whether students identified in the fall who returned for the second semester were again identified as requiring support. These data should be seen in a comparative context that includes students who were not part of the intervention.

Benefit Analysis

An institution can quantify revenue gains resulting from higher rates of first-to-second-semester persistence, which is likely to mean that fewer students needed to repeat failed classes. That is likely to reduce the number of second-semester sections of those classes, which can lower instructional costs. Higher rates of retention to the second year and student persistence to degree have major impacts on tuition revenue, an increasingly critical revenue stream in contemporary higher education. Additional institutional costs or gains in terms of personnel and supply and expense budgets can be totaled and then measured against the net revenue gain from tuition. Positive gains in student persistence to degree also can be tracked.

Higher levels of student satisfaction are another potential benefit. If students believe that the institution is concerned about them and their academic success, they are more likely to persist and to speak positively about their experience. A word-of-mouth reputation for being a university that truly cares about students and does its best to assist them should help reputation and recruiting. It also might attract additional support from the outside, including, for example, contributions for scholarships and providing internship opportunities for students. Positive working relations forged as a result of this initiative will have numerous spillover effects, improving morale and promoting a more widely shared sense of community, especially around the goal of supporting student success. These relations also should increase students' sense of connection to the campus, an important factor in their satisfaction and retention. In this regard, a study that indicated relatively positive academic gains for students in an early alert program also suggested the program had value "in keeping advisors informed, building trust between different parties within the institution and the message that professors are paying attention to students" (Hanover Research Council,

2008, pp. 17–18). Donnelly (2011) found that "the data reveal differences in academic performance between those flagged for an intervention and similarly prepared students not so identified" (p. 42), even though the ACT scores and high school grade point averages were similar for both groups.

Institutional Practices

St. Mary's University

A Catholic and Marianist liberal arts institution in San Antonio, Texas, St. Mary's is a selective, highly residential Hispanic-serving private university with an enrollment of approximately four thousand students. Primarily an undergraduate institution, it also offers twenty-one graduate programs and has a law school. St. Mary's uses two campuswide initiatives to identify at-risk students. The first, referred to as "r2r" ("refer to retain"), grew out of a long-standing program known as Early Alert Report, a paper-based report submitted during the third week of the semester. Both early alert programs originated with the director of academic advising, and then in 2011 became the responsibility of the Office of Student Retention (OSR), which had been established in fall 2008. Over time, the number of reports submitted had declined to perhaps twenty per semester for a first-year class that ranged from 575 to 630 students.

The new program benefits from an approach to better leverage technology to identify at-risk students. Early in both the fall and spring semesters, all faculty and staff members receive an e-mail that stresses the importance of the r2r program and asks them to identify students who are displaying one or more at-risk behaviors, which include nonattendance (both class and work-study), poor grades, lack of participation or engagement, and concerns regarding finances, family, or feeling isolated. These can be communicated to an OSR staff member through an r2r form on the university's intranet portal, by e-mail or telephone, or in person. While OSR emphasizes the importance of the initial three to four weeks of the semester, it has raised awareness of the fact that at-risk behaviors may manifest themselves at any time.

In fall 2012, the OSR received approximately 140 r2r referrals. It reviews these and, depending on their nature, works with a range of offices, among them the dean of students, residence life, learning assistance, academic advising, financial assistance, and faculty. The program works with all under-graduates, but most referrals are for first-year students. Approximately

70 percent of students referred respond and engage in an intervention.

As a follow-up strategy, the OSR reviews midterm grades for all freshmen who have any grades below C or have exhibited behaviors that suggest a need for intervention. The office also partners with the freshman seminar program, ND101, Academic and Personal Development. All ND101 instructors receive midterm grades for their students, and they meet with any students who have received a grade of D or F. The OSR provides a form on calculating GPA, a behavior self-inventory, and a self-assessment form that are used at those meetings. The OSR receives and scans completed self-assessment forms, and that scan is returned to the students, along with a letter thanking them for their participation and noting resources that are available to assist them. They are advised that they must meet with their ND101 instructor, and if that does not occur, they will have to meet with someone at the OSR. The office also does outreach to students experiencing financial problems. Initial results of the r2r program are encouraging: fall-to-fall retention of first-year students rose from 75 to 77 percent.

Hudson Valley Community College

Hudson Valley Community College, with campuses located in and around Albany, New York, is part of the State University of New York system. It offers over seventy degree certificate programs and enrolls about 13,500 students each semester, over 90 percent of whom attend full time. Its early warning system, which began in the 1990s, is designed to facilitate new students' transition to college through the identification of those in need of assistance and communications indicating concerns with their classroom performance. Faculty can access instructions for identifying students, and they can see a template for the letter that students will receive.

The intervention begins in the third week of both the fall and spring semesters. The official notice sent to instructors refers to research findings regarding the effectiveness of the intervention, one of which is that it can "bring students and instructors together to discuss successful learning strategies and habits." The web-based system enables instructors to download course rosters, identify students, indicate the reasons for their concern, and recommend interventions. Students receive a letter from the associate dean for instructional support services and retention that lists the instructors who have identified them and urges them to make an appointment with those instructors to discuss ways to complete the course successfully. Instructors receive an e-mail confirmation when those letters go out. Many instructors are reluctant to identify students that early in the semester because they do not yet have any grade data. The bulk of referrals occur in the fifth week of classes, with instructor participation rates of approximately 20 percent. The system remains open throughout the semester, and instructor participation increases to about 30 percent by the end of the term. While those later referrals no longer qualify as early warnings, they nonetheless capture additional students at other critical moments in the semester.

Instructional services and retention tracks process data, including the number of unique referrals, in terms of both students and faculty, and the number of letters sent. The campus information system codes all students identified by the fifth week as a cohort for retention reports. They also are automatically referred to other campus offices, including learning assistance, the disability resource center, athletics, and the Educational Opportunity Program. Academic department chairs receive a listing of students who are their majors.

Retention services, a unit within the office of instructional support services and retention, oversees evaluation of the early warning system. Satisfaction surveys sent to all instructors in fall 2007 and 2010 indicated the general reluctance of instructors to judge any behavioral issues at that point in the semester other than attendance and to make any academic evaluations prior to the initial exam. Instructors expressed concern about navigating multiple pages to participate. A new web-based form introduced in fall 2012 eliminated this issue. It allows faculty to identify students, choose the issues, and make the intervention recommendations for an entire course section from one screen. Instructors also wanted to be included as a suggested referral point for all students they had identified. Positive discussions between students and faculty have the potential to create mutually beneficial relationships.

University of North Carolina at Greensboro

Like many other colleges and universities, the University of North Carolina at Greensboro (UNCG) asks for midsemester reports on all students who are doing unsatisfactory work. Another system asks for feedback on students at several points in the semester, beginning with the fourth week. Starfish, software available in Blackboard, provides the platform for these reports. By clicking the appropriate icon, faculty and instructional staff can identify students they see as at risk and send positive feedback to students who are doing well. The university's Teaching and Learning Center website has a dedicated Starfish site that includes tutorials.

Students First Office administers the program. Part of UNCG's undergraduate studies division, Students First works with multiple offices and administrative areas to implement and coordinate interventions for students experiencing difficulties, whether academic, financial, or social. Since these factors often covary, this holistic approach enables the development of integrated strategies to address students' needs. The course-based approach includes all registered students as opposed to a discrete group preidentified as at risk. The office also provides advising to all undecided students, a category often referred to as "exploratory."

Classroom reports are completed during the fourth, eighth, and twelfth weeks of the semester—a practice that provides ongoing monitoring of students' academic progress. Students who are flagged by instructors receive an e-mail from the coordinator of academic outreach that informs them of the concerns expressed and refers them to their assigned advisors or program coordinators, who also have received the reports. They work directly with the students to assist them in addressing issues that contributed to their being identified as struggling. Whoever takes the primary role in working with the student provides feedback that is accessible to others who may be working with that student and also with the course instructor. The follow-up at the eighth and twelfth weeks provides opportunities to assess the effectiveness of the intervention and provide additional support. Throughout the process, students are encouraged to speak directly with their instructors. A survey conducted by the university's faculty teaching and learning committee indicated high levels of instructor satisfaction with the system's accessibility and identified flags for attendance and grades as the most useful feature, though they did express concerns regarding confidentiality. The committee is working to expand the system and make it more user friendly. For all students flagged in fall 2011, almost 97 percent were eligible to enroll in the spring term, and nearly 95 percent of students flagged in spring 2012 remained eligible to register for the fall semester (University of North Carolina, Greensboro, 2011–2012).

Chapter Ten

| **Probation Initiatives**

Approximately 25 percent of students are placed on academic probation during their time in college (Cohen & Brawer, 2002), and about 50 percent of those will decide to leave (Damashek, 2003). National data for 2012 indicate an overall first-to-second-year retention rate for all institutions of 66.5 percent. These ranged from 55.5 percent for two-year colleges, both public and private, to 82.2 percent for private institutions offering the doctorate. Rates for comprehensive publics were 65.2 percent, and for privates, 67.2 percent (ACT, 2012). Low grade point averages in the first year correlate strongly with higher dropout rates (Reason, 2009; Ishitani & DesJardins, 2002). Research suggests that probationary status significantly increases the dropout rate for men but does not have that impact on women (Lindo, Sanders, & Oreopoulos, 2010). Although returning students initially improve their performance, that impact diminishes over time (Lindo et al., 2010; Fletcher & Tokmouline, 2010). While demographic studies of probationary students are common, relatively few studies have focused directly on those students' experience (Shao, Hufnagel, & Karp, 2009–2010).

Institutions of higher education have long had policies specifying the conditions under which students can be placed on and removed from academic probation. Using stern language, these policies often are "strictly punitive" (Fletcher & Tokmouline, 2010, p. 3) and focus on students' personal responsibility and the time frame for raising grade point averages to an acceptable level. Policies typically apply to students throughout college and include several stages, which are defined by grade point average and credit accumulation. The process begins with an academic warning, triggered by either grade point average or credits earned. Students who do not satisfy those requirements in the ensuing semester may be placed on strict probation, which may set limits on the number of credits for which they can register and also require them to repeat courses in which they received grades of D or F. Students who do not meet those conditions must sit out for a semester before they can reapply for admission; if they are readmitted, they are automatically placed on probation. If students again fail to meet the grade point and credit requirements, they are suspended for one academic year. That notification often suggests that they consider taking courses at a technical college or community college. Despite the long-standing presence of probation policies in higher education, their impacts still remain largely unstudied (Fletcher & Tokomouline, 2010).

To a large extent, institutions of higher education have tended to explain probation as resulting from either student ability (not truly being "college material") or from students failing to take their responsibilities seriously (Habley & McClanahan, 2004). The demographic characteristics of those more likely to continue to the second year of college, for example, women, white students, and students whose parents have college degrees and well-paying jobs (Upcraft & Schuh, 1996), describe a much smaller percentage of the contemporary college population, especially in community colleges and less selective regional public universities.

Multiple factors contribute to students' lack of success during the first year of college, including poor time management and study skills (Pascarella & Terenzini, 2001) and having met only the minimal graduation standards for high school math and English (Tinto, 1993). Life circumstances, including finances, work, and child care responsibilities, may also contribute to lower levels of academic success (Ashburn, 2012). A study at Los Angeles City College found that in comparison with the general student population, students on probation had more child care responsibilities and worked more hours. They also entered with lower high school grades (Trombley, 2000). However, Cruise (2002) cautions that not all first-year students who wind up on probation were identified as at risk.

Some probation programs serve all students, and others are designed specifically for first-year students or specific student cohorts. They may be institution-wide or pertain to an individual college or major. First-year students are a target population for many probation initiatives because students who fall behind in terms of grade point average and credits earned in their initial semester of college attendance are less likely to persist and graduate. However, if students regain good standing, they are more likely to persist (Tovar & Simon, 2006). First-year students who rely heavily on financial aid typically must maintain good academic standing, so probationary status may force them to drop out of college. While financial pressures contribute significantly to students' decisions to leave college after their initial semester of attendance (Ashburn, 2012), academic skills deficiencies pose another challenge (Ryan & Glenn, 2003). Life circumstances, including time constraints due to family or work obligations, may contribute to both disengagement and low grades among first-year students. First-year students placed on probation often have poor attendance, do not complete all assigned work, and participate minimally, or not at all, in class discussions and required class activities. While multiple factors may contribute to these behaviors, they result in poor exam performance and unsatisfactory grades (Astin, 1975; Lotkowski, Robbins, & Noeth, 2004).

At many institutions, probation programs largely consist of an informational website with frequently asked questions (FAQs) and, perhaps, a suggestion that students meet with their advisor. They may also provide students with a list of available supportive programs and resources, but participation is optional, which likely reflects the view that students are adults and should assume responsibility for their academic performance.

Contemporary higher education increasingly recognizes shared responsibility for student success and the importance of creating policies and programs that reflect that commitment (Kuh, Kinzie, Schuh, Whitt, & Associates, 2005; Upcraft, Gardner, Barefoot, & Associates, 2005). Probation initiatives or academic recovery programs (a term also used for programs that assist students who are reentering a university after being forced to leave) acknowledge the seriousness of probationary status but also emphasize the institution's supportive role in assisting them to regain good standing. That commitment finds expression in an array of programs designed to increase the likelihood that probationary students will succeed academically. While some initiatives are online (Taylor & Lawrence, 2007), most are face-to-face. Robust programs recognize the importance of promoting a sense of connectedness to the institution by creating opportunities for students to interact with one another and with members of the staff and faculty. They also help students who had difficulties in high school (Snyder et al., 2002). Programs tend to take a holistic approach that recognizes the impact of nonacademic factors, for example, financial or familial challenges, that may have affected the student's academic performance. Depending on the nature of their issues, students are referred to the office best suited to provide the assistance they need.

Academic recovery programs vary widely, reflecting the characteristics of both the institution and its students. Some are prescriptive and may include one or more mandatory requirements. For example, Pasadena City College requires students to attend a probation workshop and sets a twelve-credit course limit until they regain good standing. North Carolina Central University has seen benefits from mandatory learning contracts, "which are negotiated and signed, and define responsibilities of both students and the institution" (Bradley & Blanco, 2010, p. 33). These contracts can be used with many interventions, but they are especially useful for formalizing an agreement between probationary students and advisors.

Programs may be housed in either student affairs or academic affairs, but all of them typically involve multiple offices and collaborative relationships to develop students' academic skills and awareness of the supportive services, attitudes, and behaviors that are likely to lead to success. In some cases, programs intentionally foster relationships between students on probation and academically successful students. Baylor University's Paul L. Foster Success Center provides that service for students who are experiencing academic difficulties. Both advising and counseling often play a lead role in academic recovery programs, and creating social support for students can contribute to their academic success (Arcand & LeBlanc, 2011).

The Council for the Advancement of Standards in Higher Education suggests that advising and learning assistance should engage with probation initiatives. The National Academic Advising Association provides ongoing discussions of student success on its site, Clearinghouse, Academic Advising Resources, which includes a page that focuses on advising students who are on academic probation and relevant links (Higgins, 2003). Both intrusive and appreciative advising have proven effective for students on probation (Earl, 1988; Heisserer & Parette, 2002; Kirk-Kuwaye & Nishida, 2001; Skipper, 2005), but the intrusive approach is more common (Pell Institute, 2007). Studies also indicate that counseling has a positive impact on retention. This seems to have less to do with academic performance itself (Lee, Olson, Locke, Michelson, & Odes, 2009) and largely reflects the importance of nonacademic factors, especially student attitudes (Turner & Berry, 2000). Although cooperative relations and communication are important to the effectiveness of probation initiatives, directing all students to one office—the one-stop shop model (often used by enrollment services)—is likely to prove more effective. In addition to being convenient, returning to a familiar location and seeing familiar faces can provide a sense of comfort for students.

Probation initiatives vary significantly. For example, "monitored probation" distinguishes programs that to varying degrees track students during the probationary period, including their participation rates in recommended services (Mann, Hunt, & Alford, 2003–2004). While students may participate in multiple interventions, the nature of those varies. For example, the monitored probation program at Virginia Polytechnic Institute and State University includes scheduled meetings with faculty, staff, administrators, graduate students, or peer facilitators, and student participation is tracked (Humphrey, 2006). At Tougaloo College, a church-related historically black college, the Student Academic Success Center oversees the academic recovery program. Based on initial referrals and a needs assessment, it works with students to develop a written learning agreement, which is reviewed and updated throughout the semester. Similarly, the Office of Academic Advising and Enhancement in the Franklin College of Arts and Sciences at the University of Georgia developed Collaborative

Academic and Retention Effort, which works with students to develop a plan to address their academic issues.

Approaching the Work/Critical Partners

Although there are no formalized typologies of probation programs, several critical decisions for these programs have major implications for students and institutions, and these should be identified and addressed at the start of efforts to develop or revise a probation initiative.

Investigation and Initial Review

Identification of specific desired outcomes can provide a framework for those conversations. Senior administrators might establish a task force with broad representation from student and academic affairs, including offices and individuals that already interact with students on probation. That group should review current institutional probation policy and practices and assess relevant campus data, including, for example, the size, characteristics, and success rates of students who have been placed on probation. It could then survey policies and practices at other institutions. For example, Western State Colorado University encourages students placed on probation to speak with course instructors and use services available at the Academic Resource Center, which houses first-year advising. Nebraska's Union College requires students on probation to participate in its Academic Success and Advising Program, which is administered by the Teaching Learning Center.

Based on its investigation and initial review of campus data and practice, examples from similar or aspirational institutions, and a review of scholarly literature and best practices, the task force might draft a mission statement and set of goals for the new probation program. These should be informed by institutional mission, the review of scholarly literature, and institutional student success data. As part of the larger communication process, the draft mission statement and goals should be shared with the campus community for comments and suggestions.

A review of the relevant literature on effective policies and practices to support first-year students who are on academic warning or academic probation should inform the task force's identification of critical decisions that will define the nature and scope of the program—for example:

- Will the new program serve all students on probation or target specific populations, for example, only first-year students or perhaps specific first-year cohorts?
- Will participation in program activities be required for all students on probation or only for some? If the latter, what factors, for example, GPA ranges, will inform that decision?
- Will credit load limits be established?
- Will permission be required for drops or adds?
- Will the policy require students to repeat classes they failed if those are being offered in the second semester?
- What general and specific support services will be provided?
- Will participation be monitored in an ongoing fashion? If so, how will that be done?
- What additional interventions will occur with students who continue to experience difficulties?

The primary causes for students' lack of success also need to be examined. The variability among retention initiatives in terms of organization and policies and the diversity that characterizes colleges and universities suggest the importance of following up the initial data scan with a more comprehensive and intensive review of institutional data on first-year students. Analyses of these data should provide a sense of the timing and extent of probation and how it affects student retention and graduation—for example:

- Did attendance issues play a role?
- Was course placement or selection inappropriate? Were overall credit loads unrealistic?
- What role did nonacademic factors play, for example, family, work, or transportation issues?
- If students experienced success in one or more of their classes, what factors explain that?

In sum, both a broad and a focused assessment of issues related to student failure or success that involves both quantitative and qualitative data should provide insights to inform the development of a new policy and program. Those data should inform the identification of critical partners.

Program Partners

In addition to advising and counseling, the Council for the Advancement of Standards in Higher Education suggests a role for learning assistance and developmental education professionals, who are especially helpful in identifying courses in which under-prepared students have a greater chance to succeed. Since grades define failure or success for students, faculty and instructional staff also are critical partners, especially those who teach gateway courses and others who enroll large numbers of first-year students. Their perspectives on student classroom behaviors that have a negative effect on student success should prove helpful to others who are directly engaged in working with students on probation.

The array of interventions should also provide opportunities for students on probation to interact with other support agents, including, if available, peer mentors. Successful students, especially ones who have experienced academic difficulties in the past, can provide both inspiration and student-centered advice. The Bounce Back program at the University of Colorado, Boulder, provides a support group led by a peer coach. Activities in that setting can also create a student-driven support group that meets on its own.

Depending on campus culture, faculty members may become directly involved in academic interventions, a practice that correlates positively with student success (Schreiner & Lundberg, 2004). Broad collaborative approaches provide the associational setting that Tinto (1975) suggested facilitates students' integration into and comfort with the academic environment. Positive relationships with faculty members, which also correlate positively with student success (Noel, 1985; Kuh et al., 2005), provide another potential asset. An intentional focus on relationship building between students on probation and an advisor, mentor, or coach, sometimes identified as "companioning," appears to have significant positive effects (Arcand & LeBlanc, 2012). A common element in many effective practices is reducing student isolation and creating a sense of community (Booker, 2008; Creasey, Jarvis, & Gadke, 2009; Kuh et al., 2005). Campus professionals associated with such programs as TRIO and Upward Bound can provide experience-based and data-rich perspectives that will help ground the program in practice.

Establishing a probation initiative also may require changes to current policy, such as establishing mandatory participation in one or more academic support programs, required meetings with advisors and counselors, or lowering the maximum number of credits for which probationary students can register. Whatever the specific issues, a new policy is likely to affect a broad array of offices, including the registrar, enrollment management, and advising. Additional critical partners include all administrative units or offices vested with authority to initiate changes, as well as any others whose work will be affected.

The academic dimensions of probation policies are likely to be relevant matters for one or more faculty committees, so the chairs of those should be included in the conversation. Faculty members can be conduits for sharing information about student performance, and their participation will facilitate policy implementation. Faculty engagement with students in their classes has the potential to build program effectiveness and student achievement, and faculty can also provide insight into student behaviors and classroom issues. Those who teach high-enrollment introductory classes with substantial first-year student enrollment and those in smaller introductory classes in math and English can add valuable perspectives, as can those teaching developmental education courses.

Although campus advising models vary, advisors typically work with at-risk students, and the probation policies on many campuses either suggest or require students to meet with them. Conversations with both successful students and those on probation will provide meaningful insights, and student participation in the planning process can help center their experiences and concerns.

The role of specific partners will vary depending on the nature of the program and its desired outcomes, but the experience-based perspectives from all campus offices that engage with and communicate to students who experience academic difficulties will help ground discussions in both academic and practical considerations and offer the probability of successful change. At the same time, they may identify additional stakeholders and potential roadblocks. The importance of communication and collaborations also suggests a role for campus technology services, which can facilitate communication with students, staff, and faculty by establishing discussion groups and password-protected sites to ensure privacy.

Organization/Implementation Process

The organization and implementation of the probation initiative should reflect its specific mission, goals, and objectives.

Organization

While a broad sense of engagement throughout the campus community helps to promote the development and implementation of policy, a successful academic recovery program must be housed in an appropriate office and have a dedicated leader who has the capacity to implement and monitor the policy. Institutional practices vary widely. At the University of Iowa, an associate dean for undergraduate programs and curriculum in the College of Liberal Arts and Sciences heads a unit known as academic and student development that works with students who have been placed on probation. At Occidental College, the dean of students oversees the probation program, and students typically meet with the associate dean. Probation programs are also administered through first-year programs, student success centers, and university colleges.

Since implementation requires significant cooperation from other campus offices, that should be embedded in the organizational model and include the key supportive services that have demonstrated a positive impact on this population, for example, advising, counseling tutoring, and learning assistance. While campuses vary in the mix and organization of support services for students, a broad collaborative approach is needed to address the full spectrum of issues that have a negative effect on academic performance (Prentice et al., 2009). For example, peer mentors add an important student-to-student component, and evidence suggests that their involvement can help promote the success of students who are on probation (Pagan & Edwards-Wilson, 2002–2003). A study at the University of Wisconsin-Stevens Point found that many underperforming students did not want to ask for assistance and were embarrassed by their academic record (Sage, 2010). For that and other reasons, probation initiatives focused on first-year students that have mandatory rather than optional interventions are more likely to have a positive impact (Williams & Pury, 2002; Hodges, Dochen, & Joy, 2001; Isaak, Graves, & Mayers, 2006).

Implementation

At some institutions, the size and characteristics of the student population may exceed the capacity of existing human and fiscal resources. In such cases, a pilot program could help to identify problematic process issues, such as monitoring student compliance, the timeliness of communications, and the adequacy of available services. The pilot program could include student cohorts defined by a specific first-semester grade point average (GPA) range or number of credits successfully completed. At less selective and open-enrollment institutions, the magnitude of the population placed on probation might necessitate adopting a triage approach in which all students receive a basic set of support services, while others experience more robust interventions. However, if the composition and size of that population still exceed available resources, it might make sense to identify a smaller segment whose first-semester GPA suggests they have a reasonable chance to succeed, and that could reflect credits completed and GPA. Making participation voluntary is also likely to reduce the initial cohort, but that might limit the impact of positive outcomes among campus stakeholders, since motivation is commonly assumed to contribute to positive student performance (Howey, 2008).

Although the causes of academic problems are numerous and complex, students should be encouraged to take ownership of their academic performance. Student commitment to engaging with program activities can be strengthened by having them read the probation policy and sign a contract that outlines the terms of their participation, a practice that has been shown to increase compliance with suggested behavioral changes (Williams, Bezner, Chesboro, & Leavitt, 2005). While taking into account significant differences among cohorts within the initiative, establishing some specific milestones for students should prove helpful (Offenstein, Moore, & Shulock, 2010). In all cases, both compliance and student outcomes should be monitored and used to make timely interventions and inform subsequent program development. That might include attendance, active participation, completing assignments in a timely fashion, and standard academic success measures, for example, credits earned, GPA, and drop, withdrawal, and failure rates. Focus groups with students, staff, and faculty might also prove productive.

In centering students' responsibility for academic success, colleges and universities have a reciprocal obligation to create conditions that enable students to succeed. Mohawk Valley Community College's Academic Intervention program requires students who are on academic intervention or academic probation to participate in academic success workshops designed to help them identify their strengths. It also requires them to develop an academic success plan, and they work with a designated college coach—a member of the faculty or staff who connects them with appropriate resources and acts as a mentor.

The array of interventions should be informed by analysis of campus data, which can help identify institutional practices that contribute to student failure. For example, high failure rates in specific gateway courses might result from inappropriate course selection or inadequate monitoring of drops and adds. The appropriateness of a course is not only an issue of students' skill levels, motivation, and life circumstances but also of course structure and requirements and the instructor's pedagogical approach (James, Krause, & Jennings, 2010). The academic program of first-year students typically includes one or more large lecture classes, which can produce a sense of anonymity that fosters disengagement. Providing smaller attached discussion sections can help address this issue and promote earlier identification of students who are experiencing academic difficulties. The University of North Carolina, Greensboro, developed a successful mandatory initiative for students placed on probation, Student Academic Success

100, a motivational and empowerment model that employs an "integrated model of advising/counseling and classroom/work approaches." It requires "students to work with instructors and peers to carefully examine their behaviors and goals in order to make effective long-term plans for personal success" (Hutson, 2006, pp. 37–38).

Whether the program is mandatory or voluntary, a process for monitoring compliance and active participation should be developed. This process provides opportunities to contact students and assess program effectiveness. The process should be timely and intrusive and could be linked to a second-semester early alert warning system. This might include an "early early alert" with an initial report by the end of the second week of the semester and subsequent reporting at two- or three-week intervals. Other institutional assets, such as peer tutoring and structured learning assistance or Supplemental Instruction, could be attached to specific courses, especially those in which many students are retaking the class. These interventions can help keep students on track and minimize the likelihood of subsequent failure. An Academic Quality Improvement Program team at Colorado Mountain College, a multicampus institution, focused on mathematics, specifically high rates of failure in a gateway algebra class. After investigating a range of factors that contributed to that result, they recommended pairing it with a one-credit class, Enhanced Mathematics Support. Depending on students' previous algebra grade, the course was either required or recommended (Colorado Mountain College, 2008).

The academic recovery program should be housed in an appropriate campus unit, and it needs to function as a conduit or clearinghouse for communications, since messages from multiple offices will likely confuse students or act as an additional stressor. Even if the program is not campuswide, the initial communication to students might come from the chief academic officer or the chief student affairs officer, or perhaps both. The message should emphasize both the seriousness of probationary status and the possibilities for positive change, perhaps citing success data from national studies or campus data. That communication might urge, or even require, students to schedule a meeting with an administrator or staff person in the office that serves as the primary contact for the probation initiative. That office would then send a follow-up message to the student.

The pace and scope of the implementation also merit consideration. Retention data and second-semester grades can help identify the number of students who are not well served by the existing policy. The size and characteristics of that group should inform program implementation decisions. Qualitative data are particularly important because students' poor academic performance may be related to other pressures in their lives, whether financial, personal, or familial. Academic advisors, counselors, residence hall advisors, and financial aid officers can provide valuable intelligence about those issues. The institutional mission may also inform decisions. For example, if the mission identifies a special commitment to specific student cohorts, implementation decisions should reflect that.

Leadership Roles/Communication

Engaging Major Stakeholders

It is important to identify and bring together all major campus stakeholders. That said, since many of the offices providing support services for students are in student services, the chief administrative officer of that area should play a major leadership role. And since academic probation is based on poor performance in the classroom, the chief academic officer also needs to be associated with the initiative.

Communication should include all offices and committees concerned with first-year students. That acknowledges their interest in and commitment to student success and can add allies and ideas while minimizing ownership issues. Depending on campus culture, student government or a student leadership council might also have representatives on the leadership team. Students who have been on probation and regained good standing can provide important real-world insights on the multiple factors that impede success in the classroom and can be engaged with this initiative either informally or as part of a peer mentoring program. Student success may also be affected, both positively and negatively, by a professor's teaching style and strategies, and peer mentors are likely to add experience-grounded strategies to promote probationary students' success. In addition, engagement with successful students will likely strengthen their sense of connectedness to the institution and provide positive role models. Indiana University-Purdue University, Indianapolis's STAR program (Students Taking Academic Responsibility) uses peer mentors in its work with students on probation (Gilbert, 2007), as does the University of North Carolina at Charlotte.

The active engagement of faculty and instructors is critical to the success of probation programs. Academic deans, department chairs, and chairs of relevant academic committees can initiate discussions about the positive educational and fiscal benefits that effective probation initiatives have produced at peer institutions. Campus opinion leaders who are seen as advocates for both high academic standards and student success can play an important role in promoting faculty participation. In an evidence-based culture, institutional research data can create a sense of urgency and facilitate consensus on this issue.

Communication

Communications to students are an important aspect of the program. Semester transcripts from the registrar's office are likely to be the first communication that students receive about their probationary status. Once the initiative is in place, in addition to indicating the student's probationary status, the transcript might include a message about the university's probation initiative and direct the students to the appropriate office. A follow-up joint communication from student affairs and academic affairs underscores the seriousness of the situation. The tone and substance of these and follow-up messages from the office or unit overseeing the problem should convey both the seriousness of probation and the support that students will receive to help them regain good standing.

A task force could develop a document to define the parameters of the problem in terms of student retention and graduation. That document might also address the individual, institutional, and broader societal costs of student failure. Local and regional institutions might focus on the negative impact of high attrition rates on their service region and their implications for institutional image and campus morale. This information could then be presented to the student and faculty senates and major campus leadership groups that represent students, faculty, and academic staff. At that point, the task force could consider adding members to make it more broadly representative. While a larger membership creates challenges in terms of scheduling meetings, it ensures that all major constituencies have a voice. Establishing subcommittees or working groups can minimize scheduling issues and provide an efficient way to address specific issues.

Resource Needs/Personnel

Resource and personnel needs vary with program focus and scale. For example, the program might include only a specific cohort of first-year students placed on probation after their initial semester of attendance or a larger population defined by a first-semester GPA. The program might be campuswide or limited to a specific college, department, or major. A mandatory program, that is, one that requires students to participate in one or more supportive interventions, will have higher resource and personnel needs than one in which participation is voluntary. The number and nature of specific interventions included in the probation program will also affect workload, and the capacities of academic and student support offices have fiscal implications.

The initial implementation stage is a major responsibility, and to be effective, the program must have a director. If that responsibility is assigned to an individual who already has major responsibilities or is housed in an office that already has workload challenges, it is unlikely to be successful. Faculty and staff who teach large introductory courses with heavy first-year enrollment, especially those in which first-year students have high rates of drop, withdrawal, incomplete, or failure, also may need additional support. The structure of the program is likely to necessitate monitoring attendance and having earlier or more frequent graded assignments, which may require the use of student assistants or the provision of released time for faculty teaching large gateway classes. Mandatory monitored programs prove more successful, as do those that link to a full array of support services, including peer mentors and tutors, so capacity issues must be addressed. Other costs include funding for collecting and assessing data and compensation for students serving as mentors or in other capacities. Analysis of assessment findings might suggest optimal sizes for introductory classes and perhaps the need to support faculty who teach them by making adjustments to load.

Assessment

The mission and goals of the program should guide assessment. Formative assessment of program organization and processes, including, for example, communication among participating offices and with students and classroom instructors, may identify issues related to timeliness and barriers to compliance. In some cases, students may ignore campus e-mail because they use other providers. Since the major purpose of the initiative is to reduce failure and dropout rates among students placed on probation, it becomes important to track student progress throughout the semester through ongoing attendance and grade reports for exams, papers, and class participation to provide opportunities for early interventions. Assessment might also identify capacity issues in participating offices. High energy and enthusiasm for a new initiative may sustain it for a while, but not over the long run. Similarly, problematic relationships within and among participating offices that may temporarily have been put on hold are likely to resurface. These issues may be identified through interviews and focused discussions with personnel in key participating offices, including their directors. A summative assessment at the end of the semester could include final grades, credit completion, and the percentage of students who regain good standing, move to strict probation, or leave the institution.

These results could be disaggregated in terms of the degree to which students actively participated in the program and by the extent to which they achieved academic success. Comparisons of the success rates of those groups might be followed up with focus groups or interviews to identify potential changes, one of which might be to make the policy mandatory. An institution could also focus on student cohorts of particular interest, for example, returning adults, students of color, first-generation students, or veterans. Interviews and focus groups with successful and unsuccessful students should provide helpful qualitative data. For example, students with significant child care and work responsibilities may simply have insufficient time for a full-time program but need that status to qualify for financial aid. Interviews with faculty members teaching critical gateway courses also may provide insights regarding student performance.

It also makes sense to find out if the initiative had a positive effect on nonprobationary students in 100-level courses. For example, earlier graded experiences and other positive educational practices may have deepened their learning as well. Positive outcomes could promote higher levels of faculty participation and support for the program. Moreover, a successful program promises to boost morale among all participating staff and faculty.

Students' reflections on the mix of activities and the communication process should form part of the assessment, as should those of student mentors, coaches, or tutors. Affective issues also are an important component of student engagement (Appleton, Christenson, & Furlong, 2008). An intervention may be well designed from an academic perspective but delivered in a fashion that does not engage students. And, as noted earlier, the experience of nonprobationary students in those classes also merits consideration.

A close focus on success rates in individual classes, especially those with multiple sections, could yield intelligence regarding course-based practices and teaching approaches that lead to student success. At the course level, it also would be instructive to compare the performance of first-year students in the program with those who are second-year or upper-class students. That analysis might indicate that the student mix in some 100-level class may be a contributing factor to poor performance by students who are in their initial semester of college. Tracking student inputs, especially attendance and class participation, also should yield useful data.

Benefit Analysis

Over time, a successful initiative should reduce the need for additional second-semester sections of 100-level courses caused by high rates of D, F, and W grades in the first semester. A reduction in incomplete grades would minimize the number of incompletes that lapse to failures. This might enable institutions to reduce adjunct budgets and class size or expand the range of course offerings. A successful academic recovery program will also minimize the number of course withdrawals and repeats, which increases the likelihood that students will complete a degree (Adelman, 2006; Chen & Carroll, 2005).

An effective program will likely promote higher rates of student engagement with their peers and with the university, which should boost first-year students' grades, which correlates positively with first-to-second-year retention (Kuh, Kinzie, Cruce, Shoup, & Gonyea, 2006). Higher rates of student persistence produce monetary benefits for the institution and its students. Pointing to the costs associated with recruiting and educating students who leave after their first year, Cuseo (2010a) suggests that expenditures that support student success are more cost effective than recruiting new students to replace those who have dropped out. The broadly collaborative approach in which professional staff from student and academic affairs offices partner with faculty and instructional staff should foster a greater sense of community, raise campus morale, and improve recruiting and institutional reputation. Moreover, successful students are positive ambassadors for their institution.

Institutional Practices

University of Minnesota

One of the nation's largest public research universities, the University of Minnesota's Twin Cities campus enrolls over fifty-two thousand students. In 1932, the university established General College to provide an opportunity for students who did not meet the university's standard entrance requirements. Its purpose was to increase student access and diversity, and it focused on intensive work in English, writing, and math. Having honed their skills, students then would transfer into one of the university's regular academic colleges. When a major reorganization of the University of Minnesota in 2005 resulted in the elimination of General College, it already had developed a probation initiative that provided intervention and support to promote student success. The university's College of Education and Human Development's department of postsecondary teaching and learning took on much of General College's mission and student population. It also developed a program called Access to Success and, as part of that, created a probation initiative.

University regulations place students on academic probation if their semester or cumulative GPA falls below 2.00, and a hold is placed on their registration, which can be lifted only after they have met with an advisor. The current program requires all students placed on academic probation to complete an academic contract. The contract also informs students that failure to meet the required GPA will result in their being suspended from the university. The next section details mandatory good-faith requirements that students must fulfill. These include completing a probation worksheet that asks them to identify factors that contributed to their poor academic performance. The worksheets are organized into four categories: study skills, family/social adjustment, career/major issues, and personal issues They also include an "other issues" category. The contract requires students to comment on the items they have identified, explaining how they caused academic problems and how both the university and college might help them get back on track.

Students also must provide a plan for dealing with the issues they identified and suggest what assistance they could use. They and their advisor agree on a set of academic interventions to address the major issues that contributed to their poor academic performance. The student and advisor both sign the completed form, which lifts the probation hold on the student's registration.

Advising, which employs an intrusive student-centered approach, plays a critical role in the program's operation and success. The probation initiative includes students at all levels, as does a proactive advising approach. The positive results of the probation program led the university's College of Biological Sciences to establish a similar initiative.

Purdue University, Calumet

Located in northeastern Indiana, Purdue University, Calumet, serves almost ten thousand students, and offers a wide range of master's programs. The Academic Recovery Program (ARP) began in April 2005 with approval from the university's faculty senate. Housed in the university's Center for Student Achievement, this mandatory program applies to the most academically at-risk tier of students on probation. It serves first-, second-, and third-year students.

Students placed on probation meet with an academic advisor and develop an academic success plan. Advisors receive a list with the names of these students and get in touch with them if they do not make an appointment in a timely fashion. Probationary students may not enroll for more than twelve credit hours, and they are required to repeat any courses in which they received a failing grade. Students who have declared a major must repeat any courses in that major in which they received a grade of D. All students who register for nine or more credits must enroll in GNS29000, Learning Strategies, a course designed to help them identify and reflect on the reasons they did not achieve satisfactory grades and help them succeed in college-level work.

Probationary students automatically have holds on their records, which are lifted after they have met with their advisors. After they register, the holds are restored, which means that ARP students need advisor approval to withdraw from a course or take an incomplete. Students must enroll in tutoring or supplemental instruction if it is available for any of their courses. GNS29000 instructors monitor compliance. The Center for Student Achievement's website has an extensive probation FAQ list which also includes a list of related campus resources. Students in GNS29000 are registered as a group in the university's myPUC portal through which they receive communications on a range of topics related to academic success. These occur weekly and are also sent to course instructors, who then reference them during class.

Data indicate that implementation of the ARP has significantly increased the percentage of students who return to good standing. For example, in the 2007–2008 academic year, 37 percent of the students participating in ARP during the spring semester returned to good standing. For 2010–2011, 56.7 percent regained good standing.

Chaffey College

A community college in Southern California, Chaffey's main campus is in Rancho Cucamonga, with campuses in Chino and Fontana as well. Its enrollment totals nearly 19,500 students, of whom 77 percent are classified as minority and historically underrepresented. In 2002, Chaffee was one of several community colleges that received support from MDRC (formerly the Manpower Demonstration Research Project), which partnered with it to develop a data-based student success initiative.

Chaffey chose to focus on developing a probation program. After an eighteen-month strategic planning effort, it began a one-semester voluntary program known as Opening Doors. It had negligible impact and was followed by a two-semester program, Enhanced Opening Doors to Excellence, that resulted from a collaborative effort of administrators, student affairs counselors, and faculty. It required students to take a college success course, essentially an orientation to the college's requirements, and to become familiar with the college's success centers, which offered several support programs, including, for example, group and individual supplementary instruction in math, reading, and writing (Scrivner, Sommolt, & Collado, 2009). The new program required students on probation to register for College Success, a course that focused on essential study skills and familiarized them with the college's requirements. Students also were required to work on their skills by participating in programs at the college's success centers.

Designed as a research project, the new version tracked eight hundred students, half of whom were in a control group. Students who participated in the required activities achieved significant gains in credit completion and GPA as compared to the control group. For example, they regained good standing at twice the rate of the control group. A five-year data run (2002–2007) indicated that students who used the success centers made significant gains (Scrivner et al., 2009). Chaffey institutionalized mandatory participation in Enhanced Opening Doors for probationary students in spring 2007. Assessment indicated that the voluntary program had negligible impact. However, mandatory participation in the two-semester program did produce meaningful gains in terms of credits earned, GPA, and the number of students who regained good standing (Scrivner et al., 2009).

Chaffey has continued its emphasis on out-of-class instruction and assistance to students. This includes Smart Start, a program that uses predictor variables to identify students who would profit by participating in a set of supportive activities, including workshops, directed learning activities, diagnosis of skills and learning styles, time management, effective use of resources to promote in-class success, and testing strategies. It has identified thirty predictor variables to preidentify students who are more likely to end up on probation (Diaz et al., 2007).

Chapter Eleven

Peer Leadership

Higher education research and student development theory have documented the profound impact of peers on the undergraduate experience. Fellow students are a significant influence on intellectual development, academic engagement, moral development, clarification of political and social values, determination of academic and social self-concept, and interpersonal skills (summarized in Pascarella & Terenzini, 1991, 2005; Skipper, 2005). Peers not only influence developmental processes and skill acquisition but are a factor in the transition of students to college, satisfaction with the collegiate experience, learning and academic performance, and persistence to graduation (Cuseo, 2010a). In fact, the influence of fellow students can even outweigh the effect of faculty and staff on students' experiences. Astin (1993b) concluded that "the student's peer group is the single most potent source of influence on growth and development during the undergraduate years" (p. 398).

Given that informal peer interaction has such a significant influence on the adjustment, development, learning, and success of undergraduate students, it is not surprising that educators are seeking to harness this power in more formal ways through peer leadership, mentorship, and education. Peer education and leadership draw generally from the fundamental principles of student interaction but also have specific characteristics and parameters as a form of interpersonal relationships. Newton and Ender (2010) define *peer educators* as "students who have been selected, trained, and designated by a campus authority to offer educational services to their peers . . . [which] . . . are intentionally designed to assist in the adjustment, satisfaction, and persistence of students toward attainment of their educational goals" (p. 6). This definition clearly identifies the general intent of these student relationships as advancing the personal and academic outcomes of college for fellow undergraduates. It also summarizes the fundamental and common features of peer leader programs (Keup, 2012; Latino & Ashcraft, 2012; Newton & Ender, 2010):

- Intentional recruitment and selection
- Initial training and ongoing support
- Clearly defined roles and responsibilities
- Challenging duties
- Opportunities for reflection and self-evaluation
- Supervision, support, and feedback from qualified staff

Although there are shared characteristics of peer leader positions, there are several pathways of influence for these student relationships. First, the scope of the peer-to-peer relationships ranges from micro to macro (Cuseo, 2010c). More specifically, Cuseo indicates that peer leadership can "promote positive personal change or individual empowerment" on an individual level; enables "collective change" and agency for a group or classroom; advances "change in campus policies, programs, practices, or procedures" on an organizational level as is common for peer leaders in student government, organizations, and activities; or provides "civic leadership or political change" on a community or social level (2010c, p. 4). Second, there are several roles that student leaders may assume in their interaction with their peers such as personal support agent, academic success agent or learning coach, role model, resource and referral agent, college success agent, and life success coach. Third, the domain of the collegiate experience in which the peer interaction takes place delineates the peer leader experience, most notably with respect to its foundation in the academic or cocurricular forums.

Each of these three aspects of formalized peer relationships must be identified and considered in order to properly recruit, train, and support peer leaders. Moreover, their intersection affects what we call these peer relationships and programs:

- *Peer mentors.* These are almost exclusively individual in scope, tend to be ongoing role models or support agents, and often provide advisement that extends beyond academic guidance and tends toward holistic student support (Cuseo, 2010c).

- *Peer educator.* This role may serve an individual (e.g., a tutor) or a group (e.g., a co-instructor or supplemental instruction leader), is characteristically found in the academic domain of college, and generally serves as an instructional or academic support agent.
- *Peer leader.* This has the greatest flexibility and broadest application with respect to scope, student role, and campus domain. Furthermore, it aligns closely with the notion of leadership and engaged citizenry as key outcomes of college (Association of American Colleges and Universities, 2007).

Other names for undergraduates in formal positions to help other students are *peer counselor, ambassador, student coach, student assistant, peer advisor, student facilitator, instructor,* and *tutor* (Cuseo, 2010c; Newton & Ender, 2010; Keup, 2012).

Peer leadership has the longest history in student services and is still heavily used in support areas such as orientation and residential life. As these areas became professionalized in the mid-1950s with the emergence of student affairs as a subspecialty of higher education, student roles as peer leaders in orientation and residential life were introduced. Today student orientation leaders play a critical role in fostering a successful transition for first-year students at their respective institutions by creating a safe space for new students' orientation experience, helping to communicate institutional expectations, clarifying campus culture and traditions for entering students, and beginning to forge a sense of community (Ganser & Kennedy, 2012; Ward-Roof, 2010).

Student staff members in residence life, often called *resident assistants* or *resident mentors,* take on the mantle of peer leadership with respect to nurturing the sense of community that begins for first-year students in orientation. Resident mentors or assistants also develop cocurricular programming in the residence halls, oversee the logistical elements of a functional and safe living space for students, and provide channels for undergraduate involvement on campus (Ganser & Kennedy, 2012; Johnson & Parker, 2008).

As the number of students and the need for support increases, many institutions face the challenge of providing more student services, particularly for first-year students, in an era when resources are shrinking. Thus, "in order to maintain and even increase the level of services and support provided with limited professional staff, many institutions turn to [student] paraprofessionals to fill the gaps" (Ganser & Kennedy, 2012, p. 18). Paraprofessionals in student services like orientation and residential life also face new challenges, such as communicating with students' family members, managing the expectations of a new generation of entering students, and serving students from different backgrounds. Finally, due in part to the successful integration of peer leaders in orientation and residential life, other student service areas have expanded their use of student paraprofessionals and peer leaders, such as judicial affairs, placement centers, crisis intervention, student counseling, and religious centers (Cuseo, 2010c; Ender & Kay, 2001).

Historically, undergraduate peers were not heavily engaged in the instruction or academic support of fellow students. If they were involved in such activities, it was typically considered a marginal pursuit offered for students who needed to be "fixed." Now, involvement of peers in the classroom and in academic support functions has become the norm and evolved into "a mainstream enterprise that improves teaching and learning experiences for all students" (Latino & Unite, 2012, p. 31; Shook & Keup, 2012). The most common ways that peers are engaged in the classroom are as co-instructors or teaching assistants in freshman composition, introductory mathematics, and gateway courses to majors. First-year seminars are another curricular space where peer leadership and instruction has gained traction, as with the University 101 Peer Leader Program at the University of South Carolina. Other peer leader roles in the academic domain are tutors, peer advisors, academic coaches, health educators, peer advisors, and academic mentors (Keup & Skipper, 2010; Latino & Unite, 2012; Newton & Ender, 2010). Furthermore, as Supplemental Instruction (SI) has grown in both the United States and internationally, SI leaders offer another opportunity for peer education. As both the home of the International Center for Supplemental Instruction and an early adopter of this academic resource, the University of Missouri, Kansas City, represents a gold standard for the administration of a robust SI program and the integration of peer leaders into its delivery.

Student organizations and campus activities represent yet another common opportunity for peer leadership in the first year, especially since recent data show that half of entering students at four-year colleges and universities expect to participate in student clubs and groups during college, 33 percent expect to play intramural or recreational sports, 12 percent intend to join a Greek letter organization, and 7 percent anticipate participating in student government (Pryor, DeAngelo, Palacki Blake, Hurtado, & Tran, 2011). Higher education has now embraced participation in student organizations and campus activities, once considered ancillary to student learning in college, as having the potential to be an educationally purposeful endeavor (Wooten, Hunt, LeDuc, & Poskus, 2012) and a means toward advancing twenty-first-century learning outcomes and leadership competencies (National Association for Campus Activities, 2009). Both appointed and elected positions within student organizations, as well as the participation of student leaders in institutional governance, offer myriad peer leader roles as well as meaningful learning opportunities for these students. For example, at "the University of South Florida, the University of Georgia, and the University of West Georgia, the student government has primary authority for the distribution of student fees in support of student organizations, support services, and student affairs offices. Students become more aware of the many sources of input that go into making decisions about what programs or departments are most important to ensuring [fellow] student success" (Wooten et al., 2012, p. 52).

One of the most significant trends with respect to the peer leadership movement in higher education is the wide range of leadership roles that undergraduate peer leaders assume. Many of these roles staff student success initiatives targeted to new students and represent significant support agents for first-year students. National data show that use of peer leadership in the academic domain now rivals that of student services and campus activities (Shook & Keup, 2012). Although fewer peers are engaged in leadership, mentorship, and instructional roles in counseling, mental and physical health support, judicial affairs, and study-abroad programs, these peer leader programs are growing as well. Overall, "the number of institutions reporting the use of students in leadership roles has increased" and "the number of campus settings and services using campus helpers has increased substantially" (Ender & Kay, 2001, p. 5).

Approaching the Work/Critical Partners

As with any other first-year program, even initial efforts at the development of a peer leader program should consider the long-range sustainability of the program. Thus, it is critical to pay early attention to the programmatic elements that are core to success and sustainability, such as institutional context, organizational structure, program goals, and buy-in across all segments of the campus (Esplin, Seabold, & Pinnegar, 2012; Lynch, 2001). A firm understanding of the program with respect to these issues and parameters will clarify the vision, direct decisions, and inform structural solutions. The ultimate goal of any first-year initiative, including peer leader programs, is to ensure the centrality of the program to the learning experiences, administrative activities, and strategic direction of the institution. The most successful and long-standing peer leader programs situate themselves securely within the institutional context and address student needs. A peer leader program that resides on the margins is likely to lose visibility and become vulnerable.

There are a number of common reasons for creating peer leader programs—for example (Esplin et al., 2012; Ganser & Kennedy, 2012):

- Addressing a gap in professional staffing
- Expanding program scope and reach
- Enhancing persistence for all students as well as among historically at-risk populations
- Facilitating the orientation and integration of students coming to the institution as first-year or transfer students
- Fostering student engagement in the campus community
- Providing specialized program-level support

Although "the basic principles of peer education, leadership, and mentoring are highly transferable, . . . the specific characteristics of programs that provide consistent, organized, and efficacious outcomes-based delivery of peer leadership . . . [are] rarely transferable as a whole from one institution to another" (Esplin et al., p. 86). Therefore, it is important to identify how these issues are operationalized within a specific campus context, how these priorities may shift based on the student populations at a particular institution, and what other challenges and opportunities peer leader programs might address at a specific college or university. If a peer leader program fits well with the mission, vision, and strategic direction of an institution, it is more likely to become part of the campus culture and traditions, a significant contributor to programmatic sustainability.

Alignment between the peer leader program and institutional context also provides a foundation for evaluating administrative aspects of the program. For instance, placement of the peer leader program within the larger organizational structure depends on the goals of the program and needs to consider proximity to faculty, staff, peer leaders, and targeted student populations. Some examples of possible administrative homes for the peer leader program are student affairs, academic affairs, a school or college, enrollment management, or housing and residential life. Resource decisions, budget models, and funding channels will flow from the position of the program within the organizational structure and its connection to the institutional context and culture.

Gaining institutional buy-in from cross-campus partners is another aspect of the initial and long-term success of a peer leader program. Like many other first-year initiatives, peer leadership tends to draw support from all sectors of the institution and fosters a strong sense of shared ownership. As such, "peer leader programs can create a high degree of cooperative goodwill between academic departments and campus support units that transcends physical separation, perceived isolation, and political tensions" (Esplin et al., 2012, p. 87). Critical campus partners are largely determined by the goals and administrative home of the peer leader program. For example, peer leaders in the academic domain of the undergraduate experience are likely to draw support from faculty; support staff from colleges or majors; honors programs; university colleges; academic advisors; study-abroad programs; student preprofessional societies; and the leadership of Supplemental Instruction, first-year seminar programs, and student success centers.

Peer leadership programs situated in student services often collaborate with other units, including orientation programs, residential life, housing, student health services, judicial affairs, offices of community service, admissions, and visitor services. Opportunities in campus activities and student life will likely find engaged partnership from student life, student productions and media, Greek life, the athletic department, recreational activities, and student religious organizations. Although not as frequently used as other campus units, alumni affairs, career services, development offices, parents' associations and offices of parent programs, and community partners may also yield fruitful collaborations in support of peer leader programs. Finally, students themselves, either those who were previously served by a peer leader program or those who are in a peer leader, mentor, or educator role, are a treasure trove of information about how to plan and deliver these programs in a way that is relevant to students.

Campus partners may emerge based on the administrative needs of the peer leader program. For example, if students are being paid for their service, the office of personnel and human resources will be instrumental to the processing of hiring and employment paperwork for potentially large cohorts of new student paraprofessionals entering these roles each year. In addition, in an era when students have high expectations about the integration of technology into their collegiate experience, staff from information technology services can help infuse peer leader programs with computer technologies and social networking features in a way that fulfills students' expectations and advances twenty-first-century learning outcomes and media literacy among the students being served by the program (Johnson, 2012).

The diversity of peer leader programs makes it difficult to determine a single formula for campus partnership. However, chances of programmatic success are related to two conditions. First, institutional leadership must be visibly supportive of the effort within the campus community. Second, it is important that more than one campus unit or office, and preferably several, are invested in the success of the peer leader endeavor. Both of these conditions contribute to the centrality of the peer leader program to the core educational endeavors of the college or university.

Organization/Implementation Process

The basic components of any peer leader program—whether it is in the classroom, cocurriculum, or student life—are the effective implementation of recruitment, selection, and training processes for peer leaders. However, before these processes begin, it is necessary for those who are overseeing the program to ask themselves some questions about the program (Esplin et al., 2012):

- What are the intended goals of the peer leader program?
- What needs are the peer leaders fulfilling within the institution?
- What is the scope of their roles and responsibilities in pursuit of program goals and toward addressing institutional needs?
- Will the peer leaders be working with students individually or in groups?
- What are the best means to motivate and support peer leaders?
- What resources are available to execute these motivational and support strategies?

Thorough consideration of these questions and an analysis of their answers will help identify the type of peer leader program necessary, the appropriate organizational structure to support it, and potential partners for the program.

Peer Leader Description

The answers to the questions about the program also provide a framework for the peer leader position description. The characteristics for the position should "reflect the goals of the program and the expectations the program director has of the students who will serve as peer leaders" (Hunter & Heath, 2001, p. 38). Since peer leaders serve as both a role model and a resource for students, there are some common position requirements:

- A minimum grade point average or other index of academic performance

- A history of involvement on campus
- Leadership skills or interest
- Successful experiences with the program in which they will serve as a peer leader
- Class level (commonly juniors or seniors)
- Strong interpersonal and communication skills
- Affiliation with a particular department, major, or student organization

If there are specific training requirements (e.g., summer training workshop) or an expected time investment (e.g., enrollment in a peer leadership course), it is wise to include those commitments as requirements in the position description (Esplin et al., 2012).

Recruiting and Selecting Peer Leaders

Advertising these requirements to attract potential candidates for the peer leader positions is the next step in the implementation process. Standard channels of communication for student employment are available for peer leader positions that are paid. Nominations from faculty, staff, and current peer leaders are additional resources to generate a pool of potential peer leaders. Social media are yet another way to reach a large number of students who may be interested in serving as peer leaders. However, often the most fruitful means of recruiting students is through the culture of informal student-to-student marketing (Hunter & Heath, 2001).

When circulating these calls for participation, there are a few issues to address that will increase the chances that the recruitment process and peer leader service will be successful. First, it is important to differentiate characteristics that must be innate in peer leaders and, thus, part of the recruitment phase, from skills that can be realistically taught in training. Since peer leader positions are valuable learning experiences for the students in those roles as well as for the students they serve, it is unreasonable to expect peer leaders to possess at the outset all of the knowledge and capabilities necessary for long-range success in the position. Second, peer leader program administrators must direct a critical eye toward the language and expectations articulated in the advertisements to ensure that they are explicit and accurate. "Sometimes, in an effort to attract students, peer leader program staff members focus on the fun aspects of the role and inadvertently misrepresent the high expectations associated with the position . . . [which] may create challenges when peer leaders are unhappy in a role that they misunderstood" (Esplin et al., 2012). Third, successful recruitment must pursue practices that draw on the diversity of potential student leaders, particularly with respect to historically underrepresented student populations. The requirements for the position, desired characteristics, clearly articulated expectations for roles and responsibilities, and evidence of a commitment to recruiting a diverse pool of peer leader candidates should all be present on the peer leader application form.

Upon completion of the recruitment and application phase of the peer leader program, efforts during the selection phase will determine if the applicants possess the necessary skills and commitment to fulfill the expectations and duties of the position. Clearly the peer leader program administrator should provide oversight for the selection process. However, inclusion of other colleagues as members of a selection committee will likely yield a stronger cohort of peer leaders. The campus partners identified earlier in this chapter are all excellent additions to any selection committee for a peer leader program and provide yet another opportunity for the program to serve as an example of cross-campus collaboration.

After initial introductions and a review of the responsibilities of the selection committee, the first task for these individuals is to undertake a systematic review of the applications against a predetermined set of criteria. Then the committee can decide to interview all candidates who meet the basic criteria or invite only select candidates to participate in an interview process. This decision will be influenced by resource limitations, institutional hiring policies for peer leader positions that draw a stipend or salary, and academic guidelines for peer educator positions that earn credit or have responsibilities in the classroom. Interviews may be conducted individually or in a group; in-person, online, or by phone; follow a prescribed set of questions or engage a more unstructured protocol; or include role-play scenarios and activities. Regardless of the structure, the primary goal of the interview process is to provide candidates the "opportunity to demonstrate the skills needed for the peer leader role" (Esplin et al., 2012, p. 93). Predetermined criteria, well-structured evaluation sheets, and time parameters for the interview will help "interviewers systematically think about the alignment between a candidate's skills and abilities and the position requirements" (Esplin et al., 2012, p. 93). The members of the selection committee should clarify the selection categories, determine whether there is a need or capacity for a wait list or alternates, and discuss issues of overselection to account for attrition.

Training for Peer Leaders

Once the peer leaders have been selected, it is crucial that they engage in an intentional and comprehensive training program that fully equips them for success in their new role. Initial training often includes an intense training workshop, course, retreat, required reading, or online modules (Newton & Ender, 2010; Esplin et al., 2012; Hunter & Heath, 2001). However, it is also important to consider ongoing training and support for these leaders in order to help them "continuously reflect upon and learn from their experiences, troubleshoot while in their role, stay updated on timeline issues, steadily improve skills, and receive encouragement" (Jacobs, Hurley, & Unite, 2008, in Esplin et al., 2012, p. 94). Models for such continued support include regular meetings, refresher workshops, online interactions, written reflections, and ongoing and attentive supervision (Esplin et al., 2012).

The content of the initial and ongoing training depends on the domain of the peer leader experience, the range of duties in the role, and whether the position is an individual mentor or group leader. Regardless of these issues, a number of topics are commonly addressed (Newton & Ender, 2010):

- Problem solving
- Understanding interpersonal dynamics
- Communication and facilitation skills
- Conflict resolution
- Campus resources
- Referral techniques

- Ethics
- Setting professional boundaries

Reflection activities and engagement of active learning strategies in peer leader training are nearly universal and allow the training experience to model strategies that the peer leaders will draw on in their roles with fellow students. Although the structure, duration, and content of training depends on the nature of the peer leader position, the most significant factor in these decisions is that the needs of the peer leaders are being met and that they are well equipped to be successful in this role.

Leadership Roles/Communication

Typically peer leader, mentor, and educator programs are components of a larger initiative such as a first-year seminar, residence life, orientation, advising, supplemental instruction, learning communities, health education, campus activities, bridge programs, or student life. Therefore, while there usually is an administrator overseeing the first-year initiative, the scope of that person's role typically encompasses much more than the peer leader program. Connecting the goals of the program to the larger initiative and communicating it as part of the initiative's mission and strategic direction, rather than appearing like an add-on project, make oversight of the peer leadership piece more effective and efficient.

Two trends in the management of peer leader programs are worth noting. The first represents an extension of the peer leadership concept to include opportunities for advanced positions for experienced peer leaders (Ganser & Kennedy, 2012; Lynch, 2001). Resulting from a range of institutional forces, such as "further budget cuts resulting in greater reliance upon paraprofessionals, oversight of more services with no additional professional staff, and increased enrollment numbers," there is a move to engage students to provide overall leadership among the peer leaders (Ganser & Kennedy, 2012, p. 22). As another alternative, peer leader programs have matured to the point where greater numbers of trained and experienced student paraprofessionals are in a position to embrace professional advancement in these roles.

Thus, more experienced peer leaders are in a position to contribute to the training, guidance, and oversight of new and more junior peer leaders. Titles for these positions include team captain, assistant director, peer trainer, and peer leader advisor, and they are most often found in programs that serve a large number of students such as first-year seminars, orientation, and residence life. Students in these advanced positions often serve as trainers, supervisors, and mentors for the peer leaders, as well as provide administrative assistance to the professional staff leading the program.

A second trend in the oversight of peer leader programs is an interest in coordination of these roles across campus. Because peer leadership is a component of many student support and success initiatives, it is very easy for several programs to be engaged in similar activities with respect to the recruitment, selection, training, and support of these student leaders. Without proper communication, these parallel processes can result in duplication of effort, internal competition among peer leaders for different campus positions, and recruitment of the same pool of talented and involved students for various peer leader opportunities across campus. More institutions are forming peer leader support networks or peer leader advisory committees, which include staff members who oversee programs engaging peer leaders, as well as representation from the peer leaders themselves. These groups help provide a forum for communication among peer leader programs on campus and "are a structure through which to align practices, maximize the benefits of the peer leader experience, create resource efficiencies, and increase campus collaboration" (Ganser & Kennedy, 2012, p. 27). Members of these groups can share recruitment time lines, application forms, selection criteria, training resources, and pay scales in an effort to minimize costly errors, redundancy of effort, and competition among programs. They also "allow for sharing, reflection, and processing of peer leadership experiences, which leads to greater meaning making of the experience" (Ganser & Kennedy, 2012, p. 27). Finally, peer leadership support networks and advisor committees can work together toward a common set of learning outcomes for these practices, as well as identify economies of scale in assessment and evaluation practices for their respective programs.

Resource Needs/Personnel

Oversight of peer leaders is often only one component of a position for the directors of student support programs, so additional staff may be needed, especially for larger programs. In some instances, other professional staff members support the work of the director with respect to peer leaders. There also is a trend toward engaging undergraduate paraprofessionals in leadership, supervisory, or training roles for peer leaders. These key leadership roles may be complemented by involvement of critical partners across campus in areas that are aligned with the domain and purpose of the peer leader program. Other common personnel roles for these programs are fulfilled by centralized campus services such as instructional technology services, centers of teaching excellence and faculty and instructor development, and human resources. Although not all of these professional positions are noted as line items in the peer leader budget or are represented on the staff roster for the program, it is beneficial to understand fully the web of professional, volunteer, and centralized personnel support that is necessary to develop and administer a peer leader program.

Beyond personnel, one of the greatest investments of resources for a peer leader program occurs in recruitment, selection, and training. The human resources and time investment of the program administrator to create the position description, application, and review criteria is substantial. Developing and disseminating recruitment materials, print or electronic, is a perennial expense to consider. Furthermore, the costs associated with the service of the selection committee in application review, interviewing, and peer leader selection can be significant, especially for larger programs. Even if these colleagues are not paid, they are diverting their time and expertise away from other activities, which can represent a considerable investment. Other costs are for supplies, facilities, and collateral material for the training process, as well as the potential to pay for guest speakers, textbooks, and in-person or online training modules. Some peer leader positions are also afforded a small budget to help them bond with, instruct, and otherwise address the needs of the students they serve. These costs are often embedded within the larger budget of a first-year program but must be accounted for nonetheless.

Another expense for peer leader programs is in the form of recognition and compensation for the peer leaders. National data indicate that peer leader positions most often receive recognition for their service in the form of financial compensation such as hourly pay, stipends, scholarships, or room and board. Especially for larger programs, these costs can be extensive and must be included in the program budget. Other compensation models may not include remuneration but do provide incentives that require budgetary investment. The most significant example is the allocation of class credit, which requires an investment in facilities, instructional staff, and learning resources to offer the course from which the peer leaders draw credit. Another example is the development and management of formalized leadership programs or cocurricular transcripts, which require resources to develop, oversee, and track. Even small tokens of appreciation for volunteer peer leader positions, such as T-shirts, pizza parties, recognition events, and certificates, require some funding.

Much like most other aspects of developing, implementing, and managing a peer leader program, the source of funding for the program is largely dependent on the type of program, those it serves, and where it resides in the organizational structure. Initial funding may come from a grant, a one-time investment of institutional funds, or a reallocation of resources from another program. However, it is important to the development of the program to ensure that a sustainable resource stream is identified. For academic programs, these funds may come from tuition allocations, student fees, or departmental budgets. For fee-based programs such as orientation, student health services, and residence life, peer leader programs are likely to draw from the revenue collected for those programs. Peer leadership opportunities within student organizations and campus activities are often funded by budget allocations from the division of student life or membership fees. Careful consideration of scalability, constant communication about return on investment for these programs, and consideration of renewable funding sources are vital to the success and sustainability of peer leader programs.

Assessment

Assessment is a substantial component of communicating the message that peer leader programs yield positive outcomes and are a worthy investment.

Latino and Ashcraft (2012) recommend that assessment activities for peer leader programs represent a three-pronged effort:

- Evaluate the effectiveness of the peer leader program on the students being served.
- Examine the impact of the experience on the peer leaders themselves.
- Address the effectiveness of peer leadership on the overall success of the program.

A critical point of consideration in an effective and efficient assessment plan for peer leadership programs is to leverage data that the institution is already collecting. For example, although there is not yet a standardized questionnaire for peer leader experiences, peer leadership assessment data may include an extraction of data from a national survey of the first-year experience or locally developed student surveys. Course evaluations can be another rich resource of assessment data for peer leadership experiences that are connected to the classroom, such as peer-led instruction, tutoring, or Supplemental Instruction. Whether these instruments are focused on the peer leadership experience or merely have a few items to indicate participation in a peer-led initiative or service as a peer leader, mentor, or educator, these data will help provide connections between the experience and important student outcomes such as persistence, satisfaction, adjustment, integration, and the development of academic, leadership, communication, intercultural, and interpersonal skills.

If it is possible to connect institutional data from admissions offices and the registrar, as well as facility use statistics, to peer leader experiences, these data may yield important information about the relationship between peer leadership experiences and student outcomes. For paid peer leader positions, standard human resource processes such as employee reviews, supervisor documentation, and professional development plans may provide assessment data. Annual reports from student organizations may provide insight into the patterns and impact of students serving in leadership roles within those groups. Finally, as student portfolios, cocurricular transcripts, and leadership curricula grow in popularity and use, they may also serve as resources for assessment of peer leadership experiences.

Esplin et al. (2012) state that "strong peer leader programs use a variety of methods and approaches to collect and analyze data" (p. 97). As such, it is important not to overlook qualitative methodology, which is also valuable to a peer leadership assessment plan. Focus groups and individual interviews with peer leaders and the students they serve will likely provide bountiful information on the developmental process resulting from the peer leader experience. In addition, these methods will yield greater feedback on psychological and affective outcomes that are more difficult to measure, such as intercultural competence, leadership skills, social and academic self-confidence, and student motivation. Similar data may be drawn from reflection processes that are often included in peer leader training both initially and in ongoing supervision and support. The narratives derived from these reflection processes provide a rich resource for understanding the developmental gains and the challenges experienced as a result of peer leader experiences.

Esplin et al. (2012) identify common assessment practices among successful peer leader programs. The first of these is clear articulation of program goals. While peer leader programs, and thus their assessment plans, are very process oriented, ultimately there needs to be a measurable outcome. Often these outcomes are similar to goals articulated for any other first-year initiative (Cuseo, 2010b; Keup & Skipper, 2010):

- Persistence
- Academic achievement in the form of grades and receipt of honors
- Increased academic and social self-concept among first-year students
- Greater knowledge and use of campus resources
- A strong sense of belonging and institutional affiliation

- Satisfaction with the individual program and overall collegiate experience
- Increased interaction with students

These programs may also address other outcomes that are more specialized to peer leader experiences (Keup & Skipper, 2010):

- Leadership development
- Increased appreciation for diversity
- Emotional development
- Interpersonal skills
- Organization skills
- Time management

The second good assessment practice among successful peer leader programs is the ability to connect these program outcomes and their evaluation strategies to a vision and mission that is meaningful to program and campus stakeholders. This can be done through alignment with accreditation goals, strategic plans, or institutional self-study processes.

A third common assessment practice is a commitment to ongoing assessment and a dedication to continuous program improvement. Finally, successful peer leader programs are transparent in their assessment practices and findings. Wide dissemination of assessment findings to all program constituents is a valuable step in the process of evaluation and program improvement. All of these assessment practices converge to create a culture of accountability and data-driven decision making about peer leadership.

Benefit Analysis

Developing, administering, and expanding peer leadership, mentorship, and education programs involve significant investments in personnel, facilities and supplies, outreach and recruitment, training resources, and the time of professional and volunteer personnel. One of the greatest features of peer leadership and education is that it provides benefits at multiple levels. As we noted with respect to assessment practices, "the first is the impact of the peer educator on the students served" and the "second represents the impact of the peer education experience on the peer educators themselves" (Latino & Unite, 2012, p. 40). The final level of impact is at the programmatic or even institutional level.

Not surprisingly, the primary beneficiaries of peer mentorship, leadership, and education are the students who are the recipients of these programs. Research findings and assessment data have repeatedly shown the important impact of formalized peer interactions on students' development of "a stronger sense of community, [and a] greater social and academic integration" (Shook & Keup, 2012, p. 7). Undergraduates also benefit from their interaction with peer leaders as advocates of academic support and as resource and referral agents. In addition, the role of formalized peer mentorship has been shown to be a valuable catalyst for community building, adjustment, and success among historically underrepresented and potentially marginalized students, such as women and minority students in science, technology, engineering, and math (STEM) fields (Chesney, 2011); African American and Hispanic students on predominantly white campuses (Cole, 2008; Guiffrida, 2003, 2006); and first-generation students (Davis, 2010).

Although peer leader programs are designed primarily to address the needs of the students being served, their power lies in the mutual benefit to both peer leaders and students. Through intense training and fulfillment of the roles and responsibilities of their positions, peer leaders become more involved students and are exposed to integrative and active pedagogies. More specifically, Harmon (2006) found that peer mentors for first-year students reported increases in their ability to manage groups, empathize with students, and facilitate learning. Peer leaders also report a greater sense of belonging at their institution, gain a deeper understanding of institutional processes and governance, build stronger relationships with faculty and staff, become more responsible, increase their appreciation of diversity, and gain in awareness of professional and ethical standards (Keup & Skipper, 2010; Latino, 2010). Still other research has shown that peer leaders report development in their communication and leadership skills; applied learning; knowledge of campus resources; interaction with faculty, staff, and peers; critical thinking; problem solving; and interpersonal skills (Astin, 1993b; Newton & Ender, 2010; Keup, 2012). Finally, national data indicate that peer leaders report gains in organization, time management, and general academic skills (Shook & Keup, 2012).

On an institutional level, peer leadership and education programs provide a reasonable staffing alternative in resource-sensitive times: "Student paraprofessionals provide a cost-efficient and yet high-quality alternative to better accommodate the large number of students who need services" (Shook & Keup, 2012). In addition to being cost-effective, peer leaders are often more valuable as a resource to fellow students than professional staff are due to their proximity to the students and the fact that they are perceived as a more accessible authority figure than faculty and staff (Cuseo, 1991). The success of both the students and peer leaders in the program increases the overall retention and graduation rates for the institution, thereby contributing to the reputation of the school and creating a pool of engaged graduates who go on to be active alumni (Shook & Keup, 2012).

Institutional Practices

University of Wisconsin-Madison

As the main campus of the University of Wisconsin system, the Madison campus is a four-year public, land grant institution that serves nearly twenty-nine thousand undergraduate students. The institution is dedicated to a three-pronged mission of research, teaching, and service and strives to create "a learning environment in which faculty, staff and students can discover, examine critically, preserve and transmit the knowledge, wisdom and values that will help ensure the survival of this and future generations and improve the quality of life for all" (University of Wisconsin, 2013). The university seeks to attract and serve a diverse body of students and is especially committed to serving students from historically underrepresented and underserved groups. In pursuit of this mission, it hosts a number of initiatives to assist students in their transition into and progress through the university, including orientation, living-learning communities, first-year seminars, service-learning, advising, and a common reading program.

As a primarily residential campus, the university offers residence hall space to over seven thousand students each year, 77 percent of whom are first-year students. In order to support the full range of student support programming and campus life activities for all residential students, the office of university housing employs a number of resident assistants called *house fellows*. Similar to many other institutions, house fellows are on-site staff members who live in the residence halls with a group of students who remain under the house fellow's supervision for the duration of the students' stay in the residence hall. The responsibilities of house fellows focus on four core values of university housing: academics, involvement, community, and diversity. Duties may include personal and academic advisement, community building, safety and crisis management, roommate negotiation and mediation, and cocurricular programming.

While most campuses with residential housing employ students as resident assistants or resident mentors, fewer campuses engage peer leaders as mentors, advocates, and resources to students from underrepresented identities who live on campus. The University of Wisconsin represents an example of this type of peer leadership through its lesbian, gay, bisexual, transgender, and queer (LGBTQ) diversity coordinators on the university housing staff. These coordinators reach out to students in the residence halls who self-identify as members of LGBTQ community to provide them support and advocacy. They also serve the entire residential community on LGBTQ issues, including making the residence halls LBGTQ "safe zones," providing ally training, sponsoring gay-straight alliance organizations for students, and contributing to general programming in the residence halls. Through the efforts of these peer leaders, LGBTQ students in the residence halls have a specialized resource and an advocate for a safer living environment. Moreover, the awareness of the entire residence life community is increased with respect to LGBTQ issues in particular and diversity considerations in general.

University of Texas at Dallas

Founded in 1969 but admitting freshmen only since 1991, the University of Texas at Dallas is a diverse, urban four-year institution that is on its way to becoming a tier 1 research university. It serves over fifteen thousand students and maintains a commitment to excellence in all areas of undergraduate education, with a special emphasis on science, technology, engineering, and math (STEM) programs. Due to this focus, "success, retention, and persistence in gateway science and mathematics courses . . . play a critical role in influencing student decisions not only to continue their studies in related degree programs but to continue their college careers" (Chesney, 2011, p. 8).

Historically, STEM gateway courses at UT Dallas had a high failure and withdrawal rate. In order to address student challenges in STEM gateway courses, UT Dallas introduced peer-led team learning (PLTL) in fall 2008. PLTL is a "zero credit, ninety-minute small-group session of eight to ten students, which is facilitated by another student who has already successful passed the course" (Chesney, 2011, pp. 8–9). PLTL leaders meet with students weekly in which they serve as discussion leaders, foster students' active engagement with the material, and "effectively reduce the distance between leader and learner" by creating an accessible resource in the PLTL leader (Chesney, 2011, p. 9). The peer educators who lead the PLTL sections are encouraged to interact with one another to provide peer support. More important, they are connected to a faculty liaison to help connect the PLTL sections to the course content, develop curriculum and content for the PLTL sessions, and provide guidance to the PLTL peer leaders. The key to success in this peer-led support program appears to be the focus on process by providing students with learning tools for self-sufficiency with the material rather than just providing answers to challenging problems. Assessment data provide empirical evidence of this success in the form of precipitous drops in the rate of students receiving Ds and Fs and withdrawing from these previously problematic STEM gateway courses.

The program was initially launched with only twelve peer leaders for one course, General Chemistry I, which served as a requirement for more than a dozen majors and had a 37 percent failure and withdrawal rate. The pilot group served by those leaders had only a 19 percent drop, withdrawal, and failure rate, which fell to 9 percent for the following cohort of students in General Chemistry I (Chesney, 2011). These initial and subsequent success rates for the program have led to its growth to 125 sections of PLTL serving over one thousand students enrolled in different STEM gateway courses (Chesney, 2011). In order to meet this demand, the process for recruiting and supporting PLTL leaders has become more streamlined and is managed by the UT Dallas Gateways to Engagement, Mastery, and Success Center. The greatest source for new PLTL leaders are students who were previously enrolled in a PLTL section, thereby providing yet another measurement of the program's success.

Florida International University

Located in Miami, Florida International University (FIU) is a public, four-year, Hispanic-serving institution with over forty-six thousand students, which makes it one of the twenty-five largest public universities in the country. It is primarily a commuter campus, and the average age of its students is twenty-two. Offering bachelor's, master's, and doctoral degrees, FIU maintains a focus on research as a significant component of its institutional mission and identity.

Piloted in 2006, Panther Camp is a three-day orientation retreat for incoming FIU students that is held camp style, with cabins and bunk beds, at Lake Placid Camp and Conference Center in Lake Placid, Florida. The camp has three educational programs that are focused college life, balance and time management, and academic life. Camp participants are divided into teams that are called "families," with two peer facilitators per family (Glisson, 2009). The families engage in team-building activities, discuss academic and personal strategies for their transition to college, and provide opportunities for processing and reflection. Four identical sections of Panther Camp are offered over the summer: three for freshmen and one for transfers.

The unique aspect of this orientation program is that it is entirely coordinated by current FIU peer leaders, including the development of educational programming, learning outcomes, and camp activities. Over thirty current FIU students serve as facilitators, and the executive board is made up of eight peer leaders who previously served as facilitators. Students who serve as peer leaders for Panther Camp must maintain a 2.5 grade point average and participate in training workshops, retreats, and regular meetings that focus on group dynamics, learning outcomes, facilitation skills, introduction to student development theory, team building, campus traditions and resources, intercultural awareness, and leadership skills (Glisson, 2009).

Results of assessments conducted in 2012 indicated that Panther Camp participants were extremely satisfied with their experience: 97 percent would recommend the camp to future FIU freshmen, and 80 percent expressed interest in serving as a camp facilitator. In addition, the participants reported significant gains in their ability to make new friends, manage their time, develop their communication skills, engage in teamwork, and appreciate diversity. These same students also noted substantial self-reported gains on all measures related to knowledge of campus resources, traditions, student organizations, and involvement opportunities. Previous assessment data indicate that these gains translate into positive decisions and engagement during the first year. For example, 100 percent of students who participated in Panther Camp in 2011 became involved in at least one club or activity at the institution (Florida International University, 2011). Other data show that 100 percent of students who participated in the camp in previous years persisted to their second year of college (Glisson, 2009).

In 2008, the evaluation of Panther Camp included an assessment of the peer leader experience. Quantitative results showed that "their peer educator role resulted in their having increased confidence in all 20 of the functional areas assessed" (Glisson, 2009, p. 5) Focus group results with camp peer leaders supported these findings, especially in the areas of leadership development, diversity skills, and affinity for the campus and its traditions. Finally, camp peer leaders reported that the success of their experience led them to consider pursuing a career in higher education.

Chapter Twelve

| Second-Year Transitions

Upcraft, Gardner, and Barefoot (2005) helped center the concept of first-year transitions and the importance of both "challenging and supporting" students (Sanford, 1962) through innovative teaching and learning strategies and robust academic and student support services. The success of those collaborative initiatives suggested that a similar focus on the second year of college might ease another challenging transition for students, and that sparked efforts to identify the critical needs of second-year students from both academic and student development perspectives.

Historically, the term *sophomore* applied to students who successfully completed thirty or more credits during their initial year, but in contemporary higher education, many returning second-year students fall below that threshold. Some may have tested into one or more developmental education courses, which generally do not count as credits toward degree. Others may have registered for the minimum number of credits required for full-time status because of family or work responsibilities or dropped courses that they found overly challenging. Course failures also reduce credits earned. A study by the National Center for Education Statistics (2009) that focused on family background found that students whose parents did not have a college degree "earned about 18 credits in the first year, compared with 25 credits for those whose parents had a bachelor's degree or higher." Both student cohorts graduated within five years, and in both cases, the earned credits in the first year fell below the traditional benchmark for sophomore status. Well-prepared students who have taken Advanced Placement courses or participated in International

Baccalaureate programs in high school might achieve junior status prior to the second semester or fourth quarter. Further complicating the implementation of effective living-learning programs are the developmental needs of nontraditional students, which differ from those of traditionally aged college students (Macari, Maples, & D'Andrea, 2006), as do needs related to gender and ethnic identity.

The 2008 National Resource Center for The First-Year Experience and Students in Transition's Survey of Sophomore Initiatives received 315 responses, and 41.6 percent of those included second-to-third-year retention rates. Two-thirds of the institutions with sophomore programs had second-to-third-year retention rates that ranged from 75 percent to 100 percent, compared to only 38 percent for those without programs. And while cautioning that correlation does not necessarily prove causation, it appeared that "institutions that develop and deliver sophomore-year success initiatives generally yield higher third-year return rates from their students, suggesting that such second-year programming is a worthy investment" (Keup, Gahagan, & Goodwin, 2010, p. 26). The survey also found little active engagement by academic affairs, even though contemporary literature on second-year programs emphasizes the importance of broad campus collaborations that build on existing programs as a key to successful implementation (Hunter et al., 2010).

Although student affairs and student support offices have established a variety of collaborative sophomore initiatives, the partners are either largely or solely with other student affairs professionals. However, programs that actively engage faculty and students and include opportunities for formal and informal student-faculty interactions promote a sense of community and contribute to student and academic development goals (Schreiner, 2010; Kuh, Kinzie, Schuh, Whitt, & Associates, 2005; Lundberg & Schreiner, 2004; Kuh & Hu, 2000; Anaya & Cole, 2001; Alderman, 2008; Astin, 1993b), which suggests that this is an area that merits attention in planning, implementing, and revising second-year programs (Fischer, 2007; Graunke & Woosley, 2005).

Retention concerns have prompted institutions to engage with this initiative. National data indicate that other than the first year, the second year has the highest number of dropouts (Lipka,

2006), confirming long-standing references to the "sophomore slump" (Freedman, 1956; Feldman & Newcomb, 1994; Lemons & Richmond, 1987; Gump, 2007). Tobolowsky (2008) observed that "when Freedman coined the phrase 'sophomore slump' he characterized the second year as one of student inertia and confusion," and referring to the work of Gansemer-Topf, Stern, and Benjamin (2007) she pointed out that "contemporary educators note similar behaviors among today's sophomores" (p. 60). Tobolowsky and Serven (2007) observed that both Evenbeck et al. (2000) and Gardner (2000) had remarked on the divergence between expectations and reality as being prevalent among second year students, and Schaller (2007) discussed various developmental needs of sophomores.

The belated identification of sophomores as a group meriting additional attention and support reflects the fact that achieving sophomore status seemed to suggest they had succeeded and therefore, as Schreiner and Pattengale (2000) suggested, they became "invisible." Pointing to the relative absence of national research instruments and data focused on both sophomores and juniors, Tobolowsky (2008) referred to sophomore transitions as "the forgotten year." Gahagan and Hunter (2008) suggested the importance of identifying needs that are specific to second-year students and addressing those through an integrated program. Multiple dimensions of the sophomore year that affect students' level of engagement and academic success have been identified, including academic, financial, emotional, and inspirational (Gohn, Swartz, & Donnelly, 2001). Chickering and Reisser (1993) included establishing a sense of identity and purpose as important developmental needs for second-year students, and Chemers, Hu, and Garcia (2001) noted that academic self-efficacy, a goal for many first-year programs, contributes to student success and suggested that as an ongoing focus for second-year students.

Pattengale and Schreiner (2000) identified three major categories of challenges for second-year students: academic, developmental, and institutional. Schaller (2005) posited three critical dimensions of student experience—friendships, self, and academics—and discussed how they changed during the four stages of sophomore transition: random exploration, focused exploration, tentative choices, and commitment. Random exploration is characteristic of first-year students and is marked by "exuberance" accompanied by nonreflective decisions, but some second-year students have not yet moved beyond that. During focused exploration, "students began to express a level of frustration with their current relationships, with themselves, or with their academic experience [and] began to question the choices they had made during random exploration and wondered out loud about the mistakes they had made" (Schaller, 2005, p. 18). Students who complete that sequence are prepared to make choices about their future, including their major course of study and career goals. Most students in Schaller's study did not reach the final stage, but those who did expressed confidence in their choices and were ready to move ahead. Supporting and facilitating students' journeys to that final stage should be a guiding aspirational goal for all sophomore-year experience (SYE) programs, and those should be informed by assessment of students' "needs and experiences," including "academic, career development, and personal development" (Schaller, 2006, p. 18). Schreiner (2010) highlighted the importance of investigating the relationship between institutional structure and the student experience by focusing on "issues of persistence, engagement, satisfaction, and major choice, including academic self-efficacy and motivation" (p. 13).

Focus groups conducted with first- and second-year high-risk students in community colleges, technical colleges, and four-year institutions identified critical concerns related to finances and debt levels, time management (particularly balancing work, family, and academic demands), and the need to develop their nontechnical or soft skills, such as leadership and working collaboratively in groups (Lake Research Partners, 2011; Johnston & McGregor, 2005).

Schaller (2010) described the second year as a "journey into self"—a time when "students become more critical of self and of the information they have taken as 'truth', [and] begin a search for directions and ... the process of becoming open to multiple perspectives about the world" (pp. 66, 70). Schreiner (2010) concluded that nonpersisting second-year students "were significantly less satisfied with the campus climate, intellectual growth, and spiritual fit" (p. 44). Evidence also indicates that the drop in supportive services in the second year contributes to sophomore dissatisfaction (Graunke & Woosley, 2005). In sum, perceived as less at risk and on the path to academic success, sophomores became "the academy's middle children" (Gahagan & Hunter, 2006).

While the terms *second-year experience* and *sophomore-year experience* are used in many institutions, those programs vary widely in terms of organizational models, percentage of students served, their mix of activities, and the breadth and intensity of collaborations, especially in terms of the active role of faculty and other academic affairs administrators and staff.

As noted, the development of SYE (sophomore-year experience) programs has largely been a student affairs initiative, and those have tended to focus mostly or exclusively on student development goals. According to the 2008 National Resource Center survey, the most common second-year initiatives were career planning (76.7 percent) and leadership development (58.8 percent). Vladosta State University's Academic Quality Improvement Plan, which focused on the second year, asked juniors for their reflections on information and experiences they would have liked more of during their sophomore year. They identified "Service Learning, Global Perspectives, and Interpersonal Connection created by an SYE program or research with faculty" (Peguesse, 2008, p. 2). In terms of academics, the National Resource Center survey results placed advising first (57.4 percent), followed by peer mentoring by sophomores (38.6 percent). Sanchez-Legulinel (2008) highlights the positive impact of peer mentoring on student success and retention. Columbia City College in Chicago has a peer support program whose mission is "to increase the success and retention rates of first-year minority and underrepresented students" and provides "personal, academic, social and cultural experiences" (Columbia City College, 2013). Only 27 percent of institutions included undergraduate research, and 16.1 percent had curricular learning communities. However, some institutions do focus on academic outcomes. Institutions that require second-year students to live on campus often have SYE living-learning programs. Seattle University's Sophomore Step-Up provides a residential program that has strong connections to its Center for Service and Community Engagement and several other campus areas, and fosters links with faculty.

Institution-specific data should be interpreted within a broader context of scholarly literature that identifies risk factors for second-year students and suggests ways to address them. For example, Schreiner (2010) provides five specific recommendations to increase sophomore satisfaction and success:

- Promoting connections with faculty
- An advising approach that connects students' present with their aspirational futures
- Promoting positive relationships with their peers
- Access to student-friendly services
- Programs that assist them in identifying their academic strengths

In addition, second-year students often need academic support, since they find their classes more challenging in terms of concepts and workload than those they took the previous year. That underscores the importance of providing programs directed to strengthening students' academic skills. These might include workshops on individual and group study strategies, preparing for essay exams, and writing research papers. Time management is another critical skill area.

Approaching the Work/Critical Partners

Since SYE programs are concerned with student development and retention, guidelines from the Council for the Advancement of Standards in Higher Education (CAS) are an important reference and guide in that they "integrate student learning and development outcomes into six broad categories (called domains): knowledge acquisition, construction, integration and application; cognitive complexity; intrapersonal development; interpersonal competence; humanitarianism and civic engagement; and practical competence." Compliance requires that "institutional programs and services ... identify relevant and desirable learning from these domains, assess relevant and desirable learning, and articulate how their programs and services contribute to domains not specifically assessed" (CAS, 2009). More recent CAS guidelines indicate that both curricular and cocurricular activities "must promote student learning and development outcomes that are purposeful, contribute to students' realization of their potential, and prepare students for satisfying and productive lives" (CAS, 2012, p. 4), and they also emphasize collaborations as critical to promoting student success. Programs that begin with respectful partnerships between student and academic affairs are likely to design programs that address these standards by focusing on both student and academic development needs.

Identifying appropriate outcomes and the program activities that promote them is critical to the success of SYE programs, and a rich and growing scholarly literature exists to guide program design and development. Schaller (2006) affirms that all SYE programs should include "academic, career development and personal development components" (p. 9). Schreiner (2010) notes the scholarly literature's emphasis on three basic themes:

- Positive connection between campus climate and student success, which suggests that by focusing on the sophomore year, institutions will communicate both a sense of concern and supportive programs to help students achieve their goals.
- "The importance of instructor effectiveness, intellectual growth, faculty interaction, and advising as sophomores engage in focused exploration of their career and life goals" (p. 44).
- A focus on high levels of student dissatisfaction among second-year students, which exceed those of any other class. In fact, Schreiner (2009) suggests that "increasing student satisfaction—particularly with the campus climate—can increase their odds of persisting, as well as significantly influence students' opinion that if they had the chance to do it all again, they would choose their present institution" (p. 8).

Program Design and Development

Gardner, Tobolowsky, and Hunter (2010) recommended establishing an inclusive second-year task force to lead the development of an SYE program. This provides opportunities to engage a larger number of administrators, staff, faculty, and students in productive discussions and promotes a broader sense of ownership for the initiative. South Dakota State University took that approach, which was led by the vice president for student affairs and the vice president for academic affairs, both of whom were concerned about retention of second-year students. Implementation began in the 2012–2013 academic year, and plans include residential learning programs, international engagement, service-learning, and the development of "semester by semester academic plans for all majors" and will emphasize civic engagement, service-learning, and leadership development (South Dakota State University, 2012).

Institutional data on second-year student success should help determine the scope, scale, and staging of the proposed program, and targeted surveys of second-year students, perhaps supplemented by focus groups, can identify critical issues and challenges that students perceive. For example, in planning its SYE program, the University of Massachusetts, Amherst, analyzed student success data, reviewed scholarly literature, and examined best practices at peer institutions. It also conducted a campus climate study.

Focusing on developmental tasks for second-year students, for example, developing a greater sense of identify and autonomy, clarifying values, and identifying a major and career goals, should help identify offices and, perhaps, individuals who need to be engaged. The importance of a sense of community and positive relations with faculty members suggests that developmental goals for students cannot be fully realized in the absence of a respectful working partnership between student and academic affairs. Those in turn should inform the development of a mission for the SYE program. For instance, the mission of the College of New Jersey's SYE program, which serves twelve hundred residential students, is to "create an environment that fosters self-exploration, ethical and value development and goal setting to help our sophomores refine their identity, explore their purpose and understand their roles within the community at large" (Perkowsky & Williams, 2011, p. 13). Butler University's Year 2 at BU, organized by student affairs, developed a mission statement that stressed its support for students to make use of the university's resources to help them identify and fulfill their academic goals. New Jersey's Caldwell College focused on three goals: clarifying and selecting majors, identifying potential occupations, and fostering more student engagement with campus life.

Campus Partners

Gardner et al. (2010) suggested that "students will be more successful in the second year transition if they are recipients of thoughtful and intentional curricular and co-curricular initiatives that are delivered through a partnership among faculty, academic and student affairs administrators, institutional researchers, and students" (p. 252). The identification of critical campus partners should be informed by scholarly literature and a campus scan that includes an analysis of student success data, the program mission, and a set of potential goals and outcomes. For example, the importance of identifying career goals and selecting majors suggests roles for advising, career services, and academic departments. Fostering a sense of community among students and with the institution, including positive relations with faculty members, suggests that developmental goals for students cannot be fully realized in the absence of a respectful working partnership between student and academic affairs. The classroom provides an important setting for promoting community and a commitment to learning, which underscores the importance of faculty partners. Similarly, given the powerful learning experiences provided by study abroad, service-learning, and community-based learning, professionals from those areas are also critical partners.

Students should be recognized as critical partners in the identification, planning, and implementation of programs. A sense of ownership promotes both efficacy and responsibility for productive outcomes. Tobolowsky and Cox (2007) emphasized the importance of student voices in terms of grounding the program in the realities of the student experience and designing and implementing programs to address student needs; one of their key recommendations is to recognize and be guided by student wisdom.

Organization/Implementation Process

With regard to process, Tetley, Tobolowsky, and Chan (2010) point to the importance of institutional commitment and of identifying and gaining the support of critical stakeholders, building assessment into the program, and carrying out a campus audit. They also stress that programs should link academic and student affairs. This advice in part reflects suggestions from Tobolowsky and Cox (2007) for developing an effective SYE program: "Learn from the students themselves" and "don't work alone" (pp. 95–96). The specific mix of offices and individuals will reflect differences in institutional history, culture, size, and complexity. For example, the 2008 National Resource Center survey indicated second-year programs administered through residence life, student life, career services, advising, retention, and transitions, with the most common position titles including "dean, associate/assistant dean, director, coordinator, or manager" (Keup et al., 2010, p. 15). Programs should begin with a collaborative approach that brings together student and academic affairs and, at least initially, includes active participation from their chief administrators.

Institutions whose second-year populations include a substantial number of students in academic difficulty, whether in terms of grade point average or credit completion, might target most of its programming to support that group. Those with large second-year residential student populations could develop living-learning communities for second-year students, while programming for a largely commuter student population might focus on learning communities that include both advising and career exploration. Transition issues suggest the importance of strengthening students' sense of connection to the campus. Operationally, that includes connections with other students, as well as with faculty and staff, and participation in campus-based social and cultural opportunities. Both commuter and residential campuses should think strategically about programs and activities to address those issues.

As with first-year programs, within a general framework of supporting student success, second-year initiatives can take many forms. A program might focus on one or several student cohorts—for example, returning full-time students who earned fewer than thirty credits in their first year, students who have work or family responsibilities (or both), or high-achieving students who have indicated an interest in occupations that require graduate or professional school degrees. The broader institutional mission should inform the development of a mission statement for the second year (Koring, 2005), and that focus facilitates the identification of core SYE activities, teaching-learning strategies, and potential links between social and academic activities. Drury

University crafted a comprehensive SYE mission statement that identified several student cohorts and stressed the need to "educate students, parents, faculty and staff on the unique needs of sophomore students; assist sophomores in making a successful transition from first year to second year and help sophomores to make more informed and thoughtful decisions about their academic and professional future." These would contribute to "the quality of life and academic satisfaction for all Drury sophomore students" (Farnum & Associates, 2010, p. 24).

Determining a home and an organizational structure for the SYE program, including its leadership, are initial critical decisions. The broader integration of SYE programs with university mission and educational goals and with student experiences in an FYE program is more likely to occur at institutions where both programs share an administrative home. Beloit College initially established an independent sophomore-year program but then merged it with the first-year program. Now called the Initiatives Program, its overall goal is to enable students to "design their own educational trajectory" and understand why it makes sense for them. Students retain the same academic advisor during those four semesters, which fosters an ongoing advising relationship for students that builds on and extends the first-year experience (FYE) and the synergies that might result from identifying initiatives and collaborations that would benefit both first- and second-year students. Institutions that have not yet established any first-year initiatives might consider the example of CSU-Channel Islands, which established a task force to develop programs for the first two college years.

A sense of community can be fostered across multiple dimensions of the student experience. Tobolowsky and Cox (2007) identified many such possibilities, including second-year seminars, living-learning communities, themed learning communities, sophomore-specific student governance officers or councils, and sophomore retreats. They also centered the importance of engaging students in "educationally purposeful activities," for example, leadership development, study abroad, and mentoring (p. 97). The 2008 National Resource Center Survey of Sophomore Year Initiatives found that the most common second-year

programs are career planning (76.7 percent), leadership development (58.8 percent), and academic advising (57.4 percent). Other
common initiatives were sophomores as peer mentors, residence
life, study abroad, community service and service-learning, and
faculty and staff mentors. Some campuses have created "sophomore summits" as a kick-off event for the second year. Emory
University uses a convention-style approach, with multiple booths
that focus on programs and resources for second-year students.

Since commuter and nontraditional second-year students generally spend less time on campus, fostering a sense of community
among them requires a different approach. Cocurricular activities
that are connected to classroom learning and provide opportunities for collaborations between professionals in student affairs
and academic affairs have a positive impact on student learning
and overall success (Chickering & Reisser, 1993; Lundberg &
Schreiner, 2004). Through the use of a cocurricular transcript
program that specifies specific leaning outcomes, all students,
including nontraditional and commuter students, can be encouraged to engage in positive learning experiences that can take
place both on and off campus (Gutkowski, 2006). These might
emphasize collaborative projects that include several students,
which will help build a sense of community and strengthen a
sense of belonging to the institution.

Developing and sponsoring activities that promote interactions among students, faculty, and staff could be a major focus
for creating an SYE seminar and could foster the personal relationships that contribute to student identity development (Boivin,
Fountain, & Bayless, 2000). Advising provides another collaborative opportunity. For example, in 2010, San José State University's
Advising Liaisons and Student Academic Success Services sponsored the campus's first annual sophomore advising exposition,
which included booths set up by student services and academic
departments. Advising offices could build on that type of program
by hosting group discussions of the challenges and issues of the
second year, followed by one-on-one advising sessions. Career
services offices could employ that same approach by developing
workshops focused on general career areas and specific occupations. Faculty participants would have an opportunity to provide
information about their major field and its appropriateness for

various occupations, and community members could discuss their education and careers. Academic departments could explain their various majors, and promote community by hosting open houses for sophomores (Koring, 2005).

Everything does not need to, nor should be, developed and implemented at the same time. Informed by specific critical student needs, the program's mission, goals, and objectives should help identify target populations. For example, a retention focus might identify specific student cohorts identified as at risk and provide academic support linked to specific student needs. A goal to engage all second-year students could be implemented in phases over several years using a triage approach that focuses on students most at risk or on providing one or two new services seen as most critical to second-year success. Strengthening the capacity of advising and career services also might be essential to developing and implementing a comprehensive program.

Institutional strategic plans often include ongoing reviews of existing campus programs, services, and human and fiscal resources. As has been noted, the critical nature of student transitions suggests that institutions with a well-developed FYE program could merge the two into an office of first- and second-year programs, thereby creating a seamless student experience focused on developmental tasks for each of those years. The centrality of decisions regarding majors and careers during the sophomore year underscores the importance of both advising and career services, and those offices could function as the program's organizational core.

Leadership Roles/Communication

Support from the campus's senior leadership could begin with identifying the development of a second-year program as a campus priority. Although most of these programs originate in student affairs, the critical role of faculty as well as the gains from more broadly collaborative programs suggests that the chief officers in both areas should endorse and support planning for the second-year program. A united front at the highest levels affirming the need to plan, develop, and implement the program will boost its possibilities for success.

Leadership from the heads of offices with special importance to second-year students' concerns, such as advising, career centers, and study abroad, should be complemented by faculty members with interests and experience in community-based learning and service-learning. Involving student leaders is especially important given the focus on student success. Meetings with committees and offices whose purview includes the types of activities likely to form part of the program will facilitate a broader sense of ownership and minimize concerns regarding issues of ownership. This initiative is unlikely to thrive without support from students, so representatives from student government and other relevant student organizations must be included. While this preparatory work takes time, it should create broader support throughout the campus.

The next stage, transforming those general conversations into a set of specific initiatives, is unlikely to occur without broader campus conversations to modify and flesh out program details, develop a plan with target dates, and set the parameters for a budget. The vehicle for those conversations could be a second-year steering committee or task force. Alternatively, depending on campus culture, the next step might take the form of a set of conversations within the areas most likely to play significant roles in a second-year program. That additional process step can create broader support. The campus chief executive officer or the heads of academic affairs and student affairs then could call a general campus meeting, focusing on the challenges and opportunities surrounding the development and implementation of the new program, while also highlighting its potential benefits to students, staff, and faculty and the institution itself.

As with any other important initiative, transparency should characterize the task force's work. Posting meetings and minutes on a dedicated SYE website and presenting updates at faculty and staff meetings and those of relevant campus committees creates awareness throughout the campus community. At appropriate points in the process, the task force might host a series of campus forums to provide updates and respond to questions and concerns. Members of the task force can also report on the initiative at their own staff or committee meetings. Similarly, the task force's final report and recommendations could be presented in various venues, prior to formal approval of the new second-year program.

Resource Needs/Personnel

Costs will vary depending on program design, including, for example, the size of the target population, the mix of curricular and cocurricular activities, enrollment limits for specific classes, and the need for additional personnel. A new campuswide program should not diminish the effectiveness of other important services, so it is important to develop a realistic initial budget. Overseeing the ongoing development and implementation of a comprehensive second-year program requires a full-time administrator at a level consonant with the importance of the task. To ensure ongoing collaboration between student affairs and academic affairs, the program is likely to need a steering or executive committee that reflects that partnership, and, depending on the nature and range of its responsibilities, the director or perhaps codirectors of that committee may need to be released from some of their existing responsibilities. Increased student use of campus resources may create capacity challenges for advising, career services, study-abroad offices, and other academic and student affairs offices. If the initiative is conjoined with an existing first-year program, the administrative capacity of that office would need to be upgraded. Organizing and staffing events on campus and in the community also may require additional personnel and funding.

Teaching and learning strategies that include small group discussions with reports back to the entire class provide opportunities for students to connect with their peers, and collaborative projects can help build community within the classroom (Davis, 1993; Howe & Strauss, 2003; Pascarella, & Terenzini, 2005). These pedagogical approaches, which provide benefits to students at any point in their college experience, can be especially effective for second-year students in terms of raising their satisfaction, which is perhaps the most critical variable in student retention (Schreiner, 2009). This underscores the importance of providing professional development both on and off campus for personnel who teach in the second-year program. Smaller class size facilitates interactions among students and between students and instructors and provides more opportunities for whole-class discussion (Knott, 2009; Arias & Walker, 2004).

The number and enrollment limits of sections for the targeted populations will have fiscal and personnel implications. A program approach that incorporates activities both on campus and in the community also requires additional resources. To sustain an SYE program, participants need ongoing professional development, and that might include travel to national meetings and bringing speakers and consultants to campus. Social programming that involves students, staff, and faculty is likely to increase, and off-campus activities for students may involve expenses for travel and food. Funding for a robust program of formative and summative assessment, which might include the services of an outside evaluator, is another expense category. A successful program is likely to increase student use of such campus services as advising, career services, peer mentoring, and study-abroad offices, which could create capacity issues. Providing ongoing professional development for those engaged directly in the initiative might involve sending teams to relevant national and regional conferences and perhaps bringing consultants to campus. These should also be budgeted.

Assessment

Evaluating responses to the 2008 survey by the National Resource Center for The First-Year Experience and Students in Transition, Keup et al. (2010) noted that "more than 40% of respondents indicated that they did not assess long-standing sophomore success initiatives, illustrating a significant area of vulnerability for the sustainability of these programs" (p. 10). The survey also indicated that the majority of institutions did not provide robust, comprehensive data and that they mainly relied on surveys (Keup, Gahagan, & Goodwin, 2010).

The term *institutional effectiveness* implies progress toward achieving a set of anticipated outcomes that impelled the development of an initiative, and this became a common element in accreditation. For example, in 2005, the Middle States Commission on Higher Education noted important changes in two standards—institutional effectiveness and student learning. It described institutional effectiveness as a process characterized by "defining clearly articulated institutional and unit-level goals; Implementing strategies to achieve those goals; Assessing achievement of those goals; and Using the results of those assessments to improve programs and services and inform planning and resource allocation decisions" (p. 3). At one level, the goals and objectives of all second-year programs are similar in that they seek to enhance the student experience and create higher levels of student academic success and student development, thereby increasing rates of student satisfaction, persistence, and graduation. At other levels, programs may vary significantly because of differing institutional missions and priorities and differences in the size, preparedness, and characteristics of their student populations. However, they all should be informed by Schreiner's (2010) discussion of factors that promote the success and satisfaction of second-year students.

Activities defined in terms of anticipated outcomes and their relationship to overall mission, goals, and objectives provide a focus for ongoing program development and assessment. This degree of specificity also enables discussion about meanings and outcomes with regard to each of the program areas, which informs the development of programs designed to achieve those ends. Incorporating an assessment strategy and a time line into the overall program design provides multiple benefits, not the least of which is that ongoing collection and analysis of data establishes a culture of evidence (Dwyer, Millett, & Payne, 2006).

In addition to tracking grade point average, course completion rates, and retention, qualitative aspects of the student experience merit attention. Social media can provide a platform for student perspectives and suggestions. Focus groups and interviews also can yield valuable insights and may identify unanticipated positive and negative outcomes. Linking qualitative and quantitative data should contribute to a holistic assessment of the student experience. Engaging student affairs in the assessment approach would strengthen the process because of their concerns with and perspectives on student learning and development (Schuh & Gansemer-Topf, 2010).

A comprehensive overview and analysis also should include the perspectives of students, staff, and faculty. With regard to students, Schreiner (2009) suggests "we can better understand the challenges of sophomore retention by using student satisfaction indicators—and the more specific those indicators are, the better. And . . . we learned that satisfaction levels not only differ across class level, but contribute differently to student persistence at each level. As a result . . . disaggregating SSI (Student Satisfaction Inventory, Noel-Levitz) data by class level provides your most detailed road map of how to strategically address the retention challenges your institution faces'' (p. 9). In addition to posting data on a dedicated program website, program updates can be shared at relevant faculty, staff, and student meetings.

Benefit Analysis

While specific program goals and activities vary, an effective second-year program promotes student development and academic success. SYE programs foster commitment to the institution and to an academic program (Graunke & Woosley, 2005). Students who clarify their career objectives, select appropriate majors, and are engaged with their peers and the institution are more likely to persist and have higher levels of academic performance (Gardner, 2000; Dixon & Chung, 2008). Engagement with the institution, fellow students, and academics results in fewer repeated courses, dropouts, and probationary students as well as significant efficiency gains for both students and the institution. Students who experience success are likely to remain engaged with campus activities, and many will likely want to volunteer to work on individual programs or serve as peer mentors for participating students. They also may help develop and support new SYE programs. Successful students are good ambassadors for the institution, which can lead to enrollment gains, increased external support, and a larger and more engaged alumni association. Campus morale also should rise. These benefits, which can be quantified, should factor into decisions regarding the breadth and reach of the program. In general, a smaller program done well will yield greater benefits than a larger program done poorly. The collaborative nature of the program is likely to benefit campus climate and overall morale. Greater workplace satisfaction can bring numerous benefits on campus and in the community.

Institutional Practices

Miami University (Ohio)

Founded in 1809, Miami University is a public residential university, with its main campus in Oxford, Ohio, and branch campuses in Hamilton and Middleton. The main campus enrolls approximately fifteen thousand students, which includes about twenty-three hundred graduate students. In 2009, concerns about second-year retention, which at that point was two percentage points below the first-year rate, led Miami to launch a sophomore initiative. A 2008 decision that required all second-year students to live on campus facilitated programming with residence life and fraternities and sororities. It also sparked the development of a residential curriculum that spans the full undergraduate experience. This curriculum is a student development model that reflects the learning partnership approach, which stresses the social construction of knowledge and its relationship to the self. In this formulation, peers share authority and collaboratively create knowledge (Baxter Magolda & King, 2004). The residential curriculum established four outcomes: "academic success, effective community engagement, intrapersonal development, and cultural proficiency" (Miami University, 2012). These are approached through three stages: "Moving In, Moving On, and Moving Through"; the second of these applies to sophomores. Residence life staff collaborate with their supervisors to develop a set of appropriate activities to address those needs. The program's guiding themes are local and global citizenship, career exploration and commitment to majors, connected academic experiences, and health and wellness.

The Office of Second Year Programs supports sophomores in terms of both academic and personal success. It also coordinates university resources to strengthen connections between second-year students and the university. Launched in 2009, the second-year program website is a primary tool for providing information to students, and it has an active Facebook presence. A second-year student advisory council provides leadership opportunities and a strong student voice with regard to programming. Modeling the partnership approach, it participates in and publicizes a broad array of initiatives. For example, it provides support for the campus housing fair, an event primarily organized by student government, which offers an opportunity for sophomores to become familiar with available community rental properties to inform their choice off of-campus housing prior to junior year. Other activities include a recognition event for student leaders, a coffee club to promote interactions between students and faculty, career chats with recruiters, a set of video interviews with seniors that includes reflections and advice about student success, and a recognition event for sophomore leaders.

A data-rich environment includes information on classes with high sophomore enrollment, major declarations, and second-to-third-year retention statistics that is used to inform programming. Studies conducted by leading theorists and practitioners in the field of student development and student success guided the work of a faculty group, led by the associate provost for academic affairs. Its overarching goal was to make the second-year experience part of the university's academic mission. In addition, a faculty committee developed a sweeping set of second-year curriculum suggestions to support, complement, and extend the existing sophomore programs. Miami has participated in national surveys of second-year programs and a survey that is being distributed to second-year students.

University of West Georgia

Founded in 1906, and located in Carrollton, the University of West Georgia's student population numbers about eleven thousand. It houses its sophomore program in EXCEL—the Center for Academic Success, whose motto is "Explore, Expand, Engage." In addition to organizing the second-year program, it includes a broader array of student support and development services, including Supplemental Instruction, advising, tutoring, and mentoring. The program seeks to strengthen students' engagement with the campus and develop an understanding of how their individual lives are connected to local, national, and international communities. Organized into five networks, program components focus on specific issues of importance to sophomores, including academic success and choosing a major and career. Second Year Networks provide opportunities for students to identify and interact with other sophomores who share interests. Second Year Challenge uses an online form that lists areas of concern, such as selecting a major, time management, and community service. Students can select any three of the listed concerns, set a specific date for accomplishing their goal, and choose up to six departments (units) whose assistance would enable them to meet the challenge; in addition to EXCEL, these are Career Services, the Center for Student Involvement, Department of Foreign Languages and Literature, International Services and Programs, and the Student Development Center. They also have the option to create a personal challenge. A locally developed online survey tool, created in Survey Monkey, provides a platform for student feedback.

Students also can choose to participate in several campus events, which strengthen their connection to the university and provide opportunities to interact with other second-year students. Fall semester events include a homecoming tailgate, a second-year outdoor adventure series (this occurs in the spring too), a canned food drive for the homeless, and a sculpture competition. The Second Year Finals Breakfast takes place on two mornings and offers a free breakfast and door prizes, and tutors are available at the event. EXCEL Center data for 2011 indicated that participants in the second-year program achieved higher grade point averages (2.77 versus 2.66) and rates of retention (95 percent versus 83.5 percent) than those who did not participate.

Loyola University, Maryland

Founded in 1852 and located in Baltimore, Loyola University, Maryland, is the oldest Catholic-Jesuit educational institution in the United States. The Carnegie Foundation for the Advancement of Teaching classifies it as "highly residential" and as "balanced arts and sciences/professions." Its College of Arts and Sciences, School of Education, and Sellinger School of Business and Management offer both undergraduate and graduate programs. It serves some thirty-eight hundred undergraduates, and total enrollment exceeds six thousand.

Institutional concerns regarding first-to-third-year retention prompted the inclusion of programming for sophomores in the university's 2002–2007 strategic plan. Student development took the lead in planning second-year programs, but some initiatives originated in academic affairs. The initial set of programs, known as the Crossroads Sophomore Initiative, began in 2003 and included a three-day retreat known as "Road-Trip" that focused on "vocational discernment," the identification of a specific personal calling. Crossroads also established a residential learning community. Now known as the "Ad Infinitum Living Learning Community," it includes "studying abroad, career and internship exploration, strengthening friendships, personal reflection, spiritual guidance and vocational discernment" (Loyola University, 2013).

Loyola also created a student development position, director of sophomore initiatives, and an academic affairs position, associate dean for second-year students, with the understanding that they would collaborate in developing program activities. This resulted in a number of collaboratively developed and spoonsored programs, including Discovery, Discover Your P.A.T.H, Dessert and Discernment, and SophoMORE Week (Loyola University, 2013). Dessert and Discernment, a monthly discussion series, has focused on such topics as selecting majors, study abroad, and issues related to spirituality. SophoMORE Week includes both academic and social events and concludes with "Navigating Your Sophomore Year," a conference that addresses selecting a major and provides information about internships and experiential learning.

Several programs focused on building community among students, including a program common to many second-year programs, "mystery bus," where students sign up for a bus trip without knowing its destination or the others who will be participating. The Sophomores Initiative program includes *Sophomore Spotlight*, a newsletter published monthly during the academic year that lists upcoming events. For example, the October 2012 edition listed sophomore workshops on selecting majors, service and involvement, and internships, all of which are free and are led by upper-class students, staff, faculty, and administrators. Assessment of the program includes sophomore focus groups, student surveys, tracking participation in SYE programs, and focus groups with juniors and seniors who participated in the program. Evaluation processes "are still relatively new, but data support that learning outcomes for each program are being met" (Farnum & Associates, 2010, p. 41).

Conclusion: Lessons Learned

In writing this book, we were mindful that its readers would be diverse in terms of their professional positions, the nature of their institutions, student mix, fiscal and human resources, and existing array of student success programs. Therefore, we did not present a one-size-fits-all formula but instead sought to present a way to conceptualize, organize, and operationalize a process to develop and implement sustainable, successful programs. Our inclusion of a range of institutional references and examples of institutional practices also reflects that approach, because we know that good ideas and effective practices exist throughout higher education. In keeping with its practitioner approach, we conclude with lessons learned, suggesting that program development, implementation, and sustainability will be strengthened by an approach that incorporates the following principles and practices:

- *Align program goals with institutional mission, goals, and strategic priorities.* Think about and be able to articulate how the program supports the general mission of the college or university and the select missions of one or more of its functional areas. The perception and reality of that alignment transform the proposed program from being something "extra" to being something integral to the institution.
- *Identify specific outcomes for programs* in terms of their positive impact on shared institutional goals for students and use these to inform program development and assessment activities. Outcomes should address both academic and student development goals, while recognizing that academic success remains central to retention and graduation. It is also important to share drafts of these outcomes with relevant

campus offices and committees, encourage them to provide feedback, and use that feedback to review and perhaps revise program outcomes.

- *Be mindful of campus culture,* which both implicitly and explicitly defines values, appropriate behaviors, and acceptable ways of doing things. Below that broad level, institutions of higher education include multiple subcultures both within and across functional areas. The presence and impact of these multiple cultures are often manifest in issues related to ownership and buy-in.
- *Gain support from relevant administrators.* When staff and faculty speak about senior administrative support, it often is transactional, such as released time or additional funding, in return for a program. Consider thinking in terms of administrative engagement, which suggests a more active role that can help facilitate the ongoing development of programs. Clearly defined mission-relevant outcomes increase the likelihood of administrative buy-in and support. Given variations in institutional complexity, culture, and the specific nature of the proposed program, the relevant administrators vary across campuses, but perceived fit of program outcomes with mission usually is a critical initial factor in decisions.
- *Effective, sustainable programs need an administrative home and dedicated leadership.* A focus on program outcomes and the range of offices and personnel that would need to participate can help identify the office best positioned to house the program. Our stress on leadership recognizes that one or two individuals ultimately need to assume responsibility for the program's success. In the case of coleaders, lines of responsibility and authority should be specified. At the same time, a team approach that encourages staff members to take ownership of key roles and responsibilities for specific program elements promotes their engagement with the program and facilitates its implementation.
- *Carry out an internal institutional campus scan or audit.* This can identify the campus offices and personnel who might

contribute to or be affected by a proposed program and suggest potential partners and areas where ownership issues need to be recognized and addressed. We also have emphasized the importance of an external scan to identify peer or aspirational institutions that have similar programs. That may minimize campus skepticism about its institutional fit and practicality.

- *Connect with the broader academic world,* including networks of peer practitioners who have experience with the programs you are interested in building at your campus. Think also of the regional, national, and international organizations and associations that might provide information and resources for planning and implementing program initiatives and for professional development, including consultants who have worked with such programs at institutions similar to yours. Most of these organizations sponsor conferences and workshops that promote professional development. An external scan should also include relevant scholarly literature, including assessment studies that attest to benefits likely to result for students and the institution.

- *An approach and rationale that speaks to multiple constituencies opens up the potential for collaborations, which can contribute resources and ideas to the program.* The student experience spills across the boundaries of campuses' official organizational structure, and a focus on that can help identify additional collaborations and partnerships. The participation of people from different areas in itself is a powerful statement about the program's importance, and their support should help with implementation and sustainability.

- *Explore ways to partner with students.* Students play important roles as peer leaders, mentors, tutors, and advisors. Students can enrich teaching and learning in other ways too. For example, members of discipline-based, ethnic, and gender-related clubs can provide presentations relevant to many classes, as could students who engaged in study-abroad and cocurricular activities. These students would be modeling many of the skills and dispositions that colleges seek to develop and also help to create community. Student government can be a powerful partner for student success programs. For example, it can serve as an advocate for the program to students, administrators, and alumni, and it also could contribute fiscal and human resources for specific events.

- *Pilot and assess programs by focusing on a specific student cohort or outcomes.* Confronted with limited resources and multiple commitments, institutions may be reluctant or unable to commit to a full program launch. A pilot provides an opportunity to begin the program and assess its impact. Positive results for students who participated in the pilot then provide a justification for continued or expanded funding.
- *Be mindful of the role and authority of standing committees, especially faculty committees.* All colleges and universities have committees whose purviews include specific areas, practices, and processes and focus on a wide array of campus concerns. Given the breadth of committees and their charges, almost any significant change is likely to involve the work of one or more committees, so failing to consult with colleagues early on can derail or impede the development of a proposal.
- *Think strategically about both fiscal and human assets.* Focus on ways that a portion of existing revenue streams in other areas could contribute funds and services to the new initiative that would advance shared goals. Ultimately, however, sustainable programs must have adequate personnel and consistent fiscal support. That support becomes counterproductive if it weakens other important services.
- *Develop a communication plan that speaks to critical partners and provides a road map for engaging them as the process develops.* Consider the forms of communication that would be most effective at different stages of planning and implementation. Transparency relies on a strategy that uses multiple approaches to keep people in the loop. That can include dedicated websites, social media,

and presentations to committees and at all-campus events. Ongoing communication helps sustain collaborations.

- *Engage in robust formative and summative assessment that provides data to help frame, develop, and modify the program.* As the program is implemented, formative assessment can identify problem areas and improve program development, while summative assessment provides evidence on program effectiveness. Positive assessment results provide evidence that the program is meeting its goals and is making a difference for students and the institution. Assessment also informs ongoing program development.

- *Planning and implementation is likely to be a lengthy process, so while remaining mindful of what needs to be accomplished, recognize and celebrate accomplishments as you move ahead.* Also anticipate that partners may change over time as the program develops. As that occurs, it is important to honor the contributions of departing partners, while warmly welcoming new colleagues as team members.

The leadership and vision of one individual is often responsible for the development of new programs. That person's passion and commitment includes a willingness to assume responsibility for program success, which helps bring other colleagues to the table. However, an important aspect of that leadership is to encourage new colleagues to assume responsibility for program success. Sustainable programs recognize the importance of multiple levels of leadership, and they encourage and celebrate the contributions of new and continuing partners. Long-term sustainability implies the need for ongoing change. Programs that fail to respond to new knowledge, changing student populations, or new accreditation requirements diminish their relevance to present needs and may lose funding and administrative support.

We know that practitioners are vital to institutional success and that their dedicated work with students often goes unrecognized. To some extent, that reflects the fact that administrators often focus on putting out fires and a quietly effective program falls off their screen. Programs contribute to this situation when their communication plan fails to include ongoing messages to the campus community to highlight program events and successes and, at times, because the program's leaders become less concerned with bringing in new people. Programs that remain identified with one or two people are unlikely to become institutionalized.

Practitioners are the face of the institution to its most important population, students, and its most important function, education. We hope you find ideas of value in this book and encourage you to share your thoughts with us.

References

Ackerman, S. P. (1991). The benefits of summer bridge programs for underrepresented and low-income students. *College and University, 66*(4), 201–208.

ACT. (2010a). *Trends and tracking charts: 1983–2010.* Retrieved from http://www.act.org/research/policymakers/reports/graduation.html

ACT. (2010b). *What works in student retention? Fourth national survey.* Iowa City, IA: Author.

ACT. (2011). *National collegiate retention and persistence to degree rates.* Retrieved from http://www.act.org/research/policymakers/reports/graduation.html

ACT. (2012). *National collegiate retention and persistence to degree rates.* Retrieved from www.act.org/research/policymakers/pdf/retain_2012.pdf

Adelman, C. (2006). *The tool box revisited: Paths to degree completion from high school through college.* Washington, DC: US Department of Education.

Aiken-Wisniewski, S. A., ed., with Campbell, S., Higa, L., Kirk-Kuwaye, M., Nutt, C., & Robbins, R. (2010). *Guide to Assessment in Academic Advising* (2nd. ed.) (CD). Manhattan, KS, National Academic Advising Association.

Aiken-Wisniewski, S. A., Smith, J. S., & Troxel, W. G. (2010). Expanding research in academic advising: Methodological strategies to engage advisers in research. *NACADA Journal, 30*(1), 4–11.

Alderman, R. V. (2008). *Faculty and student-out-of-classroom interaction: Student perceptions of quality of interaction* (Unpublished doctoral dissertation). Texas A&M University, College Station.

Allen, J. M., & Smith, C. L. (2008). Importance of, responsibility for, and satisfaction with academic advising: A faculty perspective. *Journal of College Student Development, 49*(5), 397–411.

Allens, J., Robbins, S. B., & Sawyer, R. (2009). Can measuring psychosocial factors promote college success? *Applied Measurement in Education, 23*, 1–22.

Anaya, G., & Cole, G. D. (2001). Latina/o student achievement: Exploring the influence of student-faculty interactions on student grades. *Journal of College Student Development, 42*(1), 3–14.

Appleby, D. C. (2008). Advising as Teaching and Learning. In V. N. Gordon, W. R. Habley, & T. J. Grites (Eds.), *Academic advising: A comprehensive handbook* (2nd ed.) (pp. 85–100). San Francisco: Jossey-Bass.

Appleton, J. J., Christenson, S. L., & Furlong, M. J. (2008). *Psychology in the Schools, 45*(5), 369–386.

Aragon, S. R. (2003). Creating social presence in on-line environments. *New Directions for Adult and Continuing Education, 100*, 57–68.

Arcand, I., & LeBlanc, R. (2011). Academic probation and companioning: Three perspectives on experience and support. *Mevlana International Journal of Education, 1*(2), 1–14.

Arcand, I., & LeBlanc, R. (2012). *L'expérience de la probation académique ou "C'tua juste e moi qui est pas capable au niveau universitaire? Une étude de cas."* Canadian Journal of Education/Revue Candiene de L'Education, *35*(4), 31–61.

Arendale, D. (2005). Terms of endearment: Words that define and guide developmental education. *Journal of College Reading and Learning, 35*(2), 67–82.

Ariand, I. (2012). "Creating a relationship": The characteristics of a companioning relationship in the context of academic probation. *International Journal of Humanities and Social Sciences, 2*(4), 28–49.

Arias, J. J., & Walker, D. M. (2004). Additional evidence on the relationship between class size and student performance. *Journal of Economic Education, 35*(4), 311–329.

Ashburn, E. (2012, January 9). Why do students drop out? Because they must work at jobs too. *Chronicle of Higher Education.* Retrieved from chronicle.com/article/Why-Do-Students-Drop-Out-/49417/

Association of American Colleges and Universities. (2007). *College learning for the new global century.* Washington, DC: Author.

Association of American Colleges and Universities. (2011). *The LEAP vision for learning: Outcomes, practices, impact, and employers' views.* Washington, DC: Author.

Astin, A. W. (1975). *Preventing students from dropping out.* San Francisco, CA: Jossey-Bass.

Astin, A. W. (1993a). *Assessment for excellence.* Phoenix, AZ: American Council on Education and Oryx Press.

Astin, A. W. (1993b). *What matters in college? Four critical years revisited.* San Francisco, CA: Jossey-Bass.

Austin, A. M., & Gustafson, L. (2006). Impact of course length on student learning. *Journal of Economics and Finance Education, 5*(1), 26–37.

Austin, M., Cherney, E., Crowner, J., & Hill, A. (1997). The forum: Intrusive group advising for the probationary student. *NACADA Journal, 17*(2), 45–47.

Bailey, T. R. (2009). Challenge and opportunity: Rethinking the role and function of developmental education in community college. *New Directions for Community Colleges, 29*(145), 11–30.

Bailey, T. R., & Alfonso, M. (2005). *Paths to persistence: An analysis of research on program effectiveness at community colleges* (New Agenda Series, Vol. 6, No. 1). Indianapolis, IN: Lumina Foundation for Education.

Bailey, T. R., Wook Jeong, D., & Cho, S.-W. (2009). Referral, enrollment, and completion in developmental education sequences in community colleges. Community College Research Center, Columbia University, Working Paper #15, pp. 1–32. acadcmiccommons.columbia .edu/download/fedora . . . /ac/ . . . /332_659.pdf

Bailey, T. R., Wook Jeong, D., & Cho, S.-W. (2010). Referral, enrollment, and completion in developmental education sequences in community colleges. *Economics of Education Review, 29*(2), 255–270.

Baker, V. L., & Griffin, K. A. (2010). Beyond mentoring and advising: Toward understanding the role of faculty "developers" in student success. *About Campus, 14*(6), 2–8.

Banta, T. W., & Kuh, G. D. (1998). A missing link in assessment: Collaboration between academic and student affairs professionals. *Change, 50*(2), 40–46.

Barefoot, B. O. (1992). *Helping first-year college students climb the academic ladder: Report of a national survey of freshman seminar programming in American higher education* (Unpublished doctoral dissertation). College of William and Mary, Williamsburg, VA.

Barefoot, B. O., Gardner, J. N., Cutright, M., Morris, L. V., Schroeder, C. C., Schwartz, S. W., Siegel, M. J., & Swing, R. L. (2005). *Achieving and sustaining institutional excellence for the first year of college.* San Francisco, CA: Jossey-Bass.

Barefoot, B. O., Griffin, B. Q., & Koch, A. K. (2012). *Enhancing student success and retention throughout undergraduate education: A national survey.* Brevard, NC: John N. Gardner Institute for Excellence in Undergraduate Education.

Barefoot, B. O., & Koch, A. K. (2011, February). *Preliminary findings from a national survey of efforts to improve undergraduate student success and retention.* Concurrent session presented at the 30th Annual Conference on the First-Year Experience, Atlanta, GA.

Barefoot, B. O., Warnock, C. L., Dickenson, M. P., Richardson, S. E., & Roberts, M. R. (1998). *Exploring the evidence: Reporting research on first-year seminars, Vol. 2* (Monograph No. 25). Columbia: University of South Carolina, National Resource Center for The First-Year Experience and Students in Transition.

Barr, R. B., & Tagg, J. (1995). From teaching to learning: A new paradigm for undergraduate education. *Change, 27*(6), 12–25.

Baxter Magolda, M. (2004). Self-authorship as the common goal of 21st century education. In M. Baxter Magolda & P. M. King (Eds.), *Learning partnerships: Theory and models of practice to educate for self-authorship* (pp. 1–35). Sterling, VA: Stylus.

Baxter Magolda, M. B., & King, P. M. (2004). *Learning partnerships: Theory and models of practice to educate for self-authorship*. Sterling, VA: Stylus.

Beck, H. P., & Davidson, W. D. (2001). Establishing an early warning system: Predicting low grades in college students from survey of academic orientations. *Research in Higher Education, 42*(6), 709–723.

Bedford, M. H., & Durkee, P. E. (1989). Retention: Some more ideas. *NASPA Journal, 27,* 168–171.

Bell, B. J. (2006a). Wilderness orientation: Exploring the relationship between college preorientation programs and social support. *Journal of Experiential Education, 29*(2), 145–167.

Bell, B. J. (2006b). Social support development and wilderness pre-orientation experiences. *Journal of Experiential Education, 28*(3), 248–249.

Bell, B. J., & Vaillancourt, C. (2011). When college outdoor orientation programs end: A grounded theory investigation of program discontinuation at four-year college in the United States. *Journal of The First-Year Experience & Students in Transition, 23*(1), 103–117.

Bettinger, E. P., & Long, B. P. (2005). *Addressing the needs of under-prepared students in higher education: Does college remediation work?* (Working Paper No. 11325). Cambridge, MA: National Bureau of Economic Research.

Bickford, D. J. (2002). Navigating the white waters of collaborative work. In N.V.M. Chism & D. J. Bickford (Eds.), *The importance of physical space in creating supportive learning environments. New Directions for Teaching and Learning*, 43–52.

Bickford, D. J., & Wright, J. D. (2006). Community: The hidden context for learning. In G. D. Oblinger (Ed.), *Learning spaces* (pp. 1–22). Boulder, CO: EDUCAUSE. Retrieved from http://net.educause.edu/ir/library/pdf/PUB7102d.pdf

Binder, C. (2005). Learning, teaching, and an evolutionary imperative. A summary of remarks made by Carl Binder upon receiving the Fred

S. Keller Award for Contributions to Behavioral Education. *The American Psychological Association Division 25 Recorder, 38*(1), 10–1.

Blackhurst, A. E., Akey, L. D., Bobilya, A. J. (2003). A qualitative investigation of student outcomes in a residential learning community. *Journal of The First-Year Experience & Students in Transition, 15*(2), 35–59.

Bloom, J. L., Hutson, B. L., & He, Y. (2008). *The appreciative advising revolution*. Champaign, IL: Stipes Publishing.

Bloom, J. L., & Martin, N. A. (2002). Incorporating appreciative advising into academic advising. *Mentor*. State College: Pennsylvania State University, Division of Undergraduate Studies.

Boise State University. (2012). *Living-learning communities*. Retrieved from http://housing.boisestate.edu/livinglearningcommunities/program-information

Boivin, M., Fountain, G. A., & Bayless, B. (2000). Meeting the challenges of the sophomore year. In L. Schreiner & J. Pattengale (Eds.), *Visible solutions for invisible students: Helping sophomores succeed*. Columbia: University of South Carolina, National Resource Center for The First-Year Experience and Students in Transition.

Booker, K. C. (2008). The role of instructors and peers in establishing classroom community. *Journal of Instructional Psychology, 35*(1), 12–16.

Bowles, P., Falk, D. R., & Strawn, D. L. (1994, December). *Collaboration pays off: An advance program for at-risk college freshmen teaches a few lessons to students, faculty, and the institution*. Paper presented at the Annual Meeting of the National Reading Conference, San Diego, CA.

Bowling Green State University. (2013). *The Residential Learning Communities International Clearing House*. Retrieved from http://pcc.bgsu.edu/ricch/

Boyer, E. L. (1990). *Scholarship reconsidered*. Princeton, NJ: Carnegie Foundation for the Advancement of Teaching.

Boylan, H. (2004). Accelerating developmental education: The case for collaboration. *Inquiry, 9*(1).

Boylan, H. (2007). Developments: American Council of Developmental Education Associations (ACDEA) changes its bylaws and name. *Journal of Developmental Education, 31*(2), 34.

Boylan, H. (2009). *Targeted Intervention for Developmental Education Students (T.I.D.E.S.)*. Boone, NC: National Center for Developmental Education.

Boylan, H., Bliss, L., & Bonham B. (1994). Characteristic components of developmental programs. *Research in Developmental Education, 11*(1), 1–4.

Boylan, H., Bliss, L., & Bonham, B. (1997). Program components and their relationship to student success. *Journal of Developmental Education, 20*(3), 2–9.

Boylan, H. R., & Saxon, D. P. (2009). *What works in remediation: Lessons from 30 years of research.* Prepared for the League for Innovation in the Community College. Retrieved from http://www.ced.appstate.edu/centers/ncde/reserve reading/what works.htm

Bradley, J.A.P., & Blanco, P. D. (2010). *Promoting a culture of student success. How colleges and universities are improving retention.* Southern Regional Education Board. Publications.sreb.org/2010/10EO2_Promoting_Culture.pdf

Brill, J. M., & Park, Y. (2008). Facilitating engaged learning in the interaction age: Taking a pedagogically-disciplined approach to innovation with emergent technologies. *International Journal of Teaching and Learning in Higher Education, 20*(1), 70–78.

Brower, A. M. (2008). More like a home than a hotel: The impact of living-learning programs on college high-risk drinking. *Journal of College and University Student Housing, 35*(1), 32–49.

Brower, A. M., & Dettinger, K. M. (1998). What is a learning community? Toward a comprehensive model. *About Campus, 3*(5), 15–21.

Brower, A. M., & Inkelas, K. (2010). Living-learning programs: One high-impact educational practice. *Liberal Education, 96*(2), 36–43.

Brown, J. L., & Hernandez, C. L. (2010). Technology in orientation. In J. A. Ward-Roof (Ed.), *Designing successful transitions: A guide for orienting students to college* (Monograph No. 13, 3rd ed., pp. 117–129). Columbia: University of South Carolina, National Resource Center for The First-Year Experience and Students in Transition.

Brown, T., & Rivas, M. (1994). The prescriptive relationship in academic advising as an appropriate developmental intervention with multicultural populations. *NACADA Journal, 14*(2), 108–111.

Brownell, J. E., & Swaner, L. E. (2010). *Five high-impact practices: Research on learning outcomes, completion, and quality.* Washington, DC: Association of American Colleges and Universities.

Buckingham, M., & Clifton, D. O. (2001). *Now, discover your strengths.* New York, NY: Free Press.

Burton, J., & Wellington, K. (1998). The O'Banion model of academic advising: An integrative approach. *NACADA Journal, 18*(2), 13–20.

Busby, R. R., Gammel, H. L., & Jeffcoat, N. K. (2002). Grades, graduation, and orientation: A longitudinal study of how new student programs relate to grade point average and graduation. *Journal of College Orientation and Transition, 10*(1), 45–57.

California Polytechnic State University. (2013). Residential Life and Education. Living Learning Program (LLP). Retrieved from www.residentiallife.calpoly.edu/rl_lco/living_learning.html

Campbell, S., & Nutt, C. (2008). Academic advising in the new global century: Supporting student engagement and learning outcomes achievement. *Peer Review, 10*(1), 4–7.

Casazza, M. E. (1999). Who are we and where did we come from? *Journal of Developmental Education, 23*(1), 2–4, 6–7.

Cavote, S. E., & Koprere-Frye, K. (2004). Subject-based first-year experience courses: Questions about program effectiveness. *Journal of The First-Year Experience & Students in Transition, 16*(2), 85–102.

Chemers, M. M., Hu, L., & Garcia, B. F (2001). Academic self-efficacy and first year college student performance and adjustment. *Journal of Educational Psychology, 93*(1), 55–64.

Chen, X., & Carroll, C. D. (2005). *First generation students in postsecondary education: A look at their college transcripts.* Washington, DC: US Department of Education

Chenoweth, K. (1998). The new faces of Vassar: The Seven Sister college has tapped into an often overlooked resource of minority undergraduates: Transfer students. *Black Issues in Higher Education, 14*(2), 22–23.

Chesney, T. D. (2011). Transforming science education through peer-led team learning. *Peer Review, 13*(3), 8–10.

Chickering, A. W. (1969). *Education and identity.* San Francisco, CA: Jossey-Bass.

Chickering, A. W., & Gamson, Z. F. (1987). Seven principles for good practice. *AAHE Bulletin, 39*(7), 3–7.

Chickering, A. W., & Riesser, L. (1993). *Education and identity* (2nd ed.). San Francisco, CA: Jossey-Bass.

Chism, N.V.M., & Bickford, D. J. (2002). *The importance of physical space in creating supportive learning environments.* San Francisco, CA: Jossey-Bass.

Church, M. (2005). Integrative theory of academic advising: A proposition. *The Mentor: An Academic Advising Journal, 7*(2). Retrieved from nacada.ksu.edu

Clifton, D. O., & Anderson, E. (2002). *StrengthsQuest: Discover and develop your strengths in academics, career, and beyond.* Washington, DC: Gallup Organization.

Cohen, A., & Brawer, F. B. (2002). *The American community college* (4th ed.). San Francisco, CA: Jossey-Bass.

Cohen, A. M., & Kisker, C. B. (2010). *The shaping of American higher education: Emergence and growth of the contemporary system* (2nd ed.). San Francisco, CA: Jossey Bass.

Cole, D. (2008). Constructive criticism: The role of student-faculty interactions on African American and Hispanic students' educational gains. *Journal of College Student Development, 49*(6), 587–605.

College Board Advocacy. (2009). *How colleges organize themselves to increase student persistence: Four-year institutions.* Retrieved from professionals .collegeboard.com/profdownload/college-retention.pdf

Collins, C. C. (2007). LSU's summer scholars program grooms exemplary minority first-year students. *E-Source for College Transitions, 4*(3), 3–4.

Colorado Mountain College. (2008). *AQIP in-class engagement strategies action team, MAT 121 College Algebra.* Retrieved from www.coloradomtn.edu/File/aqip/InClassStudentEngagement.pdf

Columbia City College. (2013). *Student life.* Retrieved from http://www .colum.edu/Students/Multicultural_Affairs/Peer_Support _Program

Commander, N. E., Valeri-Gold, M., & Darnell, K. (2004). The strategic thinking and learning community: An innovative model for providing academic assistance. *Journal of The First-Year Experience & Students in Transition, 16*(1), 61–76.

Community College Survey of Student Engagement. (2012). *About the Community College Survey of Student Engagement (CCSSE): Brief history.* Retrieved from http://www.ccsse.org/aboutccsse/aboutccsse.cfm

Complete College America. (2012). *Remediation: Higher education's bridge to nowhere.* Retrieved from http:www.completecollege.org/docs /cca-Remediation-final.pdf

Cooperrider, D. L., Sorenson, P., Whitney, D., & Yager, T. (2000). *Appreciative inquiry: Rethinking human organization toward a positive theory of change.* Champaign, IL: Stipes Publishing.

Cooperrider, D., & Srivastva, S. (1987). Appreciative inquiry in organizational life. *Research in Organizational Change and Development, 1,* 129–169.

Council for the Advancement of Standards in Higher Education. (2005). *The role of academic advising, CAS Standards Contextual Statement.* http://www.cas.edu/getpdf.cfm?PDF=E864D2C4-D655-8F74-2E647CDECD29B7D0

Council for the Advancement of Standards in Higher Education. (2006). *Self-assessment guide for housing and residential life programs.* Washington, DC: Author.

Council for the Advancement of Standards in Higher Education. (2007). *The role of learning assistance programs. CAS standards contextual statement.* Retrieved from www.cas.edu/getpdf

Council for the Advancement of Standards in Higher Education. (2009). *CAS professional standards for higher education* (7th ed.). Washington, DC: Author.

Council for the Advancement of Standards in Higher Education. (2012). CAS General Standards, Part 2. Program. CAS General Standards. http://www.cas.edu/Index.php/cas-general-standards

Cox, R. D. (2009). *The college fear factor. How students and professors misunderstand one another.* Cambridge, MA: Harvard University Press.

Creasey, G., Jarvis, P., & Gadke, D. (2009). Student attachment stances, instructor immediacy, and student-instructor relationships as predictors of achievement expectancies in college students. *Journal of College Student Development, 54*(4), 353–372. doi:10:1353/csd.0.0082

Creamer, E. C., & Scott, D. W. (2000). Assessing individual advisor effectiveness. In V. N. Gordon, W. R. Habley, & Associates (Eds.), *Academic advising: A comprehensive handbook* (pp. 339–348). San Francisco, CA: Jossey-Bass.

Crissman Ishler, J. L., & Upcraft, M. L. (2001). Assessing first-year programs. In J. H. Schuh, M. L. Upcraft, & Associates, *Assessment practice in student affairs: An application manual* (pp. 261–274). San Francisco, CA: Jossey-Bass.

Crissman Ishler, J. L. (2005). Today's first-year students. In M. L. Upcraft, J. N. Gardner, B. O. Barefoot, & Associates (Eds.), *Challenging and supporting the first-year student: A handbook for improving the first year of college* (pp. 15–26). San Francisco, CA: Jossey-Bass.

Crookston, B. B. (1994). A developmental view of academic advising as teaching. *NACADA Journal, 14*(2), 5–9. (Originally published 1972)

Cross, P. (1998). Why learning communities, why now? *About Campus, 3*(3), 4–11.

Cruce, T., Wolniak, G. C., Seifert, T. A., & Pascarella, E. T. (2006). Impacts of good practices on cognitive development, learning orientations, and graduate degree plans during the first year of college. *Journal of College Student Development, 47*(4), 365–383.

Cruise, C. A. (2002). Advising students on academic probation. *Mentor.* Retrieved from www.psu.edu/dus/mentor/021028cc.htm

Cuseo, J. B. (1991). *The freshman orientation seminar: A research-based rationale for its value, delivery, and content* (Monograph No. 4). Columbia: University of South Carolina, National Resource Center for the Freshman Year Experience.

Cuseo, J. B. (2003a). Red flags: Behavioral indicators of potential student attrition. (n.p.) Retrieved from http://www.uwc.edu/sites /default/files/imce-uploads/employees/academic-resources /esfy/_files/red_flags-behavioral_indicators_of_potential_student _attrition.pdf

Cuseo, J. B. (2003b). Comprehensive academic support for students during the first year of college. In G. L. Kramer & Associates, *Student academic services: An integrated approach* (pp. 271–310). San Francisco: Jossey-Bass.

Cueso, J. B. (2007). The empirical case against large class size: Adverse effects on the teaching, learning, and retention of first-year students. *Journal of Faculty Development, 21*(1), 5–21.

Cuseo, J. B. (2009). The first-year seminar: A vehicle for promoting the instructional development of college faculty. *E-Source for College Student Development, 7*(1), 4–5, 7.

Cuseo, J. B. (2010a). Fiscal benefits of student retention and first-year retention Initiatives. *Ohio University.* Retrieved from http://www.ohio.edu/fye/upload/retention-fiscal-benefits.pdf

Cuseo, J. B. (2010b). Peer power: Empirical evidence for the positive impact of peer interaction, support, and leadership. *E-Source for College Transitions, 7*(4), 4–6.

Cuseo, J. B. (2010c). Peer leadership: Definition, description, and classification. *E-Source for College Transitions, 7*(5), 3–5.

Damashek, R. (2003). *Support programs for students on academic probation.* (ERIC Document Reproduction Service No. ED 475 734).

Davis, B. G. (1993). *Tools for teaching.* San Francisco, CA: Jossey-Bass.

Davis, J. (2010). *The first-generation student experience.* Sterling, VA: Stylus Publishing.

Deering, C. G. (2011). Managing disruptive behavior in the classroom. *College Quarterly, 4*(3). Retrieved from www.collegequarterly.ca /2011-vol14-num03-summer/deering.html

Diaz, R., Wurtz, K., Molina, M., Jabalera, K., Villalpando, A., & Arner, T. (2007). *Smart start: A collaborative model for reducing the likelihood of academic probation.* Retrieved from 3csn.org/files/2012/06/0708 -Smart-Start.pdf

Dickson, G. L., & McMahon, T. R. (1989). *Developmental advising inventory* (collegiate ed.). Kettering, OH: Developmental Advising Inventories.

Dillon, J. (2003). Bringing counseling to the classroom and the residence hall: The university learning community. *Journal of Humanistic Counseling Education and Development, 42*(2), 194–208.

Dillon, R. K., & Fisher, B. J. (2000). Faculty as part of the advising equation: An inquiry into faculty viewpoints on advising. *NACADA Journal, 20*(1), 16–23.

Dixon, R. A., & Chung, K. (2008). Revisiting first-year college students mattering: Social support, academic stress, and the mattering experience. *Journal of College Student Retention: Research, Theory and Practice, 9*(1), 21–37.

Donnelly, D. L., & Boreland, K. W., Jr. (2002). Undeclared students' patterns of declaration: Practical and political implications for orientation and transition programs. *Journal of College Orientation and Transition, 10*(1), 5–13.

Donnelly, J. E. (2011). Forum: Use of a web-based academic alert system for identification of underachieving students at an urban research institution. *College and University, 85*(4), 39–42.

Drake, J. K. (2011, July-August). The role of academic advising in student retention and persistence. *About Campus, 16*(3), 8–12.

Dwyer, C. A., Millett, C. M., & Payne, D. G. (2006). *A culture of evidence: Postsecondary assessment and learning outcomes.* Princeton, NJ: Educational Testing Service.

Dwyer, J. O. (1989). A historical look at the freshman year experience. In M. L. Upcraft, J. N. Gardner, & Associates, *The freshman year experience.* San Francisco, CA: Jossey-Bass.

Earl, W. R. (1988). Intrusive advising of freshmen in academic difficulty. *NACADA Journal, 8*(2), 23–27.

Eggleston, L. E., & Laanan, F. S. (2001). Making the transition to the senior institution. In F. S. Lanaan (Ed.), *Transfer students: Trends and issues. New Directions for Community Colleges, 114,* 87–97.

Elgin Community College. (2012). *Early alert program.* Retrieved from www.elgin.edu/faculty.aspx?id=13214

Elliott, J. L., & Decker, E. (1999). Garnering the fundamental resources for learning communities. In J. H. Levine (Ed.), *Learning communities: New structures, new partnerships for learning* (Monograph No. 26, pp. 19–28). Columbia: University of South Carolina, National Resource Center for The First-Year Experience and Students in Transition.

Ender, S. C., & Kay, K. (2001). Peer leader programs: A rationale and review of the literature. In S. L. Hamid (Ed.), *Peer leadership: A primer on program essentials.* Columbia: University of South Carolina, National Resource Center for The First-Year Experience and Students in Transition.

ERIC Clearinghouse on Higher Education. (2001). *Critical issue bibliography (CRIB) sheet: Summer bridge programs.* Washington, DC: ERIC Clearinghouse on Higher Education, George Washington University.

Erickson, B. L., Peters, C. B., & Strommer, D. W. (2006). *Teaching first-year college students.* San Francisco, CA: Jossey-Bass.

Erikson, L. (1998, February). *At-risk student perceptions of the value of their freshman orientation week experiences.* Paper presented at the annual meeting of the Eastern Educational Research Association, Tampa, FL.

Esplin, P., Seabold, J., & Pinnegar, F. (2012). The architecture of a high-impact and sustainable peer leader program: A blueprint for success. In J. R. Keup (Ed.), *Peer leadership in higher education. New Directions for Higher Education, 157,* 85–100.

Evans, R. (1999). A comparison of success indicators for program and nonprogram participants in a community college summer bridge program for minority students. *Visions, 2*(2), 6–14.

Evenbeck, S. E., Boston, M., DuVivier, R. S., & Hallberg, K. (2000). Institutional approaches to helping sophomores. In L. A. Schreiner & J. Pattengale (Eds.), *Visible solution for invisible students: Helping sophomores succeed* (Monograph No. 31, pp. 79–88). Columbia: University of South Carolina, National Resource Center for The First-Year Experience and Students in Transition.

Fabich, M. (Ed.). (2004). *Orientation planning manual.* Flint, MI: National Orientation Directors Association.

Farnum, T., & Associates (2010). *Prevalence and composition of second year programs in higher education.* New Boston, NH: Author. www.teresafarnum.com/Prevalenceandcomposition2ndYear ProgrammingTFASite.pdf

Feldman K. A., & Newcomb, T. M. (1994). *The impact of college on students.* New Brunswick, NJ: Transactions.

Fidler, P. P. (1991). Relationship of freshman orientation seminars to sophomore return rates. *Journal of the Freshman Year Experience, 3*(1), 7–38.

Fidler, P. P., & Moore, P. S. (1996). A comparison of effects of campus residence and freshman seminar attendance on freshman dropout rates. *Journal of The Freshman Year Experience & Students in Transition, 8*(2), 7–16.

Fischer, M. J. (2007). Settling into campus life: Differences by race/ethnicity in college involvement, college satisfaction, and outcomes. *Journal of Higher Education Outcomes, 78*(2), 125–161.

Fitts, J. D. (1989). *A comparison of locus of control and achievement among remedial summer bridge and nonbridge students in community colleges in New Jersey.* Trenton, NJ: New Jersey Department of Higher Education. (ERIC Document Reproduction Service No. ED 315 102).

Fletcher, J. M., & Tokmouline, M. (2010). The effects of academic probation. *Lending students a hand when they need it.* Princeton, NJ: Princeton University, Office of Population Research.

Florida International University. (2011). *Panther camp's impact.* Retrieved from http://orientation.fiu.edu/?page_id=126

Ford, J. L. (2003). *Producing a comprehensive academic advising handbook for faculty utilization.* Retrieved from http://www.nacada.ksu.edu/Clearinghouse/AdvisingIssues/createhandbook.html

Fox, L., Zakely, J., Morris, R., & Jundt, M. (1993). Orientation as a catalyst: Effective retention through academic and social integration. In M. L. Upcraft, R. H. Mullendore, B. O. Barefoot, & D. S. Fidler (Eds.), *Designing successful transitions: A guide for orienting students to college* (pp. 49–59). Columbia, SC: National Resource Center for the Freshman Year Experience.

Franklin, K. K. (2000). Shared and connected learning in a freshman learning community. *Journal of The First-Year Experience & Students in Transition, 12*(2), 33–60.

Freedman, M. B. (1956). The passage through college. *Journal of Social Issues, 12,* 13–27.

Freeman, E., & Evan, W. (1990). Corporate governance: A stakeholder interpretation. *Journal of Behavioral Economics, 19*(4), 337–359.

Freeman, E., & McVea, J. (2001). A stakeholder approach to management: The state of the art. In M. Hitt, E. Freeman, & J. Harrison (Eds.), *The Blackwell handbook of strategic management* (pp. 189–207). Oxford: Blackwell Business.

Fresno City College. (2012, May). *Early alert program.* Retrieved from www.fresnocitycollege.edu/index.aspx?page=379

Friedman, D. B. (2012). *The first-year seminar: Designing, implementing, and assessing courses to support student learning and success: Vol. 5. Assessing the first-year seminar.* Columbia University of South Carolina, National Resource Center for The First-Year Experience and Students in Transition.

Fulton, M. (2008). *Getting Past Go Project.* Education Commission of the States. Retrieved from www.ecs.org/html/issue.asp?issueid=68&subissueID=217

Gabelnick, F., MacGregor, J., Matthews, R. S., & Smith, B. L. (Eds.). (1990). *Learning communities: Creating connections among students, faculty, and disciplines. New Directions for Teaching and Learning, 41.*

Gahagan, J., & Hunter, M. S. (2006). The second-year experience: Turning attention to the academy's middle children. *About Campus, 11*(3), 17–22.

Gahagan, J., & Hunter, M. S. (2008). Engaging sophomores: Attending to the needs of second year students. *AACRAO's College and University Journal, 83*(3), 45–49.

Galloway, S. P. (2000). Assessment in wilderness orientation programs: Efforts to improve college student retention. *Journal of Experiential Education, 23*(2), 75–84.

Gansemer-Topf, A. M., Stern, J. M., & Benjamin, M. (2007). Examining the experiences of second-year students at a private liberal arts college. In B. F. Tobolowsky & B. E. Cox (Eds.), *Shedding light on sophomores: An exploration of the second college year*. Columbia: University of South Carolina, National Resource Center for The First-Year Experience and Students in Transition.

Ganser, S. R., & Kennedy, T. L. (2012). Where it all began: Peer education and leadership in student services. In J. R. Keup (Ed.), *Peer leadership in higher education. New Directions for Higher Education, 157*, 17–30.

Garcia, L. D., & Paz, C. C. (2009). Evaluation of a summer bridge program. *About Campus, 14*(4), 30–32.

Garcia, P. (1991). Summer bridge: Improving retention rates for under-prepared students. *Journal of the Freshman Year Experience, 3*(2), 91–105.

Gardner, J. N. (2000). What, so what, now what. Reflections, findings, conclusions, and recommendations on service learning and the first-year experience. Preparing students for personal success and individual responsibility. In E. Zlotkowski (Ed.), *Service learning and the first-year experience: Preparing students for personal success and civic responsibility* (pp. 141–150). Columbia: University of South Carolina, National Resource Center for the First-Year and Students in Transition.

Gardner, J. N., Tobolowsky, B. F., & Hunter, B. F. (2010). Recommendations to improve sophomore student success. In M. S. Hunter, B. F. Tobolowsky, & J. N. Gardner (Eds.), *Helping sophomores succeed: Understanding and improving the second-year experience*. San Francisco, CA: Jossey-Bass.

Gardner, P. D. (2000). From drift to engagement. Finding purpose and making career connections in the sophomore year. In L. A. Schreiner & J. Pattengale (Eds.), *Visible solutions for invisible students: Helping sophomores succeed* (pp. 67–77). Columbia, SC: University of South Carolina, National Resource Center for the First Year and Students in Transition.

Gass, M. A., Garvey, D. E., & Sugerman, D. A. (2003). The long-term effects of a first-year student wilderness orientation program. *Journal of Experiential Education, 26*(1), 34–40.

Gehrke, S., & Wong, J. (2007). Students on academic probation. In L. Huff & P. Jordan (Eds.), *Advising special populations: Adult learners, community college students, LGBTQ students, multicultural students, students on probation, undecided students* (Monograph No. 17, pp. 135–150). Manhattan, KS: National Academic Advising Association.

Gentry, W. A., Kuhnert, K. W., Johnson, R. M., & Cox, B. (2006). Even a weekend works: The value of a weekend-long orientation program on first-year college students. *Journal of College Orientation and Transition, 14*(1), 26–38.

Gerlaugh, K., Thompson, L., Boylan, H., & Davis, H. (2007). National study of developmental education. II: Baseline data for community colleges. *Research in Developmental Education, 20*(4), 1–4.

Ghere, D. L (2000). Teaching American history in a developmental education context. In J. L. Higbee & P. L. Dwinell (Eds.), with D. B. Lundell, *The many faces of developmental education* (pp. 39–46). Warrensburg, MO: National Center for Developmental Education.

Gilbert, N. S. (2007, February 14). Students Taking Academic Responsibility (STAR): A mentoring program for at-risk students. *Mentor: An Academic Advising Journal.* Article retrieved from: http://dus.psu.edu/mentor/old/articles/070214ng.htm

Glennan, R. E. (2003). The importance of faculty advising: A CEO and CAO perspective. In G. L. Kramer (Ed.), *Faculty advising examined: Enhancing the potential of college faculty advisers* (pp. 40–54). San Francisco, CA: Jossey-Bass.

Glennan, R. E., Martin, D. J., & Walden, H. (2000). Summer bridge academic: A descriptive analysis and suggestions for advising academically talented students. *Journal of the National Academic Advising Association, 20*(2), 38–45.

Glisson, N. L. (Ed.). (2009). *Exploring the evidence: Reporting research on peer education programs: An online archive of campus-based research reports.* Columbia: National Resource Center for The First-Year Experience and Students in Transition, University of South Carolina. Retrieved from http://www.sc.edu/fye/resources/fyr/peers.html#case

Gohn, L., Swartz, J., & Donnelly, S. (2001). A case study of second year student persistence. *Journal of College Student Retention: Research, Theory and Practice, 2*(4), 271–294.

Goodman, K. M., Baxter Magolda, M., Seifert, T. A., & King, P. M. (2011). Good practices for student learning: Mixed-method evidence from the Wabash National Study. *About Campus, 16*(1), 2–9.

Gordon, V. P. (1989). Origins and purposes of the freshman seminar. In M. L. Upcraft, J. N. Gardner, & Associates, *The freshman year experience* (pp. 183–197). San Francisco, CA: Jossey-Bass.

Graunke, S. S., & Woosley, S. A. (2005). An exploration of the factors that affect the academic success of college sophomores. *College Student Journal, 39*(2), 367–376.

Greene, T. G. (2008). *Developmental education toolkit.* Austin: Community Colleges Central, Bridges to Opportunity Initiative, University of Texas, Austin.

Griffin, A. M., & Romm, J. (Eds.). (2008). *Exploring the evidence: Vol. 4. Reporting research on first-year seminars.* Columbia: University of South Carolina, National Resource Center for The First-Year Experience and Students in Transition.

Grites, T. J., & Gordon, V. N. (2000). Developmental academic advising revisited. *NACADA Journal, 20,* 12–14.

Grove, W. A., & Wasserman, T. (2004). The life-cycle pattern of collegiate GPA: Longitudinal cohort analysis and grade inflation. *Journal of Economic Education, 33*(2), 173–200.

Guiffrida, D. A. (2003). African American student organizations as agents of social integration. *Journal of College Student Development, 44*(3), 304–319.

Guiffrida, D. A. (2006). Toward a cultural advancement of Tinto's theory. *Review of Higher Education, 29*(4), 451–472.

Gump, S. E. (2007). Classroom research in a general education course: Exploring implications through an investigation of the sophomore slump. *Journal of General Education, 56*(2), 105–125.

Gutkowski, J. (2006). Cocurricular transcripts: Documenting holistic higher education. *The Bulletin, 74*(5).

Habley, W. R. (1994). Key concepts in academic advising. *Summer Institute on Academic Advising Session Guide,* p. 10, Manhattan, KS, National Academic Advising Association.

Habley, W. R. (2005). *Developing a mission statement for the academic advising program.* Retrieved from http://www.nacada.ksu .edu/Clearinghouse/AdvisingIssues/Mission-Statements.htm

Habley, W. R., & McClanahan, R. (2004). *What works in student retention?* Iowa City, IA: American College Testing Program.

Habley, W. R., McClanahan, R., Valiga, M., & Burkum, K. (2010). *What works in student retention? Report for all colleges and universities.* Iowa City, IA: ACT.

Habley, W. R., & Morales, R. H. (1998). Advising models: Goal achievement and program effectiveness. *NACADA Journal, 18*(1), 35–41.

Hagen, P. L., & Jordan, P. (2008). Theoretical foundations of academic advising. In V. N. Gordon, G. D. Kuh, J. Kinzie, J. Buckley, & Associates (Eds.), *What matters to student success: A review of the literature* (pp. 17–35). San Francisco, CA: Jossey-Bass.

Hanover Research Council. (2008). *Early intervention models for student success.* Retrieved from www.shawnee.edu/ . . . /New%20research/ . . .

Harmon, B. V. (2006). A qualitative study of the learning processes and outcomes associated with students who serve as peer mentors. *Journal of The First-Year Experience & Students in Transition, 18*(2), 53–82.

Harney, J. O. (2012, October 23). Developing story: A forum on improving remedial education. *New England Journal of Higher Education.* Retrieved from http://www.nebhe.org/the journal/ /developingstory-a-forum-on-improving-remedial-education

Harney, J. Y. (2008). Campus administrator perspectives on advising: Chief student affairs officer—two-year public. In V. Gordon, W. Habley, and T. Grites (Eds.) *Academic advising: A comprehensive handbook* (2nd ed.), pp. 424–430. San Francisco: Jossey-Bass.

Harward, D. W. (2008, April 15). A different way to fight student disengagement. *Inside Higher Education.* Retrieved from www.insidehighered.com/views/2008/04/15/harward

Heisserer, D. L., & Parette, P. (2002). Advising at-risk students in college and university settings. *College Student Journal, 36,* 69–83.

Hemwall, M. K., & Trachte, K .C. (2005). Academic advising as learning: Ten organizing principles. *NACADA Journal, 25*(2), 74–83.

Henscheid, J. M. (2004). Integrating the first-year experience: *The role of first-year seminars in learning communities* (Monograph No. 39). Columbia: University of South Carolina, National Resource Center for The First-Year Experience and Students in Transition.

Heiss-Arms, J., Cabrera, A., & Brower, A. M. (2008). Moving into students' spaces: The impact of location of academic advising on student engagement among undecided students. *NACADA Journal, 28*(1), 8–18.

Higgins, E. M. (2003). *Advising students on probation.* Retrieved from http://www.nacada.ksu.edu/Clearinghouse/AdvisingIssues /probation.htm

Hodges, R., Dochen, C., & Joy, D. (2001). Increasing students' success: When supplemental instruction becomes mandatory. *Journal of College Reading and Learning, 31,* 143–156.

Hoffman, M., Richmond, J., Morrow, J., & Salomne, K. (2002–2003). Investigating "sense of belonging" in first-year college students.

Journal of College Student Retention: Research, Theory and Practice, 4(3), 227–256.

Hopkins, W. H. (1988). *College success: A transitional course for freshmen.* Washington, DC: American Association of State Colleges and Universities.

Hossler, D., Kuh, G. D., & Olsen, D. (2001). Finding (more) fruit on the vines: Using higher education research and institutional research to guide institutional policies and strategies (part II). *Research in Higher Education, 42*(2), 223–235.

Howe, N., & Strauss, W. (2003). *Millennials go to college.* Great Falls, VA: American Association of Collegiate Registrars and Admissions Officers and Life Course Associates.

Howey, S. C. (2008). *Factors in student motivation.* Retrieved from http://www.nacada.ksu.edu/Clearinghouse/AdvisingIssues/Motivation.htm

Humphrey, E. (2006). Project success: Helping probationary students achieve academic success. *Journal of College Student Retention, 7*(3–4), 147–163.

Hunter, M. S., & Heath, M. M. (2001). The building blocks of the peer leader program: Recruitment, selection, and training. In S. L. Hamid (Ed.), *Peer leadership: A primer on program essentials* (Monograph No. 32, pp. 37–52). Columbia: University of South Carolina, National Resource Center for The First-Year Experience and Students in Transition.

Hunter, M. S., & Linder, C. W. (2005). First-year seminars. In M. L. Upcraft, J. N. Gardner, B. O. Barefoot, & Associates, *Challenging and supporting the first-year student: A handbook for the improving the first year of college* (pp. 275–291). San Francisco, CA: Jossey-Bass.

Hunter, M. S., Tobolowsky, B. F., Gardner, J. N., Evenbeck, S. E., Pattengale, J. A., Schaller, M., & Schreiner, L. A. (2010). *Helping sophomores succeed: Understanding and improving the second year experience.* San Francisco, CA: Jossey-Bass.

Hurtado, S., Dey, E. L., Gurin, P., & Gurin, G. (2003). College environments, diversity, and student learning. In J. C. Smart (Ed.), *Higher education: Handbook of theory and research* (pp. 145–190). New York: Kluwer Academic.

Hutson, B. L. (2006). Monitoring for success: *Implementing a proactive probation program for diverse, at-risk college students* (Unpublished doctoral dissertation). University of North Carolina at Greensboro.

Hyatt Hotels Corporation. (2011). *Hyatt and historically black colleges and universities—hospitality management consortium team up for a common cause* (press release). Retrieved from http://www.hyattpressroom

.com/hyatt/en/news_releases0/2011/hyatt-and-historically-black-colleges-and-universities-hospitality-management-consortium-team-up-for-a-common-cause.html

Indiana University-Purdue University Indianapolis. (N.d.). *Summer Bridge Program description.* Retrieved from http://www.iupui.edu/~bulletin/iupui/2010–2012/schools/univ-college/academic-program/Bridge.shtml

Inkelas, K. K., & Brower, A. M. (2007). *NSLLP National Study of Living-Learning Programs: 2007. Report of findings.* Retrieved from drum.lib.umd.edu/ . . . /1/2007%20NSLLP%20Final%20 Report.pdf

Inkelas, K. K., Daver, Z., Vogt, K., & Leonard, B. J. (2007). Living-learning programs and first-generation college students' academic and social transition to college. *Research in Higher Education, 48*(4), 403–434.

Inkelas, K. K., & Longerbeam, S. D. (2008). Working toward a comprehensive typology of living-learning communities. In G. Lina & J. Gahagan (Eds.), *Learning initiatives in the residential setting* (pp. 29–41). Columbia: University of South Carolina, National Resource Center for The First-Year Experience and Students in Transition.

Inkelas, K. K., Vogt, K. E., Longerbeam, S. D., Owen, J. E., & Johnson, D. R. (2006). Measuring outcomes of living-learning programs: Examining college environments and student learning and development. *Journal of General Education, 55*(1), 40–76.

Isaak, M., Graves, K., & Mayers, B. (2006). Academic, motivational, and emotional problems identified by college students in academic jeopardy. *Journal of College Student Retention, 8*(2), 171–183.

Ishitani, T. T., & DesJardins, S. L. (2002). A longitudinal investigation of dropout from college in the United States. *Journal of College Student Retention, 4*(2), 173–201.

Ithaca College. (2012). *Academic advising.* Retrieved from www.ithaca.edu/sacl/experience/advising/

Jacobs, B. C. (2010). Making the case for orientation: Is it worth it? In J. A. Ward-Roof (Ed.), *Designing successful transitions: A guide for orienting students to college* (Monograph No. 13, 3rd ed., pp. 29–39). Columbia: University of South Carolina, National Resource Center for The First-Year Experience and Students in Transition.

James, R., Krause, K., & Jennings, C. (2010). *The first year experience in Australian universities: Findings from 1994 to 2009.* Melbourne, Australia: Centre for the Study of Higher Education, University of Melbourne.

Jedele, R., & Tinto, V. (2011). Learning communities and community colleges: The challenges and benefits. In T. Brown, M. C. King, & P. Stanley (Eds.). *Fulfilling the promise of the community college: Increasing first-year student engagement and success* (Monograph No. 56, pp. 3–14). Columbia: University of South Carolina, National Resource Center for The First-Year Experience and Students in Transition.

Johnson, J., & Parker, J. (2008). Current staffing patterns supporting first-year students. In W. J. Zeller (Ed.), *Residence life programs and the new student experience* (Monograph No. 5, 3rd ed., pp. 107–120). Columbia, SC: University of South Carolina, National Resource Center for The First-Year Experience and Students in Transition.

Johnson, J. L. (2000–2001). Learning communities and special efforts in retention of university students: What works, what doesn't, and is the return worth the investment? *Journal of College Student Retention: Research, Theory and Practice, 2*(3), 219–238.

Johnson, M. L. (2012). Integrating technology into peer leader responsibilities. In J. R. Keup (Ed.), *Peer leadership and the student experience. New Directions for Higher Education, 157,* 59–72.

Johnston, S., & McGregor, H. (2005). Recognizing and supporting a scholarship of practice: Soft skills are hard! *Asia Pacific Journal of Cooperative Education, 61,* 1–6.

Jones, K. (2011). *Boiler gold rush.* Unpublished manuscript, Purdue University, West Lafayette, IN.

Jones, S. R., & Abes, E. S. (2004). Enduring influences of service-learning on college students' identity development. *Journal of College Student Development, 45*(1), 149–166.

June, A. W. (2011, May 16). Advising's role in tenure. *Chronicle of Higher Education.* Retrieved from http://chronicle.com/blogs/onhiring/advisings-role-in-tenure/29851

Keeling, R. P., Underhile, R., & Wall, A. F. (2007). Horizontal and vertical structures: The dynamics of organizations in higher education. *Liberal Education, 93*(4), 22–31.

Ketcheson, K. A., & Levine, J. H. (1999). Evaluating and assessing learning communities. In J. H. Levine (Ed.), *Learning communities: New structures, new partnerships for learning* (Monograph No. 26, pp. 97–108). Columbia: University of South Carolina, National Resource Center for The First-Year Experience and Students in Transition.

Keup, J. R. (Ed.). (2012). *Peer leadership in higher education. New Directions in Higher Education, 157.*

Keup, J. R., & Barefoot, B. O. (2005). Learning how to be a successful student: Exploring the impact of first-year seminars on student outcomes. *Journal of The First-Year Experience & Students in Transition, 17*(1), 11–47.

Keup, J. R., Gahagan, J., & Goodwin, R. N. (2010). *2008 National Survey of Sophomore-Year Initiatives. Curricular and cocurricular structures supporting the success of second-year students.* Columbia: University of South Carolina, National Resource Center for The First-Year Experience and Students in Transition.

Keup, J. R., & Kilgo, C. A. (in press). Conceptual considerations for first-year assessment. In R. D. Padgett (Ed.), *The first-year experience. New Directions for Institutional Research.*

Keup, J. R., & Petschauer, J. W. (2011). *The first-year seminar: Designing, implementing, and assessing courses to support student learning and success: Vol. 1. Designing and administering the course.* Columbia: University of South Carolina, National Resource Center for The First-Year Experience and Students in Transition.

Keup, J. R., & Skipper, T. L. (2010, March). *Findings from the 2009 National Survey of Peer Leaders.* Concurrent session presented at the 2010 Annual ACPA Convention, Boston, MA.

Kezar, A. (2000). *Summer bridge programs: Supporting all students.* Washington, DC: ERIC Clearinghouse on Higher Education, George Washington University. (ERIC Digest No. ED 442 421)

Kezar, A. (2005). *Promoting student success: The importance of shared leadership and collaboration.* Bloomington: Indiana University, Center for Postsecondary Research.

King, M. C. (2003). Organizational models and delivery systems for faculty advising. In G. L. Kramer (Ed.), *Faculty advising examined* (pp. 125–133). Bolton, MA: Anker.

King, M. C. (2008). Organizing of academic advising. In V. Gordon, W. R. Habley, T. J. Grites, & Associates, *Academic advising: A comprehensive handbook* (2nd ed., pp. 242–252). San Francisco, CA: Jossey-Bass.

King, M. C., & Kerr, T. J. (2005). Academic advising. In M. L. Upcraft, J. N. Gardner, & B. O. Barefoot (Eds.), *Challenging and supporting the first year student: A handbook for improving the first year of college* (pp. 320–338). San Francisco, CA: Jossey-Bass.

Kirk-Kuwaye, M., & Nishida, D. (2001). Effects of low and high adviser involvement on the academic performance of probation students. *NACADA Journal, 21,* 40–45.

Knott, L. (2009). *The role of mathematics discourse in producing leaders of discourse.* Charlotte, NC: Information Age Publishing.

Knox, M. J., & Henderson, B. D. (2010). Nontraditional is the new traditional: Understanding today's college student. In J. A. Ward-Roof (Ed.), *Designing successful transitions: A guide for orienting students to college* (Monograph No. 13, 3rd ed., pp. 193–204). Columbia: University of South Carolina, National Resource Center for The First-Year Experience and Students in Transition.

Koch, A. K. (2001). *The first-year experience in American higher education: An annotated bibliography* (3rd ed.). Columbia: University of South Carolina, National Resource Center for The First-Year Experience and Students in Transition.

Koch, A. K., Foote, S. M., Hinkle, S. E., Keup, J. R., & Pistilli, M. D. (Eds.) (2007). *The first-year experience in American higher education: An annotated bibliography* (4th ed.). Columbia: University of South Carolina, National Resource Center for The First-Year Experience and Students in Transition.

Koch, A. K., & Gardner, J. N. (2006). The history of the first-year experience in the United States: Lessons from the past, practices in the present, and implications for the future. In A. Hamana & K. Tatsuo (Eds.), *The first-year experience and transition from high school to college: An international study of content and pedagogy.* Tokyo, Japan: Maruzen Publishing.

Koring, H. (2005). *Advisor training and development.* Retrieved from http://www.nacada.ksu.edu/Clearinghouse/AdvisingIssues/adv_training.htm

Koring, H., & Campbell, S. (Eds.). (2005). *Peer advising: Intentional connections to support student learning* (NACADA Monograph Series No. 13). Manhattan, KS: National Academic Advising Association.

Kramer, G. L. (2003). *Faculty advising examined: Enhancing the potential of college faculty advisers.* Bolton, MA: Anker.

Kuh, G. D. (2001). Assessing what really matters to student learning: Inside the National Survey of Student Engagement. *Change, 33*(3), 10–17, 66.

Kuh, G. D. (2003). What we're learning about student engagement from NSSE. *Change, 35*(2), 24–32.

Kuh, G. D. (2005). Student engagement in the first year of college. In M. L. Upcraft, J. N. Gardner, & B. O. Barefoot (Eds.), *Challenging and supporting the first-year student: A handbook for improving the first year of college* (pp. 86–107). San Francisco, CA: Jossey-Bass.

Kuh, G. D. (2008). *High-impact educational practices: What they are, who has access to them, and why they matter.* Washington, DC: Association of American Colleges and Universities.

Kuh, G. D., & Hu, P. (2000). The effects of student-faculty Interaction in the 1990s. *Review of Higher Education, 24*(3), 309–332.

Kuh, G. D., Kinzie, J., Buckley, J., & Associates. (2009). *What matters to student success: A review of the literature.* Commissioned Report for the National Symposium on Postsecondary Student Success: Spearheading a Dialog on Student Success.

Kuh, G. D., Kinzie, J., Cruce, T., Shoup, R., & Gonyea, R. M. (2006). *Connecting the dots: Multi-faceted analyses of the relationships between student engagement results from the NSSE, and the institutional practices and conditions that foster student success.* Final report prepared for the Lumina Foundation, Center for Postsecondary Research, Indiana University Bloomington.

Kuh, G. D., Kinzie, J., Schuh, J., Whitt, E., & Associates. (2005). *Student success in college: Creating conditions that matter.* San Francisco, CA: Jossey-Bass.

Kuh, G. D., Schuh, J. H., Whitt, E. J., & Associates (1991). *Involving colleges: Successful approaches to fostering student learning and development outside the classroom.* San Francisco, CA: Jossey-Bass.

Kuh, G. D., Shedd, J. D., & Whitt, E. J. (1987). Student affairs and liberal education: Unrecognized (and unappreciated) common law partners. *Journal of College Student Personnel, 28*(3), 252–260.

LaGuardia Community College (n.d.a). Cooperative Education Department. Retrieved from http://www.lagcc.cuny.edu/coopedu/

LaGuardia Community College (n.d.b). Study Abroad Program: Mission Statement. Retrieved from http://www.lagcc.cuny.edu/internationalconnections/mission1.html

Lake Research Partners. (2011). *Exploring student attitudes, aspirations and barriers to success: Six focus groups among higher-risk first- and second-year community college and technical college students, and four-year university students.* Study conducted for the American Federation of Teachers. Retrieved from www.aft.org/pdfs/highered/studentfocusgrp0311.pdf

Latino, J. A. (2010). *Peer education: An overview.* Session presented at the National Resource Center for The First-Year Experience and Students in Transition's 2010 Institute on Peer Education, Indianapolis, IN.

Latino, J. A., & Ashcraft, M. L. (2012). *The first-year seminar: Designing, implementing, and assessing courses to support student learning and success: Vol. 4. Using peers in the classroom.* Columbia: University of South Carolina, National Resource Center for The First-Year Experience and Students in Transition.

Latino, J. A., & Unite, C. M. (2012). Providing academic support through peer education. In J. R. Keup (Ed.), *Peer leadership in higher education. New Directions in Higher Education, 157,* 31–43.

Laufgraben, J. L. (2005). Learning communities. In M. L. Upcraft, J. N. Gardner, B. O. Barefoot, & Associates, *Challenging and supporting the first-year student: A handbook for improving the first year of college* (pp. 371–387). San Francisco, CA: Jossey-Bass.

Laufgraben, J. L. (2006). *Common reading program: Going beyond the book* (Monograph No. 44). Columbia: University of South Carolina, National Resource Center for The First-Year Experience and Students in Transition.

Lee, D., Olson, E. A., Locke, B., Michelson, S. T., & Odes, E. (2009). The effects of college counseling services on academic performance and retention. *Journal of College Student Development, 50*(3), 305–319.

Lemons, L. J., & Richmond, D. R. (1987). A developmental perspective of the sophomore slump. *NASPA Journal, 24,* 15–19.

Lesik, S. A. (2008). *Evaluating developmental education programs in higher education.* ASHE/Lumina Policy Brief, #4.

Leskes, A., & Miller, R. (2009). *Purposeful pathways: Helping students achieve key learning outcomes.* Washington, DC: Association of American Colleges and Universities.

Lindo, J. M., Sanders, N. J., & Oreopoulos, P. (2010). Ability, gender, and performance standards: Evidence from academic probation. *American Economic Journal: Applied Economics, 2*(2), 95–117.

Lipka, S. (2006, September 8). After the freshman bubble pops: More colleges try to help their sophomores thrive. *Chronicle of Higher Education,* A34.

Logan, C. R., Salisbury-Glennon, J., & Spence, L. D. (2000). The learning edge academic program: Toward a community of learners. *Journal of The First-Year Experience & Students in Transition, 12*(1), 77–104.

Los Medanos College. (2013). *Developmental Education Program.* http://www.losmedanos.edu/deved/programeval.asp

Lotkowski, V. A., Robbins, S. B., & Noeth, R. J. (2004). *The role of academic and non-academic factors in improving college retention.* Iowa City, IA: ACT Policy Report.

Love, A. G. (1999). What are learning communities? In J. H. Levine (Ed.), *Learning communities: New structures, new partnerships for learning* (Monograph No. 26, pp. 1–8). Columbia: University of South Carolina, National Resource Center for The First-Year Experience and Students in Transition.

Love, A. G., & Tokuno, K. A. (1999). Learning community models. In J. H. Levine (Ed.), *Learning communities: New structures, new partnerships for learning* (Monograph No. 26, pp. 9–18). Columbia: University of South Carolina, National Resource Center for The First-Year Experience and Students in Transition.

Loyola University. (2013). Sophomore Living Communities\\Student Life\\Loyola University Maryland. Retrieved from http://www .loyola.edu/departments/student life/housinginformation/pro grams/sophomore.aspx

Lundberg, C. A., & Schreiner, L. A. (2004). Quality and frequency of faculty-student interaction as predictors of learning. An analysis by student race/ethnicity. *Journal of College Student Development, 45*(5), 549–565.

Lynch, C. (2001). The successful orientation of a peer leadership program. In S. L. Hamid (Ed.), *Peer leadership: A primer on program essentials* (Monograph No. 32, pp. 23–35). Columbia: University of South Carolina, National Resource Center for The First-Year Experience and Students in Transition.

Macari, D. P., Maples, M. F., & D'Andrea, L. (2006). A comparative study of psychosocial development in nontraditional and traditional college students. *Journal of College Student Retention: Research, Theory and Practice, 7*(3–4), 283–302.

MacGregor, J., & Smith, B. L. (2005). Where are learning communities now? National leaders take stock. *About Campus, 10*, 2–8.

Mack, C. E. (2010). A brief overview of the orientation, transition, and retention field. In J. A. Ward-Roof (Ed.), *Designing successful transitions: A guide for orienting students to college* (3rd ed., pp. 3–10). Columbia: University of South Carolina, National Resource Center for The First-Year Experience and Students in Transition.

Maisto, A. A., & Tammi, M. W. (1991). The effect of a content-based freshman seminar on academic and social integration. *Journal of the Freshman Year Experience, 3*(2), 29–48.

Maki, P. L. (2002). Developing an assessment plan to learn about student learning. *Journal of Academic Librarianship, 28*(1–2), 8–13.

Maki, P. L. (2004). Maps and inventories: Anchoring efforts to track student learning. *About Campus, 9*(4), 2–9.

Mangold, W. D., Bean, L. G., Adams, D. J., Schwab, W. A., & Lynch, S. M. (2003). Who goes who stays: An assessment of the effect of a freshman mentoring and unit registration program on college persistence. *Journal of College Student Retention: Research, Theory and Practice, 4*(2), 95–122.

Mann, A., Andrews, C., & Rodenburg, N. (2010). Administration of a comprehensive orientation program. In J. A. Ward-Roof (Ed.), *Designing successful transitions: A guide for orienting students to college*

(Monograph No. 13, 3rd ed., pp. 43–60). Columbia: University of South Carolina, National Resource Center for The First-Year Experience and Students in Transition.

Mann, J. R., Hunt, M. D., & Alford, J. G. (2003–2004). Monitored probation: A program that works. *Journal of College Student Retention, 5*(3), 245–254.

Mayhew, M. J., Wolniak, G. C., & Pascarella, E. T. (2008). How educational practices affect the development of life-long learning orientations in traditionally-aged undergraduate students. *Research in Higher Education, 49*, 337–356.

McCabe, R. H. (2000). *No one to waste: A report to public decision-makers and community college leaders.* Washington, DC: American Association of Community Colleges and Pew Charitable Trusts.

McCabe, R. (2003). *Yes, we can: A community college guide for developing America's underprepared.* Phoenix, AZ: League for Innovation in the Community College.

McLure, G. T., & Child, R. L. (1999). Upward Bound students compared to other college-bound students: Profiles of nonacademic characteristics and academic achievement. *Journal of Negro Education, 67*(4), 346–363.

Messia, J. (2010). *Defining advising stakeholder groups.* Retrieved from http://www.nacada.ksu.edu/Clearinghouse/AdvisingIssues /Stakeholders.htm

Metropolitan State University. (2011). *Vision, mission and core values statements.* Retrieved from http://www.metrostate.edu/msweb /choose/about/vision.html

Miami University. (2012). *Residential curriculum.* Office of Residence Life. Retrieved from www.units.muohio.edu/saf/reslife /reslife/whatwedo/rescurric.php

Middle States Commission on Higher Education. (2005). *Assessing student learning and institutional effectiveness: Understanding Middle States expectations.* Retrieved from www.msche.org/ . . . /Assessment_Expectations051222081842.pdf

Miller, M. A. (2011). *Structuring our conversations: Shifting to four dimensional advising models.* Retrieved from http://www.nacada.ksu.edu /Clearinghouse/AdvisingIssues/structure-conversations.htm

Molina, A., & Abelman, R. (2000). Style over substance in interventions for at-risk students: The impact of intrusiveness. *NACADA Journal, 20*(2), 5–15.

Mottarella, K. E., Fritzche, B. A., & Cerabino, K. C. (2004). What do students want in advising? A policy capturing study. *NACADA Journal, 24*(1&2), 48–61.

Mullendore, R. H., & Banahan, L. A. (2005). Designing orientation programs. In M. L. Upcraft, J. N. Gardner, B. O. Barefoot, & Associates, *Challenging and supporting the first-year student: A handbook for improving the first year of college* (pp. 391–409). San Francisco, CA: Jossey-Bass.

Myers, R. D. (2003). *Annotated bibliography: Perspectives in postsecondary education programs and student support interventions.* Boston, MA: Pathways to College Network.

NACADA. (2012). *Concept of academic advising.* Retrieved from http://www.nacada.ksu.edu/Resources/Clearinghouse/View -Articles/Concept of Academic Advising-a698.aspx

NADE. (2011). *About developmental education.* Retrieved from http://www .nade.net/index.html

NADE. (2013). www.nade.net/aboutnade.html

Nadler, D. P., Miller, M. T., & Dyer, B. G. (2004). Longitudinal analysis of standards used to evaluate new student orientation at a case institution. *Journal of College Orientation and Transition, 11*(2), 36–41.

National Association for Campus Activities. (2009). *Competency guide for college student leaders.* Columbia, SC: National Association for Campus Activities.

National Center for Education Statistics. (2005). *The condition of education, 2005.* Washington, DC: Author. Retrieved from http://nces.ed.gov/programs/coe/

National Survey of Student Engagement. (2007). *Experiences that matter: Enhancing student learning and success: Annual report 2007.* Bloomington: Indiana University, Center for Postsecondary Research.

National Survey of Student Engagement. (2008). *Promoting engagement for all students: The imperative to look within: 2008 results.* Bloomington: Indiana University, Center for Postsecondary Research.

National Survey of Student Engagement. (2010). *Major differences: Examining student engagement by field of student: Annual results 2010.* Bloomington: Indiana University, Center for Postsecondary Research.

National Survey of Student Engagement. (2012). *Promoting student learning and institutional improvement: Lessons from NSSE at 13.* Bloomington: Indiana University, Center for Postsecondary Research.

Newton, F. B., & Ender, S. C. (2010). *Students helping students: A guide for peer educators on college campuses* (2nd ed.). San Francisco, CA: Jossey-Bass.

Nieto, S. (1999). *The light in their eyes: Creating multicultural learning communities.* New York, NY: Teachers College Press.

Noel, L. (1985). Increasing student retention: New challenges and potential. In L. Noel, R. Levitz, D. Saluri, & Associates (Eds.),

Increasing student retention (pp. 1–27). San Francisco, CA: Jossey-Bass.

Noel-Levitz, L. (2011). Higher education benchmarks. In *Mid-year student retention indicators: Report for two-year and four-year public and private institutions.* Retrieved from www.noellevitz.com

Nora, A. & Crisp, G. (2012, July). Hispanic Student Participation and Success in Developmental Education. White paper prepared for the Hispanic Association of Colleges and Universities. Retrieved from www.hacu.net/hacu/H3ERC_Research_Initiative.asp

Nuss, E. M. (2003). The development of student affairs. In S. R. Komives & D. B. Woodward Jr. (Eds.), *Student services: A handbook for the profession* (4th ed., pp. 65–88). San Francisco, CA: Jossey-Bass.

Nutt, C. L. (2003). *Advisor training: Exemplary practices in the development of advisor skills* (NACADA Monograph No. 9). Manhattan, KS: National Academic Advising Association.

Nutt, C. L. (2004). Assessing student learning in academic advising. NACADA, *Academic Advising Today, Quarterly Newsletter, 27*(4).

O'Banion, T. (1972). An academic advising model. *Junior College Journal, 42*(6), 62, 64, & 66–69.

Oblinger, G. D. (Ed.). (2006). *Learning spaces.* Washington, DC: EDU-CAUSE.

Offenstein, J., Moore, C., & Shulock, N. (2010). *Advancing by degrees: A framework for increasing college completion.* Washington, DC: Institute for Higher Education and Policy and the Education Trust.

Ogden, P., Thompson, D., Russell, A., & Simons, C. (2003). Supplemental instruction: Short-and long-impact. *Journal of Developmental Education, 26*(3), 2–8.

Oseguera, L., Locks, A. M., & Vega, I. I. (2009). Increasing Latina/o students' baccalaureate attainment: A focus on retention. *Journal of Hispanic Higher Education, 8*(1), 23–53.

Padgett, R. D., & Keup, J. R. (2011). *2009 National Survey of First-Year Seminars: Ongoing efforts to support students in transition.* Columbia: University of South Carolina, National Resource Center for The First-Year Experience and Students in Transition.

Pagan, R., & Edwards-Wilson, R. (2002–2003). A mentoring program for remedial students. *Journal of College Student Retention: Research, Theory and Practice, 4*(3), 207–226.

Pardee, C. F. (2000). Organizational models for academic advising. In V. N. Gordon, W. R. Habley, & Associates (Eds.), *Academic advising: A comprehensive handbook* (pp. 192–209). San Francisco, CA: Jossey-Bass.

Pascarella, E. T., Cruce, T., Umbach, P. T., Wolniak, G. C., Kuh, G. D., Carini, R. M., Hayek, J. C., Gonyea, R. M., & Zhao, C. (2006). Institutional selectivity and good practices in undergraduate education: How strong is the link? *Journal of Higher Education, 77*(2), 251–285.

Pascarella, E. T., Cruce, T. M., Wolniak, G. C., & Blaich, C. F. (2004). Do liberal arts colleges really foster good practices in undergraduate education? *Journal of College Student Development, 45*(1), 57–74.

Pascarella, E. T., & Terenzini, P. T. (1991). *How college affects students: Findings and insights from twenty years of research*. San Francisco, CA: Jossey-Bass.

Pascarella, E. T., & Terenzini, P. T. (2005). *How college affects students: Vol. 2. A third decade of research*. San Francisco, CA: Jossey-Bass.

Pascarella, E. T., Terenzini, P. T., & Wolfe, L. M. (1986). Orientation to college and freshman year persistence/withdrawal decisions. *Journal of Higher Education, 57*(2), 155–175.

Pasque, P. A., & Murphy, R. (2005). The intersections of living-learning programs and social identity as factors of academic achievement and intellectual engagement. *Journal of College Student Development, 46*(4), 429–444.

Pattengale, J., & Schreiner, L. A. (2000). What is the sophomore slump and why should we care? In L. A. Schreiner & J. Pattengale (Eds.), *Visible solutions for invisible students: Helping sophomores succeed* (Monograph No. 31). Columbia: University of South Carolina, National Resource Center for The First-Year Experience and Students in Transition.

Paul, E. L., Manetas, M., Grady, K., & Vivona, J. (2001). The transitions program: A precollege advising and orientation workshop for students and parents. *Journal of the National Academic Advising Association, 21*(1&2), 76–87.

Peguesse, C. (2008). *Quality enhancement plan: Sophomore year experience plan, Vladosta State University*. Retrieved from www.valdosta.edu/sacs/qep/documents/QEPProposalforSYE_000.pdf

Pell Institute for the Study of Opportunity in Higher Education. (2007). *Demography is not destiny: Increasing the graduation rates of low-income college students at large public universities*. Washington, DC: Author.

Perkowsky, K., & Williams, K. R. (2011). *Making the fit just right: Living in a cohort model*. Washington, DC: ACPA, College Students International.

Perlman, B. M. (2011). *SYE programs and academic development: Developing an assessment for program evaluation*. Paper presented at the 18th National Conference on Students in Transition, St. Louis, MO.

Perna, L. W. (2002). Precollege outreach programs: Characteristics of programs serving historically underrepresented groups of students. *Journal of College Student Development, 43*(1), 64–83.

Petress, K. (1996). The multiple roles of an undergraduate's academic advisor. *Education, 117*(1), 90–91.

Poisel, M. A., & Joseph, S. (Eds.). (2011). *Transfer students in higher education: Building foundations for policies, programs, and services that foster student success* (Monograph No. 54). Columbia: University of South Carolina, National Resource Center for The First-Year Experience and Students in Transition.

Prentice, S., Collins, G., Couchman, J., Li, L., & Wilson, K. (2009). "It's like a blessing": A collaborative program to support students on academic probation. *Journal of Academic Language and Learning, 3*(2), 82–93.

Prola, M., Rosenburg, P., & Wright, B. (1977). The impact of a freshman orientation course. *New York State Personnel and Guidance Journal, 12*(1), 26–31.

Pryor, J. H., DeAngelo, L., Palacki Blake, L. P., Hurtado, S., & Tran, S. (2011). *The American freshman: National norms fall 2011.* Los Angeles, CA: Higher Education Research Institute, UCLA.

Pryor, J. H., Hurtado, S., DeAngelo, L., Blake, L. P., & Tran, S. (2009). *The American freshman: National norms fall 2009.* Los Angeles, CA: Higher Education Research Institute, UCLA.

Pryor, J. H., Hurtado, S., Saenz, V. B., Santos, J. L., & Korn, W. S. (2007). *The American freshman: Forty year trends.* Los Angeles, CA: Higher Education Research Institute, UCLA.

Rae, T. (2011, June 5). Just showing up: Educators focus on attendance to help students succeed. *Chronicle of Higher Education.* Retrieved from chronicle.com/article/Just-Showing-Up-Educators/127765

Reason, R. D. (2009). Student variables that predict retention. Recent research and new developments. *NASPA Journal, 46*(3), 482–501.

Reeland, B., & Jaeger, D. (2011). Measuring academic, social, and developmental outcomes. ISU housing services themed learning communities. *Progressive Measures, 6*(2), 9–10.

Reyes, N. A., & Nora, A. (2012). Lost Among the Data: A Review of Latino First Generation College Students. White paper prepared for the Hispanic Association of Colleges and Universities. Retrieved from www.hacu/ . . . net/2012

Rhodes, T. L. (Ed.). (2010). *Assessing outcomes and improving achievement: Tips and tools for using rubrics.* Washington, DC: Association of American Colleges and Universities.

Rist, A., & Allen, D. (2011). Tales from the field: Evaluating a university residential living-learning community. *Performance Xpress*. Retrieved from http://www.performanceexpress.org/2011

Robbins, R., & Zarges, K. M. (2011). *Assessment of academic advising: A summary of the process*. Retrieved from http://www.nacada.ksu.edu/Clearinghouse/AdvisingIssues/assessment-Robbins-Zarges.htm

Robert, E. R., & Thomson, G. (1994). Learning assistance and the success of underrepresented students at Berkeley. *Journal of Developmental Education, 17*(3), 4–6, 8, 10, 12, 14.

Robinson, D.A.G., Burns, C. F., & Gaw, K. F. (1996). Orientation programs: A foundation for student learning and success. In S. C. Ender, F. B. Newton, & R. B. Caple (Eds.), *Contributing to learning: The role of student affairs. New Directions for Student Services, 75,* 55–68.

Rode, D. L., & Cawthon, T. W. (2010). Theoretical perspectives on orientation. In J. A. Ward-Roof (Ed.), *Designing successful transitions: A guide for orienting students to college* (Monograph No. 13, 3rd ed., pp. 11–28). Columbia: University of South Carolina, National Resource Center for The First-Year Experience and Students in Transition.

Rothberger, R., & Zabel, L. (2012). Peer advising: Bridging the gap between professional advisor and student. *Academic Advising Today, Voices of the Global Community, 35*(2). Retrieved from http://nacada.ksu.edu/Resources/Academic-Advising-Today/View-Articles/June-2012-Vol-352-Complete-Edition.aspx

Roueche, J. E., Baker, G. A., & Roueche, S. D. (1984). *College responses to low-achieving students: A report of a national study*. Washington, DC: Community College Press.

Roueche, J. E., & Roueche, S. D. (1999). *High stakes, high performance: Making remedial education work*. Washington, DC: American Association of Community Colleges, Community College Press.

Rouse, J. E. (2011). *Social justice development: Creating social change agents in academic systems* (Unpublished doctoral dissertation). University of North Carolina at Greensboro.

Rudman, J. (1992). *An evaluation of several early alert strategies for helping first semester freshmen at the community college and a description of the newly developed early alert retention system (EARS) software.* (ERIC Document No. ED 349 055)

Ruiz, S., Sharkness, J., Kelly, K., DeAngelo, L., & Pryor, J. (2010). *Findings from the 2009 administration of Your First College Year (YFCY): National aggregates.* Los Angeles, CA: Higher Education Research Institute, UCLA.

Ryan, M. P., & Glenn, P. A. (2003). Increasing one-year retention rates by focusing on academic competence: An empirical odyssey. *College Student Retention Research, Theory and Practice, 4*(3), 297–324.

Saenz, R. (2004). *Latinos and the changing face of America.* New York, NY: Russell Sage Foundation and Population Reference Bureau.

Sage, T. L. (2010). *Academic probation: How students navigate and make sense of their experiences* (Unpublished master's thesis). University of Wisconsin, Stevens Point.

Sanchez, G. J. (2011, June). *High impact and broad reach.* Invited address at the 2011 Institute on High-Impact Practices and Student Success, Burlington, VT.

Sanchez-Legulinel, C. (2008). Supporting "slumping" sophomores: Programmatic peer initiatives designed to enhance retention in the crucial second year of college. *College Student Journal, 42,* 637–646.

Sanford, N. (1962). *The American college.* New York: Wiley.

Sanford, N. (1967). *Where colleges fail: A study of the student as a person.* San Francisco, CA, Jossey-Bass.

Santiago, D. A. (2008). *Modeling Hispanic-serving institutions: Campus practices that work for Latino students.* Washington, DC: Excelencia in Education.

Saving, K., & Keim, M. C. (1998). Student and advisor perceptions of academic advising in two midwestern colleges of business. *College Student Journal, 32,* 511–521.

Schaller, M. A. (2005). Wandering and wondering: Traversing the uneven terrain of the second college year. *About Campus, 10*(3), 17–27.

Schaller, M. A. (2006). *Complexities in understanding the experience of sophomore students.* PowerPoint presentation at the 13th National Conference on Students in Transition. National Resource Center for The First-Year Experience and Students in Transition, Nashville, TN.

Schaller, M. A. (2007). The development of college sophomores. In B. F. Tobolowsky & B. E. Cox (Eds.), *Shedding light on sophomores: An exploration of the second college year* (Monograph No. 47, pp. 1–11). Columbia: University of South Carolina, National Resource Center for The First-Year Experience and Students in Transition.

Schaller, M. A. (2010). Understanding the impact of the second year of college. In M. S. Hunter, B. F. Tobolowsky, J. N. Gardner, S. E. Evenbeck, J. A. Pattengale, M. Schaller, & L. A. Schreiner (Eds.), *Helping sophomores succeed: Understanding and improving the second-year experience* (pp. 13–29). San Francisco, CA: Jossey-Bass.

Schein, H. K. (2005). The Zen of unit one. In N. Laff (Ed.), *Liberal education at residential learning communities. New Directions for Teaching and Learning, 103*, 73–88.

Schnell, C. A., & Doekett, C. (2002–2003). First-year seminars produce long-term impact. *Journal of College Student Retention: Research, Theory, and Practice, 4*(4), 377–391.

Schreiner, L. A. (2005). Strengths-based advising: A new lens for higher education. *NACADA Journal, 25*(2), 20–29.

Schreiner, L. A. (2009). *Linking student satisfaction and retention.* Noel Levitz Research Study. Retrieved from https://www.noellevitz.com /papers-research-higher-education/2009/student-satisfaction -retention

Schreiner, L. A. (2010). Factors that contribute to sophomore success and satisfaction. In M. S. Hunter, B. F. Tobolowsky, J. N. Gardner, S. E. Evenbeck, J. A. Pattengale, M. Schaller, & L. A. Schreiner (Eds.), *Helping sophomores succeed: Understanding and improving the second year experience* (pp. 43–65). San Francisco: Jossey-Bass.

Schreiner, L. A., & Lundberg, C. A. (2004). Quality and frequency of faculty-student interaction as predictors of learning: An analysis by student race/ethnicity. *Journal of College Student Development, 45*(4), 549–564.

Schreiner, L. A., & Pattengale, J. (2000). *Visible solutions for invisible students: Helping sophomores succeed* (Monograph No. 31). Columbia: University of South Carolina, National Resource Center for The First-Year Experience and Students in Transition.

Schroeder, C. C., & Swing, R. L. (2005). Drury University: Balancing intellectual rigor with intrusive personal support in the first-year. In B. O. Barefoot, J. N. Gardner, M. Cutright, L. V. Morris, C. C. Schroeder, S. W. Schwartz, M. J. Siegel, & R. L. Swing (Eds.), *Achieving and sustaining institutional excellence for the first year of college* (pp. 145–165). San Francisco: Jossey-Bass.

Schuh, J. H., & Gansemer-Topf, A. M. (2010). *The role of student affairs in student learning assessment* (NILOA Occasional Paper No. 7). Urbana, IL: University of Illinois and Indiana University, National Institute for Learning Outcomes Assessment.

Schuh, J. H., & Upcraft, M. L., & Associates. (2001). *Assessment practice in student affairs: An application manual.* San Francisco, CA: Jossey-Bass.

Schwartz, R., & Wiese, D. (2010). Assessment and evaluation in orientation. In J. A. Ward-Roof (Ed.), *Designing successful transitions: A guide for orienting students to college* (Monograph No. 13, 3rd ed., pp. 217–228). Columbia: University of South Carolina, National

Resource Center for The First-Year Experience and Students in Transition.

Scott-Weber, L. (2004). *In sync: Environmental behavior research and the design of learning spaces.* Ann Arbor, MI: Society for College and University Planning.

Scrivner, S., Sommolt, S., & Collado, H. (2009). *Getting back on track: Effects of a community college program for probationary students.* New York: MDRC.

Shao, X., Hufnagel, P., & Karp, R. (2009–2010). The effects of Clarion Transitions on student academic performance and retention. *Journal of College Student Retention, 11*(4), 435–457.

Shapiro, N. S., & Levine, J. J. (1999). *Creating learning communities: A practical guide to winning support, organizing for change, and implementing programs.* San Francisco, CA: Jossey-Bass.

Shook, J. L., & Keup, J. R. (2012). The benefits of peer leader programs: An overview from the literature. In J. R. Keup (Ed.), *Peer leadership in higher education. New Directions for Higher Education, 157,* 5–16.

Simons, J. M. (2011). *A national study of student early alert models at four-year institutions of higher education* (EdD dissertation). Available from ProQuest Dissertations and Theses database. Retrieved from tp://gradworks.umi.com/3482551.pdf

Siriam, R., Shushock, F., Perkins, J., & Scales, T. L. (2011). Students as teachers: What faculty learn by living on campus. *Journal of College and University Student Housing, 38*(1), 40–55.

Skipper, T. L. (2005). *Student development in the first year of college: A primer for college educators.* Columbia: University of South Carolina, National Resource Center for The First-Year Experience and Students in Transition.

Skipper, T. L., Latino, J. A., Rideout, B. M., & Weigel, D. (2010). Extensions of traditional orientation programs. In J. A. Ward-Roof (Ed.), *Designing successful transitions: A guide for orienting students to college* (Monograph No. 13, 3rd ed., pp. 95–116). Columbia: University of South Carolina, National Resource Center for The First-Year Experience and Students in Transition.

Smith, J. S. (2002). Using data to inform practice: Intrusive faculty advising at a two-year college. *Community College Journal of Research and Practice, 3*(10), 813–831.

Smith, J. S. (2007). Using data to Inform decisions: Intrusive faculty advising at a community college. *Community College Journal of Research and Practice, 31*(10), 813–831.

Smith, J., & Troxel, W. G. (2008). *Infusing research into practice: Multiple pathways to conducting research in advising.* Webinar presentation for the National Academic Advising Association.

Smith, M., MacGregor, M., & Gabelnick, F. (2004). *Learning communities: Reforming undergraduate education.* San Francisco, CA: Jossey-Bass.

Snyder, C. R., Shorey, H. S., Cheavens, J., Pulvers, K. M., Adams III, V. H., & Wiklund, C. (2002). Hope and academic success in college. *Journal of Educational Psychology, 94*(4), 820–826.

South Dakota State University. (2012, July 5). Sophomore year experience plan for South Dakota State University. Retrieved from www.sdstate.edu/ . . . /Second-Year-Implementation-Team -Recommend

Sprague, R. J. (2008). Doing it all: Adding advising into faculty workloads. *Academic Advising Today, 31*(1). Retrieved from http://www.nacada.ksu.edu/AAT/NW31_1.htm#6

Stark, M. C., Harth, M., & Sirianni, F. (2001). Retention, bonding, and academic achievement: Success of a first-year seminar. *Journal of The First-Year Experience & Students in Transition, 13*(2), 7–36.

Stassen, M.L.A. (2003). Student outcomes: The impact of varying living-learning community models. *Research in Higher Education, 44*(5), 581–613.

Stein, K. (2005) Meeting the developmental needs of Latino/Latina students. *Journal of College Reading and Learning, 36*(1), 82–87.

Stone, M. E., & Jacobs, G. (Eds.). (2008). *Supplemental instruction: Improving first-year student success in high-risk courses* (Monograph No. 7, 3rd ed.). Columbia: University of South Carolina, National Resource Center for The First-Year Experience and Students in Transition.

Strayhorn, T. L. (2011). *Maximizing first-year student success in college: The paradox of transitions.* Paper presented at the Annual Conference on The First-Year Experience, Atlanta, GA. Retrieved from e.osu.edu/pdf/strayhornosufyekeynote.pdf

Stripling, W. R., & Hinck, C. L. (1993). *New student orientation: Student assessment of a program's content.* Jonesboro: Arkansas State University.

SUNY-Oswego. (2010). *First year advisor resources.* Retrieved from http://www.oswego.edu/academics/opportunities/first_year /fyadvisosresources.html

Suskie, L. (2009). *Assessing student learning: A common sense guide* (2nd ed.). San Francisco, CA: Jossey-Bass.

Swail, W. S. (2004). *The art of student retention: A handbook for practitioners and administrators.* Educational Policy Institute. Texas Higher

Education Coordinating Board 20th Annual Recruitment and Retention, Austing Texas, June 2004. www.educationalpolicy.org

Swail, W. S., with Redd, K. E., & Perna, L. W. (2003). *Retaining minority students in higher education: A framework for success* (ASHE-ERIC Higher Education Report No. 2). Washington, DC: George Washington University School of Letters and Human Development.

Swing, R. L. (2002). *Series of essays on the First-Year Initiative Benchmarking Study.* Brevard, NC: Policy Center on the First-Year of College. Retrieved from http://tech.sa.sc.edu/fye/resources/assessment/essays/FYA_Essays_view.php?editid1=41

Tallahassee Community College. (N.d.). *Mission statement.* Retrieved from https://www.tcc.fl.edu/Current/Academics/LearningCommons/Pages/Mission.aspx

Taylor, J. A., & Lawrence, J. (2007). Making students AWARE: an online strategy for students given academic warning. *Studies in Learning, Evaluation, Innovation and Development, 4*(2), 39–52.

Taylor, K., Moore, W. S., MacGregor, J., & Lindblad, J. (2003). *Learning community research and assessment: What we know now* (National Learning Communities Project Monograph Series). Olympia: Evergreen State College, Washington Center for Improving the Quality of Undergraduate Education in cooperation with the American Association for Higher Education.

Temple, D. R. (2010, February). *Developing, implementing and assessing an early alert system.* Paper presented at the 29th Annual Conference on the First-Year Experience, Denver, CO.

Terenzini, P. T., Rendon, L., Upcraft, M. L., Millar, S., Allison, K., Gregg, P., & Jalomo, R. (1996). The transition to college: Diverse students, diverse stories. In F. Stage, G. Anya, J. Bean, D. Hossler, & G. Kuh (Eds.), *ASHE Reader on college students: The evolving nature of research* (pp. 54–79). Needham Heights, MA: Ginn Press.

Tetley, J., Tobolowsky, B., & Chan, E. (2010). Designing and implementing new initiatives for sophomores. In M. Hunter, B. Tobolowsky, & J. Gardner (Eds.), *Helping sophomores succeed: Understanding and improving the second year experience* (pp. 217–233). San Francisco, CA: Jossey-Bass.

Texas Higher Education Coordinating Board. (2012). *Research and project grants: Evaluation of developmental education projects, 2010–2011.* Austin, TX: Author.

Texas Tribune. (2012). *Sam Houston State University.* Retrieved from http://www.texas tribune.org/higher-ed/explore/sam-houston-state-university/

Thelin, J. R. (2004). *A history of American higher education.* Baltimore, MD: Johns Hopkins University Press.

Thompson, B. R., & Geren, P. R. (2002). Classroom strategies for identifying and helping college students at risk for academic failure. *College Student Journal, 36*(3), 398–402.

Tinto, V. (1975). Dropouts from higher education: A theoretical synthesis of recent research. *Review of Educational Research, 45,* 89–125.

Tinto, V. (1988). Stages of student departure: Reflections on the longitudinal character of student leaving. *Journal of Higher Education, 59,* 438–445.

Tinto, V. (1993). *Leaving college: Rethinking the causes and cures of student attrition* (2nd ed.). Chicago: University of Chicago Press.

Tinto, V. (1998). Colleges as communities: Taking research on student persistence seriously. *Review of Higher Education, 21*(2), 167–177.

Tinto, V. (2000). Linking learning and leaving: Exploring the role of the college classroom in student departure. In J. M. Braxton (Ed.), *Reworking the student departure puzzle* (pp. 81–94). Nashville, TN: Vanderbilt University Press.

Tinto, V. (2009, February 5). *Taking student retention seriously: Rethinking the first year of university.* Keynote speech delivered at the ALTC FYE Curriculum Design Symposium, Queensland University of Technology, Brisbane, Australia.

Tobolowsky, B. F. (2008). Sophomores in transition: The forgotten year. In B. O. Barefoot (Ed.), *The first year and beyond: Rethinking the challenge of collegiate transition. New Directions for Higher Education, 144,* 59–67.

Tobolowsky, B. F., & Cox, B. E. (2007). *Shedding light on sophomores: An exploration of the second college year* (Monograph No. 47). Columbia: University of South Carolina, National Resource Center for The First-Year Experience and Students in Transition.

Tobolowsky, B. F., Cox, B. E., & Wagner, M. T. (2005). *Exploring the evidence: Reporting research on first-year seminars, Vol. 3* (Monograph No. 42). Columbia: University of South Carolina, National Resource Center for The First-Year Experience and Students in Transition.

Tobolowsky, B. F., and Serven, S. K. (2007). Introduction. In B. F. Tobolowsky & B. E. Cox (Eds.), *Shedding light on sophomores: An exploration of the second college year* (Monograph No. 47, pp. ix–xii). Columbia: University of South Carolina, National Resource Center for The First-Year Experience and Students in Transition.

Tobolowsky, B. F., & Associates. (2008). *2006 National Survey of First-Year Seminars: Continuing innovations in the collegiate curriculum* (Monograph No. 51). Columbia: University of South Carolina, National

Resource Center for The First-Year Experience and Students in Transition.

Tovar, E., & Simon, M. A. (2006). Academic probation as a dangerous opportunity: Factors influencing diverse college students' success. *Community College Journal of Research and Practice, 30*(7), 547–564.

Trabant, T. D. (2006). *Advising Syllabus 101.* Retrieved from http://www .nacada.ksu.edu/Clearinghouse/AdvisingIssues/syllabus101.htm

Trombley, C. T. (2000). Evaluating students on probation and determining intervention strategies: A comparison of probation and good standing students. *Journal of College Student Retention, 2*(3), 239–251.

Troxel, W. G. (2008). Assessing the effectiveness of the advising program. In V. N. Gordon, W. R. Habley, & T. J. Grites (Eds.), *Academic advising: A comprehensive handbook* (2nd ed.), pp. 386–395. San Francisco: Jossey-Bass.

Troxel, W. G., & Campbell, S. (2010). Quantitative methodologies for the academic advising practitioner-researcher. In P. L. Hagen, T. M. Kuhn, & G. M. Padak (Eds.), *Scholarly inquiry in academic advising* (pp. 73–84). Lawrence, KS: NACADA.

Troxel, W. G., & Cutright, M. (Eds.). (2008). *Exploring the evidence: Initiatives in the first college year* (Monograph No. 49). Columbia: University of South Carolina, National Resource Center for The First-Year Experience and Students in Transition.

Turner, A., & Berry, T. R., (2000). Counseling center contributions to student retention and graduation: A longitudinal assessment. *Journal of College Student Development, 41*(6), 627–635.

Twigg, C. A. (2010). *Changing the equation. Facts at a glance narrative.* Saratoga Springs, NY: National Center for Academic Transformation. Retrieved from www.thencat.org/Mathematics/CTE /CTE_FactsNarrative.html

UCLA College of Letters and Science. (2011). *Freshman cluster program.* Retrieved from http://www.uei.ucla.edu/clustersabout.htm.

University of Massachusetts, Amherst. (2001). Living-learning communities: Do they make a difference? *Assessment Bulletin, 5*(1). Retrieved from www.umass.edu/oapa/ . . . /assessment . . . /living _learning_communities.pdf

University of Minnesota. (2012). College of Education and Human Development, Jandriss Center for Innovative Higher Education. Retrieved from http://www.cehd.umn.edu/Jandris/Teaching/ EDEProgram.html

University of North Carolina, Greensboro. (2011–2012). *Faculty Teaching and Learning Commons, Annual Report, 2011–2012.* Retrieved from undergraduate.uncg.edu/about/forms/FTLC%20-%20Sum %20Annual%20Report%2011–12.pdf—2012–08–03

University of South Carolina. (2012). *History of the First University Seminar and the University 101 Program.* Retrieved from www.sc.edu/univ101 /aboutus/history.html

University of Southern California. (2013). *Writing 340 Features Class.* Retrieved from http://dornsife.usc.edu/340-featured-class

University of Wisconsin. (2013). *Mission statement.* Retrieved from http://www.wisc.edu/about/leadership/mission.php

Upcraft, M. L. (2005). Assessing the first year of college. In M. L. Upcraft, J. N. Gardner, B. O. Barefoot, & Associates, *Challenging and supporting the first-year student: A handbook for improving the first year of college* (pp. 469–485). San Francisco, CA: Jossey-Bass.

Upcraft, M. L., Crissman Ishler, J. L., & Swing, R. L. (2005). A beginner's guide for assessing the first college year. In M. L. Upcraft, J. N. Gardner, B. O. Barefoot, & Associates, *Challenging and supporting the first-year student* (pp. 486–500). San Francisco, CA: Jossey-Bass.

Upcraft, M. L., Gardner, J. N., Barefoot, B. O., & Associates. (2005). *Challenging and supporting the first-year student: A handbook for improving the first year of college.* San Francisco, CA: Jossey-Bass.

Upcraft, M. L., & Schuh, J. H. (1996). *Assessment in student affairs: A guide for practitioners.* San Francisco, CA: Jossey-Bass.

Ursinus College. (N.d.). *Multicultural services program description.* Retrieved from http://www.ursinus.edu/NetCommunity/Page .aspx?pid=455

US Department of Education. (2011). *Guide to U.S. Department of Education programs.* Washington, DC: US Department of Education, Office of Communication and Outreach.

Walker, A. A. (2003). Learning communities and their effect on students' cognitive abilities. *Journal of The First-Year Experience & Students in Transition, 15*(2), 11–33.

Walpole, M., Simmerman, H., Mack, C., Mills, J. T., Scales, M., & Albano, D. (2008). Bridge to success: Insight into summer bridge program students' college transition. *Journal of The First-Year Experience & Students in Transition, 20*(1), 11–30.

Ward-Roof, J. A. (2010). *Designing successful transitions: A guide for orienting students to college* (Monograph No. 13, 3rd ed.). Columbia: University of South Carolina, National Resource Center for The First-Year Experience and Students in Transition.

Ward-Roof, J. A., Page, L. A., Lombardi, R. (2010). Channeling parental involvement to support student success. In J. A. Ward-Roof (Ed.), *Designing successful transitions: A guide for orienting students to college*

(Monograph No. 13, 3rd ed., pp. 79–94). Columbia: University of South Carolina, National Resource Center for The First-Year Experience and Students in Transition.

Wawrzynski, M. R., Jessup-Anger, J., Stolz, K., Helman, C., & Beaulieu, J. (2009). Exploring students' perceptions of academically based living-learning communities. *College Student Affairs, 28*(1), 138–158.

Weick, K. E., Sutcliffe, C. M., & Obstfeld, D. (2005). Organizing and the process of sensemaking. *Organization Science, 16*(4), 409–421.

Weiss, M. J., Visher, M., & Weissman, E. (2011). *Learning communities for developmental education students: Early results from randomized experiments at three community colleges.* Evanston, IL: Society for Research on Educational Effectiveness.

Western Interstate Commission for Higher Education. (2008). *Knocking at the college door: Projections of high school graduates by state and race/ethnicity 1992–2022.* Boulder, CO: Author.

Williams, B., Benzer, J. P., Chesbro, S., & Leavitt, R. (2005). Using the assessing the learning strategies adults tool with older adults. Comparison based on age and functionality ability. *Topics in Geriatric Rehabilitation, 21*(4), 332–342.

Williams, S., & Pury, C. (2002). Student attitudes toward and participation in electronic discussion. *International Journal of Educational Technology, 3*(1). Retrieved from http://www.ao.uiuc.edu/ijet/v3n3/williams/index.html

Wilson, M. E., & Dannells, M. (2010). Orientation and first-year programs: A profile of participating students. In J. A. Ward-Roof (Ed.), *Designing successful transitions: A guide for orienting students to college* (Monograph No. 13, 3rd ed., pp. 149–166). Columbia: University of South Carolina, National Resource Center for The First-Year Experience and Students in Transition.

Wolf-Wendel, L. E., Tuttle, K., & Keller-Wolff, C. M. (1999). Assessment of a freshman summer transition program in an open-admissions institution. *Journal of The First-Year Experience & Students in Transition, 11*(2), 7–32.

Wooten, B. M., Hunt, J. S., LeDuc, B. F., & Poskus, P. (2012). Peer leadership in the cocurriculum: Turning campus activities into an educationally purposeful enterprise. In J. R. Keup (Ed.), *Peer leadership in higher education. New Directions in Higher Education, 157,* 45–58.

Zachary, E. M., & Schneider, E. M. (2008). *Promising instructional reforms in developmental education: A case study of three achieving the dream colleges.* New York: MDRC.

Zachary, E. M., & Schneider, E. M. (2010). Building foundations for student retention: A review of rigorous research and promising trends in developmental education. An NCPR working paper prepared for the NCPR developmental education conference: What Policies and Practices Work for Students? (Teachers College, Columbia University, Sept. 23–24)

Zakely, J. (2003). Orientation as a catalyst: Effective retention through academic and social integration. In J. A. Ward-Roof & C. Harch (Eds.), *Designing successful transitions: A guide for orientating students to college* (Monograph No. 13, 2nd ed., pp. 55–65). Columbia: University of South Carolina, National Resource Center for The First-Year Experience and Students in Transition.

Zehner, A. (2011). *Co-curricular activities and student learning outcomes.* Purdue University.

Zhao, C. M., & Kuh, G. D. (2004). Adding value: Learning communities and student engagement. *Research in Higher Education, 45*(2), 115–138.

Index